Gators, Gourdheads, and Pufflings

A biologist slogs, climbs, and wings her way

to save wildlife

Susan D. Jewell

ISBN 0-7414-4961-7

Published by:

PUBLISHING.COM

1094 New DeHaven Street, Suite 100
West Conshohocken, PA 19428-2713
Info@buybooksontheweb.com
www.buybooksontheweb.com
Toll-free (877) BUY BOOK
Local Phone (610) 941-9999
Fax (610) 941-9959

Printed in the United States of America

Printed on Recycled Paper

Published December 2008

Dedicated to the memory of my dear friend
Richard Haley (1962–2006),
who was a better naturalist, writer, educator, and
human being than I will ever be.

If you really want to feel alive,
surround yourself with living things.

Acknowledgments

I was fortunate to have honest advice and feedback from many people. I would like to extend my sincere appreciation to the following people. Literary agents Regina Ryan and Russell Galen reviewed early drafts and generously supplied valuable comments. Attorney Dan Joseph provided advice on some aspects of the manuscript, and attorney Bill Powell provided assistance with the business aspects. Mildred Mainzer, a close friend of the family, provided astute comments on an early draft. Environment writer Sally Deneen offered much-appreciated advice. Friend and naturalist Cheri Collins provided invaluable edits. Friend and writer Ceil Sinnex gave excellent feedback. Linda Purviance, a talented new writer, made astute and useful comments. Dr. Stephen Kress, a vice-president of the National Audubon Society and puffin expert, reviewed the puffin chapter and provided comments for accuracy. LeRoy Poff, stream ecologist, and Adam Zerrenner, fisheries biologist, reviewed the chapter on fishing. All these people gave generously and unselfishly of their time, and all contributed to improvements.

Miranda Spencer provided editing and comments. However, I did some revising subsequently, and I take all blame for any errors that may exist.

Most importantly, my parents, Howard and Marian Jewell, thoroughly read my manuscript multiple times and gave excellent comments. They have always been there to support my writing.

During my career with the Massachusetts Audubon Society, Savannah River Ecology Laboratory, National Audubon Society, National Park Service, and U.S. Fish and Wildlife Service, I have been privileged to work with some of this country's finest biologists and naturalists. However, this book is really about the wildlife we were all trying to save. Thus, I owe the greatest thanks to my wild patients and research subjects— the bobcats, owls, wood storks, puffins, alligators, and all the others. I am also indebted to them for making my life so rich.

Preface

When I was an undergraduate student in the wildlife biology program at the University of Vermont in the 1970s, one of my wildlife teachers was Professor Robert W. Fuller. He was slight of build and as energetic as the ducks he studied. Because of him, I learned in record time how to canoe through a marsh.

Fuller taught Wetlands Wildlife Ecology, a so-called laboratory course. Lab courses generally corresponded with science courses, and most of them did occur in a laboratory. For wildlife courses, however, the laboratory was the great outdoors.

On lab days, our class of twenty or so students would pile into the cattle trucks. That was our term of mock endearment for the oversized pickup trucks with benches on the flatbed surrounded by slatted sideboards and covered with loosely fitting canvas tarps. We felt like cattle being driven to the . . . . Oh, well, it doesn't matter, because we were actually headed to the beautiful Missisquoi National Wildlife Refuge or a remote state wildlife management area to run around the marshes and woods in search of anything that crawled, swam, or flew.

In the warm weather, we would peel back the canvas tarps and relish the sun on our faces and the wind in our hair. Warm weather didn't appear often in northern Vermont during the school year. On the contrary, our field trips often fell on frigid days. Once, when I was sitting at the open-aired tailgate-end of the cattle truck, I was mesmerized by falling snow, oblivious that my cheeks were becoming frostbitten. Because much of our studies couldn't be done from fall through spring, we even had a special summer field session.

When we arrived at the refuge for our first wetlands class, we saw a row of canoes lining the bank of the marsh. Professor Fuller jumped in one, yelled, "Follow me!" and started paddling swiftly.

I stood bewildered at the water's edge. This suburbanite had never paddled a canoe before. I soon found out that neither had many of my classmates. As we watched the back of Fuller's head vanish behind the reeds, we glanced anxiously at each other and realized that we had better get moving. I jumped into the nearest canoe with a classmate, and together we managed awkwardly to keep up.

Every week, we heard the same command. "Follow me!" echoed through the marsh, as Fuller led the flotilla. The few experienced canoeists sympathetically slipped us some paddling lessons. None of us wanted to bring up the rear, or we would miss the excitement of Fuller's discourse. Soon, we were accomplished paddlers. The crash course paid off in later years when I seriously depended on my canoeing expertise in the Everglades.

Fuller would glide silently up to a wood duck nesting box and—in one swift and smooth move—stand up, remove the porkpie hat from his head, and stuff the hat into the box's front hole like a cork. This stealthy act trapped the brooding hen gently inside. Then we would carefully reach through the hole, pull the hen out for measuring, and place an identifying band on her leg.

Dry land posed its own navigational problems. For uplands ecology studies, the cattle trucks dropped us off in the morning in teams of three in remote areas of the Green Mountains. From there, we had to find our way through rugged, trailless terrain to the pickup site several miles away on another road. Along the way, we did our wildlife survey assignment. Then we had to be waiting at the prearranged location at a certain time in the afternoon, or we would have a very long walk back to Burlington. Our only navigation tools were a magnetic compass and a topographic map. We learned how to measure the distance between our footsteps to calculate distance, whether it was across a flat surface or walking up or down a 10- or 20-degree slope. Over any terrain, we could calculate the distance quite accurately just by pacing. In those days before electronic guidance gizmos, the orienteering worked just fine—no batteries needed.

That was the start of a challenging career. Not all field studies were as much fun, however. Many a time I refrained from telling my parents of my perilous episodes in the marshes and woods. They learned of some events by reading early drafts of this book, and that was probably just as well. After months of blundering in college, I realized that I was insensitive by telling my parents on a Friday that I was going winter camping that weekend—in Vermont in January—because they would fret the entire weekend. Phoning them after I had safely returned seemed to cause them less anxiety. Later, I assumed the same was true for the paid fieldwork.

More than a few times, I have wondered how I came to be so enamored with the natural world. No one in my family had shown such an all-consuming affinity for the outdoors, although I probably inherited my penchant for science from my father, a physician. In the early years, I doubt that my parents or siblings understood my career choice. To them, I was a forest ranger or, more likely, a forest stranger—an enigma—not quite a black sheep, but something more baffling. I was the green sheep of the family.

I was fortunate to recognize the connection between people and the natural world by the time I was a teenager. The first Earth Day and a tour by Pete Seeger of his sloop *Clearwater* left indelible marks on my conscience. I joined our high school's fledgling ecology class, started recycling in our home, went on litter-collecting patrols, and haven't let up on conserving natural resources since then. Two decades later, when I was living in the Florida Keys, I cheered at learning of their philosophy for water conservation, posted in public bathrooms:

"If it's yellow, let it mellow. If it's brown, flush it down."

And, "In this land of sun and fun, we never flush for number one."

Thus, after graduating from high school, I already knew what would give meaning to my life. Off I went to college and graduate school to learn how to take care of the Earth.

Sadly, many people spend their whole lives never comprehending how deeply entwined they are with the natural world around them. They misunderstand the role of Nature, believing it an unruly force to be conquered and enslaved by and for humankind, when in fact it is the fortress of our existence. They do not recognize the repercussions of their actions upon it.

The environment is the foundation of all life. It is not a luxury—it is a necessity. To harm it is to whittle away the future of humankind. Without a healthy environment, we cannot have healthy people. Without healthy people, we cannot have a healthy economy. And, we need all of these to have a healthy society.

Our environment is the air we breathe, the water we drink, and the land we live on. These resources provide the basic ingredients we need to be healthy—if we keep them unspoiled by respecting the harmonies and rhythms of natural systems.

Environmental experts understand how crucial this balance of Nature is to the survival of the world's people. That is why environmentalists aren't just tree-huggers—they're people-huggers, too. By taking care of the environment, they take care of people, because a well-nurtured Earth provides everyone with clean air to breathe, clean water to drink, and clean soil for growing food. These are the most fundamental rights of all living things. Without them, our bodies can't function properly, and we become slaves to poor health.

Throughout time, people have lived in harmony with the air, the water, and the land, knowing that harmony kept them alive. They didn't need to know how long alligator eggs incubated or where puffins fished, as long as alligator eggs still hatched and puffins still fished.

However, for most people of industrialized nations, the connection between humans and the land was broken generations ago. Parents can no longer routinely teach their children how they are part of the natural world and how all things are connected, as their ancestors did. This information should be passed down as part of each person's legacy.

Now that we have disrupted the harmony, we need to restore it. In today's more complex world, we *do* need to know how long it takes for alligator eggs to hatch (about 56 days) and where puffins fish (we still don't know all areas) to make sure there will always be alligators and puffins and fish. While these tidbits of information may seem trivial, collecting them represents a tremendous amount of work—long, backbreaking field hours, sometimes at a risk to a researcher's life. This effort is what it takes to find the answers needed to restore harmony within the environment.

In my university days, the faculty repeatedly drilled into our heads how demanding the field of wildlife biology would be, both physically and mentally. As you will soon see by my tales from the field, they were right. To start with, even our curriculum required more credit hours than most other majors, including the pre-medical school major. Besides the expected biology courses, classes included economics, geology, statistics, chemistry, physics, soils, and a slew of other seemingly unrelated subjects.

Once I was out in the real world, the reason for the broad education became apparent. The soils and the rocks support the plant and animal life. Building livetraps, rainfall collectors, and other biologists' tools requires knowledge of physics. Hunting licenses, fishing tackle sales, and fur sales bring economics into play. We need statistics to determine hunting quotas and interpret other data we collect. And, of course, there is that famous cliché often quoted by wildlife biologists, "Managing wildlife is really about managing people." I wish I had taken a psychology class.

In addition to the occupation's physical and mental demands, the faculty impressed upon us students that, as wildlife biologists, "You'll never get rich." Those who had enrolled with visions of a romantic career in the wilderness soon found their dreams extinguished. They dropped out, one by one, until only a few die-hards remained.

The survivors were delivered into a life of grueling physical labor, shaky employment prospects, and general uncertainty about the future. The post-Earth Day environmental movement, the need for which was cemented in our own minds, was not well established in the outside world.

What would I have done if wildlife did not need saving? Instead of becoming a biologist, would I instead have become an outdoor-clothing designer, a jockey, a veterinarian? I considered each of these occupations once upon a time. However, if the environment were healthy and thriving, I'd want to spend even more time immersed in it. I would still hug trees, extol their beauty in prose, and eat dirt-specked victuals around a campfire. As the late John Denver sang, "I know he'd be a poorer man if he never saw an eagle fly." It is the soaring eagles, the spreading chestnut trees, and the bubbling mountain springs that make us rich.

Although other biologists have worked harder, suffered more, and accomplished more than I have, I feel the urge to tell my stories. The best piece of advice I ever received as a graduate student was, "Your research isn't finished until you publish it." Information is worthless if no one knows about it.

I tell these tales from the field to pass along my knowledge. Academic treatises are not the only ways to share facts and philosophies. I had forgotten yet another way, the oldest way, until a tiny tot in the Arctic reminded me.

Eski was four years old. He lived with his grandparents in a small, nondescript, government-built house in Noorvik, Alaska, a community of Inupiats enduring a mostly subsistence lifestyle. I was a guest in Eski's house, as there were no guest lodgings in the village and no roads leading elsewhere.

One day, while his family was out of the house, I stayed home alone with Eski. "Eski, do you want me to read you a story?" I inquired.

"Sure!" he replied with a cheerful smile.

"Then go find me a book to read," I instructed.

Off he went to a bedroom, returning nonchalantly to the living room several minutes later, empty-handed. Confused, I repeated, "Do you want me to read you a story?" Again, he nodded brightly. Again, I instructed, "Then go find a book."

Once more, he disappeared into the back of the house, returning minutes later, still empty-handed. I sighed and realized I would have to find a book myself. Rummaging around the house, I, too, surrendered empty-handed. *What a shame*, I thought. *These people are so poor or so far from civilization that they have no books for their children.*

Then it hit me. It wasn't poverty or isolation that kept this house devoid of children's literature. In this culture, stories came from people, not paper. Eski didn't understand what I was asking.

Sheepishly, I tried a different path. "Come sit with me, Eski. Let me tell you a story." The little boy jumped gleefully onto my lap.

If I were with you now, I'd tell you these stories myself. But I am not. So, reader, sit back and let me tell you stories of bobcats and wood storks and alligators and springs, and why we need them all.

Author's note: The opinions and views in this book are the opinions of the author only, unless expressly stated otherwise.

Contents

Prologue. Green Sheep of the Family

Born into the concrete forests of New York City, raised in a nearby bedroom community in New Jersey, I never had a chance to know Nature as a child. In suburbia, milk came from bottles that appeared mysteriously in a silvery, insulated box outside the front door in the still of the dawn. Meat came from the nice man at the corner butcher shop. Water flowed from the faucet in the sink. I do admit, however, that I knew that lettuce, radishes, and tomatoes came from the ground, because my father grew them in our backyard.

The suburban life fit me like a hat on a dog. I played outside whenever I could—at a neighborhood playground, in our yard, or in the vacant lot across the street. In grade school, I read every book I could find in my school and town libraries about Nature and the outdoors. I soaked up wild animal stories like a hungry sea sponge. I learned how rainbows form when the sunlight reflects off water droplets and how snowflakes grow as six-sided crystals. I learned how mudpots and geysers burble up from underground thermal zones in Yellowstone National Park. I believed it all, until I read about springs—how the water emerges from the ground sparkling clean and ready to drink. Ridiculous! How could water that comes from the ground be clean?

In the summer of my sixteenth year, my parents rented a Winnebago motorhome and took my brother, Steve, and me on a weeklong trip to Shenandoah National Park in Virginia. My sister, Sharon, stayed home. She was in college and had a summer job. Instead, my parents allowed me to bring a friend. I chose my pal Marcy.

Shenandoah National Park is a long, narrow strip that spans the crest of the Blue Ridge Mountains, part of the Appalachian Mountain Range that stretches from Maine to Georgia. The Appalachians are so ancient that some rocks are more than a billion years old. Although the once Rockies-sized peaks have eroded over the eons to large hills, the scenery is spectacular from Skyline Drive, the 105-mile winding road that

1

runs the crest of the park. The highest point on the road is 3,680 feet, while the peaks rise above to barely more than 4,000 feet.

The moisture-laden ground gushes forth rivers, streams, and waterfalls. Lush foliage and abundant wildlife further define the park. Nearly one hundred species of trees—a staggering diversity—grace the slopes of the park.

Our first stop in the park was at Big Meadows Campground. Always bucking the establishment, Marcy and I decided we didn't want to sleep in the cramped motorhome's bunks. I had borrowed an old canvas, A-frame Boy Scout tent, and we pitched it next to the Winnebago at the campsite. It was the closest I could come to real camping, which I had craved but never experienced.

Marcy was adventurous company. We spent many hours together on any given weekend. Once when we were bored, I told her about a game—Scissors Cut Paper—that I had read about in a James Bond book. The game's ancient origins are ambiguous, but suffice it to say, I know why it survived in various forms, in various cultures around the world, for possibly two thousand years.[1] After our initial awkwardness, we became adept and addicted. We played so fast and frenetically that we lost track of time. Throw after throw—ten or more times in a row—we would have a tie. We would repeat that scenario over and over again. Despite our blinding pace, it could take five minutes for one person to reach ten points. The amazing discovery was how we learned to think so alike. Too bad our hair was so opposite. I always envied her waist-length tresses.

The day we arrived at Shenandoah National Park, Marcy and I strolled to the nearby ranger station to inquire about hiking trails. We told the ranger that we wanted to hike a few miles, but not too far. He rattled off some trail names, each one accompanied by a verbal tour-book description. For Lewis Spring Falls, he recited, "That's where the water comes out of the ground like a spring on the side of the mountain and flows downhill into a waterfall."

My ears perked up. "What?" I exclaimed. "The water comes right out of the ground? A spring? Can you *drink* it?"

"Sure, you can drink it," replied the ranger. "It's really clean."

"Marcy, we have to go there!" I blurted. "I have to see this spring." Marcy quickly agreed. We memorized the directions to the trailhead, informed my parents, and off we went.

In 1971, people rarely carried water for a short hike. In the humid East, a thirsty hiker could imbibe at streams and springs, which were plentiful and generally potable. For a long outing, a hiker would bring a canteen filled with tap water. I had probably never seen bottled drinking water in personal sizes then. Bottled water was mostly store-brand distilled gallons used for clothes irons and car batteries.

Virginia pines, eastern hemlocks, and various oaks and hickories delightfully shaded much of the two-mile trail. The sun burned down through the canopy's openings. Only days past the summer solstice, the rays were intense.

As we approached the sign announcing Lewis Spring Falls, I suddenly forgot about the steep, rocky trail we had just labored along and the thirst I had acquired. Before me, partially illuminated by the scattered rays of sunlight that survived the battle through the dense foliage, lay the most tranquil scene I had ever witnessed. Every object seemed serene. The waterfall tumbled gaily—not roaring or crashing. Rhododendron flowers graced my view. Leaves couldn't manage a whisper in the dormant wind. The fragrance of the pine and hemlock needles nearly lulled me into a trance.

But it was the gurgling of the water that really captured my attention. I stared at the rocks, expecting to see a camouflaged drainpipe. Eventually I saw it for what it was. The water emerged mysteriously from the rocks on the mountainside and flowed downhill. In some places, it lay still in crystal-clear pools, but mostly it found a way over and around the rocks where it met its fate at the edge of the cliff. From there it disappeared again, invisible under the thick mantle of trees below. The water looked so inviting that I shucked my shoes and waded in. What a relief to feel the cool liquid numb my feet! Several times the mossy rocks loosened my footing and I landed, startled but unharmed, on my rear end.

Mesmerized by the flowing water, I almost forgot why I came—to see if it was true that the water was so clean you could drink right from the ground. I cupped my hands and dipped them in a still pool. Hesitantly, I sipped. Utter refreshment! I sipped again and again. A chill gripped me. *It's true,* I realized. *What I read about springs is true!*

Lewis Spring Falls is just one of thousands of springs across the country. Left in a natural, uncontaminated condition, spring water is nearly always pure enough to drink. Indeed, it is the ground that filters out pollutants.

Much of the Earth's fresh water is stored underground in aquifers, which are layers of soft, porous rock (such as limestone or sandstone) that may span several states. Some springs are artesian, meaning the water gushes upwards from an aquifer with great force because of the naturally high water pressure. However, other springs are seeps, like Lewis Spring, where the water oozes gently down hillsides assisted by gravity from higher elevations.

Small, local springs have provided exceptionally clean drinking water to communities around the world for thousands of years. From Alaska to Florida, from Hawaii to Maine, every state—even the District of Columbia—has springs. The names of cities reflect their presence: Palm Springs (California), Miami Springs (Florida), Colorado Springs (Colorado), Saratoga Springs (New York), Berkeley Springs (West Virginia), Chena Hot Springs (Alaska), and so on. Even the desert state of Nevada has oases where water surges up from the aquifer into glassy pools. These surface waters are isolated from other water systems, so each one may have its own species of fish that is found nowhere else. The springs are now shrinking and the pools are drying as water is drawn from the aquifer to slake the thirst of Las Vegas, Reno, and other cities. Many of these spring fish are now endangered.

In the early 1900s, people started tampering with the aquifers on a major scale by pumping out more water than could be replaced by rainfall, by letting pollutants leach through the ground to contaminate them, pumping waste material underground, or by paving the ground and blocking the downward flow of water. Most of the springs in the United States have succumbed to one of these fates—polluted, diminished, or dry. I didn't know any of this that day at Lewis Spring Falls.

While I was coming of age in the 1960s, I had heard all the most dramatic water and air pollution stories. I had seen images of Ohio's flaming Cuyahoga River that had oil slicks so broad that the water's surface caught fire. Every time my family drove across the Raritan River Bridge in northern New Jersey, I saw for myself the oil refinery smokestacks spewing black clouds. There were no fish or clams or birds left at our beaches in Monmouth County—indeed, not much natural life at all. The Clean Water Act was still six years down the trail.

It did not hit me until that minute at Lewis Spring Falls, when I breathed clean air and tasted truly clean water, what I had not comprehended before—the world the way it is supposed to be. Nature is our provider.

I gulped some more. I turned to Marcy and whispered reverently, "Everyone should have water like this."

With that magic drink, I quenched more than just my thirst. Thus began my lifelong pledge to take care of the Earth's resources.

I wanted to sit on a rock by that waterfall forever. Of course, I couldn't, but as Marcy and I walked away from the falls, the water kept tugging me back. The soft carpet of moss under my bare feet, the gentle tumbling of the water, the musical chattering of the birds, and the refreshing shade all made me feel as though no human had ever been there before me. It was my first real sensation of peace of mind.

Twenty-one years later, an exhausted and emotionally battered victim of Hurricane Andrew, I climbed into my car in Homestead, Florida, and headed north on Interstate 95. I was seeking solace and strength somewhere, and the only place I was sure I could find it was a certain waterfall in Shenandoah National Park that I had visited once before. I remembered just where it was. I drove all day and into the night until I got to Big Meadows Campground.

The next morning, I hiked down the trail and arrived at the place where the water came out of the ground like a spring on the side of the mountain and flowed downhill into a waterfall. As I reached down to scoop up the magic water, my eyes fell on a sign that wasn't there two decades earlier: "Danger—Do not drink the water. May be contaminated." But Mother Nature was my friend. I drank anyway.

Chapter 1.

The First Haunted House on the Right

To three good friends who were naturalists and correspondingly broke, the advertisement offering to rent a seventeen-room house on more than ninety acres with a barn and woods for two hundred dollars a month was magnetic. Even in 1978, when I was just out of college, that was a bargain. Who wouldn't want to live in a mansion for a pittance? As we soon learned, the gargantuan dwelling on South Road in the quaint, rural town of Hampden in the Connecticut River Valley of Massachusetts had been vacant for months (or maybe years) because nobody wanted to live there.

Nevertheless, as soon as Eileen Fielding, Rick Tuttle, and I saw the house, we couldn't wait to move in. I could even pedal my bicycle the mile to work. Little did we know the treats and tribulations that were in store for us.

As the animal care supervisor at Laughing Brook Wildlife Sanctuary, I was responsible for the care of a wide array of native critters, large and small, most of which were either permanently injured or human dependent. Human-dependent ones were usually hand-raised and unschooled in the ways of the wild. There were some exceptions to our philosophy of keeping only animals that couldn't survive on their own. These were mostly reptiles and amphibians that we retained for educational programs, since the goal of our nature center was environmental education. The sanctuary was owned and operated by the Massachusetts Audubon Society. Laughing Brook was the local field trip destination for schools in the surrounding towns. It put Hampden on the map.

All of our resident critters lived in displays that were viewable by visitors. A red fox named Tripod (missing a leg), coyotes named Shawnee and Old Man, bobcats named Priscilla and Yowler, several white-tailed deer, a permanently "decommissioned" striped skunk, owls, snakes, flying squirrels, turtles, bobwhite quails, and many other types of animals resided in our pens. Thornton W. Burgess, internationally famed author of children's nature stories, wrote a story for almost every animal that Laughing Brook later housed.

Thornton Burgess was born in 1874 on Cape Cod. From 1924 to his death in 1965, he lived in the house on the property that eventually became Laughing Brook Wildlife Sanctuary. The building, known locally as the Storyteller's House, was built in the 1780s. Many of Burgess's story ideas came from wild animals he saw in his yard.

Burgess wrote such books as *The Adventures of Peter Cottontail, Old Mother West Wind, The Adventures of Old Man Coyote,* and *Little Stories for Bedtime.* He penned 170 books, created the Radio Nature League that filled the airwaves for twelve years, and published 15,000 stories across 44 years that were syndicated in 200 newspapers. Thornton Burgess was the father of environmental education, and his legacy has been preserved at the "Storyteller's House," which is on the National Register of Historic Landmarks.

Like Laughing Brook, our rented house on South Road was steeped in history. The Smith family, whose current generation lived in eastern Massachusetts, had owned the house since it was built in 1735. It was one of the oldest in Hampden, still under the original deed from the King of England in the 1600s, so we were told. Along with the magnificent mansion, the modern Smiths inherited massive maintenance bills. No one of average means, which they were, could afford the burden. So down the path of dilapidation the once stately residence lapsed. Desperate to entice anyone to move in, they had reduced the rent.

And no one but us would want to live in that crumbling castle. No part of the venerable house had escaped the ravages of time and neglect. It was foreboding and spooky. How many decades had the wooden siding hung unpainted? Shutters dangled from missing hinges. Porch columns were rotting. So was the roof. On the northern side of the house, rain had leaked from the roof into an upstairs bedroom, then through the floor, and into the ballroom below. Because of the rot holes in the bedroom's floor and ceiling, I called it "The Holey Room" or sometimes "The Chapel."

Our "haunted house" on South Road in Hampden, Massachusetts, has room for everyone, including an owl (circa 1978).

I had never cared a whit about architecture until I moved into that house. So intriguing was the amalgamation of styles that I had to learn more. The original structure was a saltbox, a typical style in early New England. The front roof was shorter than the rear, and the rear sloped steeply, almost to the ground. In 1868, the house was turned ninety degrees to face south, with the ridgepole running east–west. How they split a house in two and swung it around I do not know. A side section (the ell) was moved to the rear, and a new section was added to the middle at that time.

We could tell by the architecture in which era different parts of the house were built. The oldest part (from the 1700s) had low ceilings and small windows. Taller rooms were added in the 1800s with nearly floor-to-ceiling Victorian windows. The rooms on the second floor were on three different levels, so you would have to step up or down between rooms, because the ceilings on the first floor were of different heights.

The foundation was constructed of flat rocks with no mortar to bind them, as was typical of the eighteenth century. A mason had fitted them together meticulously with stonewall-building skill that has nearly vanished in modern times. The basement floor was dirt with a dugout hole on one side, about two feet wide by three feet long. It was probably a sump hole, but a trio of mirthful naturalists could only refer to it as a "baby grave."

I had never dwelt much on history either, until I learned that our house on South Road was once a station on the Underground Railroad. In 1780, Massachusetts freed its slaves. However, Connecticut, a mere mile south of our house, did not. Slaves hid in the attic until their masters stopped looking for them. At one point, a struggle ensued over two slaves when their owners came after them. One slave escaped, but the other was bound and carried away.[2]

I can no longer remember what all of the seventeen rooms were. They included a kitchen, dining room, sitting room, walk-in pantry, and at least seven bedrooms. A ballroom-style living room encompassed much of the first floor, so large that it required columns to support the ceiling. Next to the ballroom was one of two staircases in the house—a grand curving staircase, the kind I had only seen in glamorous Hollywood movies. From the base of the stairs, the carved wooden banister arced gracefully upwards and out of sight.

What made Eileen, Rick, and me unconventional to our neighbors also made us a congruous team. Eileen was the staff naturalist at The Children's Museum in West Hartford, Connecticut. Rick worked at the Springfield Science Museum in nearby Springfield. He was my predecessor as the animal care specialist and naturalist at Laughing Brook and knew the captive animals better than anyone when I arrived.

Between Eileen's wildlife studies at the University of Massachusetts, her work at The Children's Museum, and volunteering at Laughing Brook, she was always bringing some needy creature home for tending. Eileen brought an unbridled sense of wit and humor to the house. Her ability to out-pun anyone was legendary. Once, while locked in verbal battle with a notorious pun foe, the volley of animal puns poured forth at lightning speed. After an unusually pensive pause by her adversary, Eileen shot back with, "Vicuña think of one faster?"

Rick chose a quiet bedroom in the isolated back-center of the house. Eileen selected a front corner room, directly above the sitting room. She was the visionary. That turned out to be the warmest bedroom in the winter, once we added a wood stove in the sitting room.

I chose a small room in the ell, between the main house and the two-story barn. The barn was attached to the house on both levels. My room had a door leading directly into the second

9

floor of the barn. How many houses do you know of that have a barn attached to a bedroom?

If the rent was a bargain, the central heating system certainly nullified it. You could easily believe that the oil furnace came with the original deed from the King of England, too, along with the leaky steam pipes. The monthly oil bills equaled half a month's rent. That was just to heat part of the house, because we closed off more than half each winter. Even then, it was barely enough to keep the water pipes from freezing. Rick once found a glass of water on his nightstand had frozen.

Much to Eileen's joy, we bought the wood stove. The heat rose directly up through the vent in her floor. However, the stove did nothing to warm my room. In winter, my thermometer often read 45 degrees. Many full nights of sleep eluded me because I couldn't warm the bed. My loathing of cold sheets was so intense I felt like a child defying bedtime, minus the kicking and screaming. Then Rick, always a thoughtful friend, gave me one very precious present—an electric blanket. Magically, slumber time lost its dread.

No sooner had we unpacked our moving boxes into the decaying mansion when strange things began to happen. As naturalists, you would think we would treat every unusual occurrence with scientific scrutiny. We tried. Eventually, we couldn't explain the cool pockets of air on sizzling summer days or the thunderlike rumblings we heard inside the house on cloudless days. Surely the foundation had settled after 250 years!

Joe Choiniere, Laughing Brook's property manager, was the only outsider who experienced the phenomena. Joe came to take care of my dog, Trapper, the only time all of us tenants were away simultaneously. Joe unlocked the side door, opened it, and heard human footsteps upstairs in the supposedly empty house. My normally sane dog was barking incessantly at the second floor from the base of the staircase, ignoring his pal who had come to feed him and walk him outside.

Wondering if one of us had returned home early, Joe called toward the footsteps, "Su? Eileen? Rick?" No one answered. He went upstairs and found no evidence of anyone there. Nothing was disturbed. Although puzzled, Joe went about his task uneventfully.

Those anomalies, combined with the history of violence when the slave owners found their missing slaves there, led us to

10

believe there are other types of creatures on this Earth that we humans cannot see. One thing we knew in our bones—whatever may have been there never tried to hurt us. It just went about its business, occasionally creaking and groaning in the process.

Giving directions to our house was easy. All we needed to say was, "Go up South Road to the first haunted house on the right." Our guests always found us. All that was missing from the scene was the proverbial hoot owl.

Neither the mansion's condition nor its possible ethereal occupants diminished its charm to us. To me as a wildlife rehabilitator, the bedroom-to-barn access was all the charm I needed. I could keep an eye on my patients day or night without going outside. And, oh, the spare rooms for hospital wards were quite a perquisite. So, too, were the ninety wooded acres where Eileen, Rick, and I could roam, complete with hiking trails and streams—a naturalist's paradise.

We accommodated a constant parade of wild things throughout the house. My job, which included running a large wildlife rehabilitation program, brought me in contact with dozens of injured animals that needed more recuperation room than the nature center could provide. Laughing Brook Audubon Sanctuary had a few vacant outdoor cages and some small indoor ones, but some of the animals needed large indoor areas in which to convalesce. Eileen brought needy animals from the Children's Museum, and even Rick came home with some ailing creatures from the Science Museum.

One autumn during bird-hunting season, two short-eared owls, both with injured wings, were delivered separately by Good Samaritans to Laughing Brook. Our local veterinarian, Dr. Donald Crouser, who kindly treated our wild creatures pro bono, confirmed that they had been shot. I can only guess that some dolts mistook them for ruffed grouse, which were legal game birds. The owls, like all birds of prey, most certainly were not legal game. However, unlike most other owls, short-eared owls frequently hunt during the day and in open fields and marshes, where their favorite prey (mice) can be found. Farmers have a great friend in the short-eared owl.

Don Crouser lived in Hampden, a short hop from Laughing Brook. He cherished his wild neighbors as much as the domestic pets he treated. He appreciated the environmental education programs we created for the public. Don and his

11

veterinary partners found many challenges in the treatment of wildlife as they tried to outwit the maladies facing our injured critters.

Don treated both of the short-eared owls and prognosed that they would be able to fly again in a few months. Until then, he prescribed a place to recover that was protected from the elements. One of our spare rooms was perfect. It was unfurnished, so Eileen, Rick, and I lined the floor with newspaper, dragged in some branches for perching, and *voilà*, we had an avian infirmary. When the birds recovered, I released them near where they had been found.

Many birds of prey (also known as raptors) came through our rehabilitation center door. I was grateful to have the advice and assistance of a local master falconer, Dick Lucius. Falconry is an ancient form of hunting, originally reserved for royalty. Typically, a falconer removes one chick from the nest of a falcon, raises it, and trains it to hunt for rabbits, squirrels, birds, and other table fare, and bring the prey intact back to the falconer. Subtracting one baby bird from a nest of two to four chicks is not necessarily harmful to the population as a whole. Often, not all the chicks in a nest survive, so reducing the brood by one may mean the remaining chicks have more food to share, which increases their chances of surviving. The trained birds are flown when they are hungry, so they are motivated to hunt. The falconer rewards them with foods that people shun, such as mice. The sport is legal in all states (except Hawaii) with state and federal permits and under careful government restrictions.

Because of the decline of peregrine falcons in this country (from DDT and other pesticides, shooting of birds, lead poisoning, and other causes), falconers seeking birds to train had to switch to more common raptors, such as red-tailed hawks. The term "falconry" now refers to the sport itself, since other types of raptors besides falcons are commonly used. Possession of all birds of prey, including red-tailed hawks, is strictly regulated under the Migratory Bird Treaty Act.

Red-tails are large hawks that have remained relatively common across North America. They are the largest commonly seen hawks in western Massachusetts. Red-tails sometimes hunt by soaring flights and sometimes by perching in a tree and watching motionlessly for unsuspecting small mammals. Their rusty-colored tails make them easy to identify. Their piercing cry is the sound most often dubbed into movies and television shows when a bald eagle is pictured. Eagle cries are wimpy chirps compared to the hair-raising scream of the red-tail. It is no surprise that red-tailed hawks are popular for falconry.

Falconry with peregrines is making a slow comeback since the species has recovered and was removed from the Endangered Species List in 1999. Federal oversight of peregrine falconry is extremely tight to ensure that the species does not end up as an endangered species again. Since 2004, the U.S. Fish and Wildlife Service has allowed falconers with permits to remove wild peregrines from their nests for use in falconry.

There are three categories of falconry licenses in the United States: Apprentice, General, and Master classes. Dick had achieved the highest rank of master falconer after the required seven years of training and inspection of his husbandry facilities.

Over the years, Dick housed and trained red-tailed hawks, prairie falcons, and kestrels (the smallest falcons). He had all the necessary permits and kept his birds in excellent health. I frequently plied him with questions when I had an injured raptor, and he patiently answered them. He also housed some of our recuperating birds if my infirmary was full. He would expend any effort to help a bird of prey.

Dick blazed the way for using permanently injured raptors for education in Massachusetts, including at Laughing Brook. Many a child thrilled to a visit by Dick, with one of his graceful avian wards perched on his arm. Some of his hawks and falcons eventually became accustomed to people and allowed the audience to stroke them gently.

Dick and I knew the bird laws and followed them precisely, which is why I was so startled when he called me one day and questioned accusingly, "How could you do that? How could you give a red-tail to a volunteer? I can't believe you would do that!"

Puzzled, I responded, "What? I never gave any bird to a volunteer."

"Yes, you did. You gave a red-tail to John Smith [not his real name], one of your volunteers. He told me you gave it to him. He called me and asked me questions about taking care of a red-tail."

"Well, I don't know what you're talking about. If I can't take care of an injured raptor, I give it to you. You know that."

Dick was so upset that it took me a few minutes to convince him that I was telling the truth. "If you give me some details," I suggested, "I can get to the bottom of this. Did John say why I supposedly gave it to him? Was it hurt? When was it?"

Dick knew the approximate date that John obtained the bird, so I started investigating at Laughing Brook. First, I checked the accession forms for the week in question. These forms were detailed records of every animal that we acquired, including contact information of the person who brought the animal in, how we treated it, and what eventually happened to it. We didn't receive many red-tails. Injured raptors usually elude helpful humans.

Our records showed that, indeed, an injured red-tailed hawk had been brought in several weeks earlier while I was on vacation. Under "Outcome," the accession form said "escaped."

I queried Joe Choiniere, the property manager and occasionally my dog-walker. Joe was a versatile guy with an ardent love of wildlife. With the help of our eager and skillful volunteers, he kept the nature center in tiptop shape on my days off.

Joe recalled the time a few weeks earlier when someone had delivered the red-tailed hawk to the nature center. Joe had wanted to send it to Dr. Crouser's veterinary clinic in Springfield, about ten miles away. Since Joe had to remain on duty at the sanctuary, he appealed for a volunteer to drive the hawk there. Many of our volunteers were teens under the driving age, but a new recruit was a few years older. John Smith had a car and eagerly offered to transport the patient. Joe tucked the bird in a carrying case, and John drove it to the clinic.

According to Joe, John said the bird became fidgety on the drive back to Laughing Brook from the clinic, and he stopped to fix its bandage. The bird escaped, and John returned with an empty carrying case. John had not been back to the nature center since.

My phone call to Dr. Crouser confirmed that he did treat the bird. He had recommended a quiet place under our care for a few weeks and felt confident the hawk would recover. He sent it back to Laughing Brook with John. I added the known facts together and concluded that John had stolen the bird.

The steps seemed to fit. After the veterinarian confirmed the bird would recover, I surmised that John drove a few miles out of his way to drop the bird off at his house. He then returned with a believable story. No one would have ever known, except for his one mistake—he did not know Dick Lucius well enough.

I explained what happened to the sanctuary director, Sally (not her real name), and advised, "Taking a hawk without a permit is a federal offense under the Migratory Bird Treaty Act. We should report this to a U.S. Fish and Wildlife Service agent and let the feds handle it."

Sally disagreed. "We don't know for sure what happened. Let's take care of it quietly ourselves, so the community won't hear about it."

My glower went unsatisfied. We had done nothing wrong. We had the required permits. Why not at least report it to a federal agent?

Sally's reason was unclear to me, but I knew she was determined to smooth ruffled feathers with the community. She had assumed the directorship from a man who rubbed many people the wrong way, except corporate donors. Patching up the staff's bruised spirits was an early goal of hers. By treating us as family, she did make progress. Every month at our staff meetings, Sally asked each of us to share some good news. While we all grumbled about doing it, I privately appreciated the sanctioned opportunity to crow. Sally's unorthodox way of dealing with the hawk did not satisfy any secret needs of mine, however.

Perhaps Sally felt the loss of the hawk would be perceived by the community as our carelessness, and she was trying to shield us from embarrassment. She told me simply, "I want you to get the hawk back yourself." I had to comply.

As a petite woman, I wasn't thrilled to waltz over to the house of a large-bodied male whom I suspected of wrongdoing, and whom I barely knew, and ask, "Would you please give me that red-tailed hawk back?"

I needed a plan. I knew that John lived with his mother in a neighboring town. I also knew that he had a job somewhere, so I phoned his house when I thought he wouldn't be home. His mother answered.

"Hello, Mrs. Smith," I said, summoning my sweetest debutante voice. "I know John from high school. One of our friends said he just got a big bird, some kind of hawk that was hurt, and he's taking care of it. Is it true? Oh, I just love birds! Do you think he'd let me see it?"

"Yes, he got that big bird. It's in the backyard," she answered.

"Oh, that's so exciting! I never saw a big bird like that close-up," I exclaimed. "Maybe I'll call him when he gets home. When will that be?"

"He'll be home around 4:15. I'm sure he'll let you see it."

Bingo! The bird was there, and John was not. Even better, I could probably get permission to take it from John's mother. I persuaded one of my trusted male volunteers to shadow me. Although just a teen, he was heftier than I. I had myself a bodyguard.

I don't remember who that helpful lad was, so I'll call him Jerry. All Jerry had to do was look tough. That sounds easy, but for a slim, perpetually smiling do-gooder, it was cause for uncomfortable squirming.

Jerry and I drove to the Smiths' house and introduced ourselves truthfully to John's mother, who fortunately was home alone. I didn't allude to any wrongdoing by John nor did I ask questions.

"We need to bring John's hawk back to Laughing Brook to tend to its injury," I explained.

"Why, of course," Mrs. Smith readily agreed. "Come right this way. I'll show you where it is." Whew! She didn't recognize my now-professional voice from my earlier sophomoric call. She showed us to the flight cage in the backyard and allowed us to take the bird without a fuss. The flight cage had not been hastily built. I wondered if John had set himself up as a volunteer for just such an opportunity.

Thankfully, the clandestine mission was uneventful, and my impromptu, peaceable bodyguard breathed a sigh of relief. We never heard from John again, and I redeemed myself in the eyes of one very conscientious master falconer.

I still feel that we should have reported John's miscarriage of justice to the authorities. If nothing else, he possessed the hawk without a permit. Sometimes when I hear about a big wildlife smuggling ring, I wonder if John is among the guilty, lured to a life of animal thievery because we did not even slap his wrist. On the other hand, perhaps he realized the close call he'd had, and, grateful for the kindness of conservationists, become a staunch advocate for conservation.

Our memorable dramas arose mostly from the ailing wild things that kindly people delivered to our nature center door. Rarely, a dilemma ensued with a longtime animal resident of Laughing Brook. Among our live exhibits were several not-so-tame predators, including bobcats and coyotes, that could seriously traumatize a careless caretaker. I had to take extra precautions with them.

Most of our live-exhibit animals were native to western Massachusetts. The coyotes were an exception. Prior to the 1800s, all lands east of the Mississippi River were coyoteless. Manmade bridges across the rivers facilitated their spread gradually eastward, fueled by easy food sources, such as open landfills, roadkills, and the perfect setup—the chicken coop. The wild canids are now found throughout the eastern states.

Shawnee, a female coyote, and Old Man, a male named for a Thornton Burgess character, were housed in attached but separate outdoor pens. Both had been hand-raised. They were accustomed to people, though not tame, and certainly not wild enough to survive on their own.

Shawnee had been sent to us from a zoo in California around 1976, before my time. The zoo folks needed to find a home for her, and they heard we already had a lone male. The match made sense—a companion for Old Man. However, the two got along more like old divorcees and had to be kept separated. The other reason Laughing Brook accepted Shawnee was that the zoo implied that she could be handled on a leash and used for educational programs. She proved the zoo staff wrong immediately upon arrival.

Old Man must have been abused with a stick before he came to us. When I started work there, Rick told me, "Always carry something resembling a stick when you enter the cage. You'll never have to use it, but I guarantee, if you don't have it with you, you'll get bitten," he counseled. He was right on both counts. The only time I forgot my prop (the hoe we used to scoop up the droppings), Old Man nipped me on my calf and broke the skin. I didn't fret because our coyotes were vaccinated for rabies every year.

Shawnee walked the line between passive and friendly, but was really neither—just wary. She retreated to a corner when someone entered her pen to clean it, change the water, or leave the food dish.

We fed the coyotes commercial dog kibble in a dish every other day and dead chicks or lab mice in between. On chick or mouse day, any one of the volunteers could toss the fluffy morsels safely through the bars. On dish day, someone had to open each pen door and place a dish inside, a task I allowed only certain volunteers to do.

The volunteers were as sacred to the operation of the nature center and rehabilitation center as if they were staff. That went triple for me. My job was the equivalent of three nearly full-time ones: maintaining the nature center exhibits and live animals, running the wildlife rehabilitation center, and presenting nature programs at Laughing Brook and elsewhere for schools, community groups, scouts, and so on.

The nature programs were never a dull chore. While you are driving down a snowy road on the way to a school program (the kids are waiting!) is not the time to realize that the carrying case you put the raccoon in was too flimsy, and he is now climbing from the back seat of the car onto your lap. Pull over, put him back in the case, cross your fingers, and keep driving. Repeat as needed. On the way home, stick the raccoon in the case in the trunk and hope the darkness keeps him quiet. Open the trunk at Laughing Brook and find the raccoon has shed the bounds of the case again and has gotten his head stuck in the hole that leads to the back seat. Pull him out gently and apologize to him for your stupidity.

Hectic schedules have a way of creating bizarre behavior out of necessity. For example, take the television shows on which I appeared for three years. Every week in alternating months, I was a guest on *Morningtown*, a Springfield, Massachusetts, children's educational show. I brought live animals, plants, taxidermy-stuffed animals, or other objects of Nature to extol their virtues to the audience. When we taped the shows, I could tape four in one day. This process was more efficient, but it certainly tested my prediction skills for what was going to happen later that month. If a show was scheduled to air around the first day of spring, I always did a "signs of spring" segment. I force-bloomed flowers that would take another month to open naturally. This I did by cutting forsythia and pussy willow twigs and setting them in a vase indoors. But, how could I chirp, "Spring is here!" if the snow was piling up in a freak March blizzard? The viewers didn't know it was taped. I would look like a blind fool.

Thus, I found it easier to do the shows live. I was always right about the weather. The drawback was that I had to arrive at the television station by "lights, camera, action" time, or else. . . .

Swinging that timing was tricky. During the school year, I rarely had weekday volunteer help, so I had a formidable schedule. My first priorities were the animals, which meant the morning ritual of cleaning the cages, indoors and out. This didn't use my college education in any manner. I freshened the outdoor pens of the coyotes, foxes, raccoons, porcupines, bobcats, and so on by scooping the droppings into a bucket with a hoe. My normal attire for this task was old clothing and work boots. On television filming days, I had no time to change my clothes. Nevertheless, I couldn't appear on television in work clothes or clean cages in dress clothes.

Enter the blessed compromise. I went to work in jeans and work boots. From the waist up, I wore a prim-and-proper blouse and blazer, protected by an overcoat or oversized shirt. My long hair was swept up in a natty bun and my cosmetics already applied. Make-up was a special event for television only, since the camera lights further washed out my bland facial features.

After scraping up the droppings, I hastened to the television station, dashed into the studio, cast off my overcoat in a smooth move, and sauntered casually behind the table-of-perfect-height, where the cameras saw only my upper torso and head. All my props, live and otherwise, were small enough to set on the table.

Mary Turley, the show's hostess, skillfully ignored the aroma emanating from my dung-filled lug soles. Fortunately, television affects only two senses for the viewers, and smell is not one of them.

On days when I had help, the volunteers would prepare the animals' food and distribute it to the pens. Volunteers who were not allowed in the coyote pen on dish day would leave the dishes on the side of the trail near the pen, out of paw-reach of the occupants, and then tell me the dishes were there. I would dash out when I had a free minute, put the dishes in each pen, and go back to whatever I was doing. This worked well, except once.

I must have been unusually bustling one day. Beth, a conscientious teen, informed me that she had set the coyotes' dishes by the pens. I kept trying to find a minute to dash out and set them in the cages and kept postponing it. Eventually, I just plumb forgot.

Around three o'clock the next morning, the phone rang at our house. The Hampden police dispatcher was calling for me.

"One of our officers saw a coyote on Main Street and he thinks it's from Laughing Brook," she explained to me.

Wild coyotes were sprawling into western Massachusetts, but they were rarely seen in the Connecticut River Valley. Many people in this small, rural town knew that the sanctuary housed coyotes. My heart skipped a beat. Could the officer be right?

Shawnee, the coyote, takes a nap at
Laughing Brook Wildlife Sanctuary.

"I'll go check it out right now!" I promised the dispatcher.

Roused awake by gut-wrenching dread, I arrived at the sanctuary minutes later and sprinted down the dark trail with a flashlight to the coyotes' pen. Oh, horror—Shawnee's side was empty! I gasped when I saw the food dish, licked clean, outside the pen, and it suddenly registered that it was my fault. The tantalizing food must have driven her crazy. In her fervor to reach it, she had dug under and out from the two-foot-deep underground fence specially installed in the pens of the digging animals.

Shawnee lacked experience with cars and strangers. She did know that chickens were tasty. In bucolic Hampden, many people raised them—including me. But unlike me, many people also kept rifles and shotguns, generally only fired during the hunting season. I shuddered to think of the damage she or the hen owners could do. I had to get her back safely!

At dawn, Joe helped me repair Shawnee's pen. Then I borrowed the Humane Society's largest dog trap. I set it up in her pen, baited it with a dead chicken, and left the pen door open. I hoped she would find her way home.

Next, I called Don Crouser for advice on tranquilizers. We kept a tranquilizer gun at the sanctuary for wildlife emergencies. I had practiced shooting it with empty darts but had never used it in earnest. I filled several darts for the tranquilizer gun; the extras were in case I missed. From a closet, I retrieved the dog-catching pole—a six-foot pole with a retractable noose at the end for catching dogs and cats safely around the body. All day I walked around the sanctuary, lugging the pole and the dart gun, while trying to carry on with my normal chores, just in case Shawnee sauntered back on her own. The other animals still needed their care.

Reports filtered in during the day from the locals. Was it Shawnee or a stray German shepherd? The police and I would check each report, but we would arrive too late to see the canids. No chickens disappeared, however, and no guns were fired. I grilled each witness if the canid ran with its tail out or down. Coyotes run with their tails hanging down and straight. Domestic dogs' tails are curled and generally held horizontally. Most people didn't notice, but a few sightings could have been Shawnee.

All evening I waited at Laughing Brook. Eventually, the sanctuary director insisted I go home. I toted my coyote-catching paraphernalia and anxiously instructed the police to call me at home if they received a report of Shawnee.

Again, in the middle of the night, the ringing of the phone echoed in the South Road mansion. This time, a police officer was sure he had spotted her and was facing off with her in the woods about a half-mile from the sanctuary. I assured the dispatcher that Shawnee wouldn't attack the officer and he needn't shoot her. I wonder how confident I sounded. After all, I was just guessing—hoping, that is.

I found the patrol car on the road minutes later. Dart gun and dog pole in hands, I ran into the woods toward the officer's voice. I recognized Shawnee instantly. She paced in circles in the officer's flashlight beam. Her steely stare pierced my heart. I don't know who was most uncomfortable—her, me, or the officer.

After cursory greetings, the officer asked curtly, "Well, ma'am, what now?" as if I had routinely captured coyotes my whole life with little more than my bare hands.

True enough, it was my call—to shoot her with a tranquilizer dart or to try catching her with the pole?

"I could shoot her with the tranquilizer, but that's risky at night. Shawnee could run off in the darkness before it takes effect and stagger onto the road. I'd rather use the pole."

I tried to slip the noose around her neck, but with my short reach, I was as effective as a clam trying to do a handstand. The officer had longer arms, and he valiantly offered to try. Dog poles are familiar tools to police officers, so no coaching was needed.

Much to his surprise, he got a ringer. Shawnee exploded in a frenzy of energy. The officer clenched the pole with both hands and hung on with all his might, casting nervous "what now, ma'am?" glances my way.

My call again. *What would Marlin Perkins do?* I wondered. The famed zoologist from *Mutual of Omaha's Wild Kingdom* would have jumped instantly into some type of action. My mind was spinning worthlessly, grateful that the night cloaked the angst on my face.

While I contemplated a plan, the officer dragged Shawnee, still on the pole, back to the road where his police cruiser was parked. He looked at the cruiser, then he looked at the writhing mass of teeth and claws, then he looked at the immaculate cruiser again. Putting her in his car was looking irrational. It was made for prisoners with shorter claws and no fangs. In the middle of the night, calling for backup from the modest force was not an option.

"Well, ma'am? How should we get her back to the pen?"

The pen was nearly a half-mile away. What I said was, "I guess we will have to walk her back to the pen." What I meant was "you will" and "drag her." He figured it out.

I had neglected to mention that she couldn't be walked on a leash, even in the best of times. The officer was brawny and brave, but it took all of his strength to tow her thirty-pound frame, writhing and howling the whole way. I doubt the police academy trained him for that.

Finally, we arrived at Shawnee's pen, and Hampden's finest peacemaker eagerly handed me the pole. He had certainly earned bragging rights back at the station.

Shawnee seemed relieved to be back in the security of her chain-link home, but not half as relieved as I was.

The saga ended happily. Shawnee was unscathed and all the neighbors' chickens came home to roost. Of course, I never forgot to feed any of the animals again.

One late winter's day, someone brought a baby great horned owl, less than two weeks old, to our wildlife rehabilitation center. I could tell its age because its eyes were milky blue. Up to this age, great horned chicks are still imprintable.

Imprinting is a behavioral term that means a chick will think that whatever feeds it is its parent, whether it really is or not. Usually, the first large animate object that a baby sees after hatching is its parent, and that becomes the object of its affection and allegiance. If that moving object is a human and shows up offering edible treats during the first few weeks, it becomes the surrogate parent. If you've ever seen barnyard ducks following a farmer around the pen, you'll know they were imprinted. It is Nature's way of teaching a baby how to recognize its own kind. Wildlife journals are replete nowadays with chronicles of captive breeding facilities that used hand puppets mimicking endangered condors, whooping cranes, and eagles to feed the chicks. The captive-raised birds are released into the wild having not lost their natural fear of humans.

I was leery of accepting an imprintable owl chick. Normally, I would have told the finder to put the chick back where she found it. I rejected many so-called orphaned baby animals because they could still be cared for by one or both parents, even without a nest, or with a crude one made by awkward human hands. I lectured people on a regular basis. "Don't worry," I'd counsel. "The parents will still take it back." People needed to learn not to interfere with Nature. This situation was no different.

"Put it in the tree as high as you can reach," I advised the owlet finder.

"But the tree was cut down, and there are lots of cats around," she whimpered.

"So find a nearby tree and get the cats away."

"There aren't any other trees, and I can't keep a bunch of cats away!" she implored.

Reluctantly, I accepted the fluffy baby, knowing that it would be a part-time job in itself to raise an owl for release into the wild. The world did not need another captive owl. Grumbling to myself about the sorry state of roving housecats destroying the lives of wild birds didn't improve the situation.

Great horned owls, commonly known as hoot owls, are the fiercest raptors in all of North America. Not even a nine-pound eagle can match the ability of a three-pound great horned owl to defend its nest or survive under adverse conditions. Much has been written in the literature, such as how they can become caught in a leg-hold trap, take flight with the trap, and still survive.

The strength of their talons is legendary. Great horned owls often kill by piercing their victim's cranium. The owls regularly prey on medium-sized mammals, like woodchucks, skunks, rabbits, raccoons, fawns, and even domestic cats, which may weigh ten to fifteen pounds. How is that for poetic justice—a bird killing a cat? The owls kill geese, swans, and turkeys, although smaller birds are more commonly victims. What is so startling is that these owls often do not eat the prey where it drops. Great horned owls may carry their hefty prey with powerful wings to a favorite perch. Once the talons sink into the prey, they lock automatically, and nothing short of killing the bird can make it relax its muscles. This provides quite a challenge for raising such a bird, especially when the best way to carry it is perched on your forearm.

Experienced outdoorspeople know that it is foolhardy to walk through the woods at night while wearing a white cap, which can be mistaken by a great horned owl for the white patch on a skunk. The same goes for other furs, such as coonskin caps. Great horned owls have been known to mistake these misleading targets for the real thing. Did I mention their talons can penetrate skulls?

Both the short-eared owl and the great horned owl are misnamed. The "ears" and the "horns" are simply feathers that project above the other head feathers. In the great horned owl, the function theoretically increases its threatening appearance. These feathers may also catch sounds better, like cupping your hands behind your ears.

Great horned owls live across most of the Western Hemisphere, making it the most widely ranging owl and the most commonly recognized. Amazingly, these birds do not migrate, and they can handle the frigid winter of the Arctic and Subarctic or the steamy summer of the tropics.

I brought the baby owl home, along with a wire cage about three feet long on each side. I set the cage on the side porch so the owlet would always know the fresh air and sounds of the outdoors. For about two weeks, the quail-sized ball of fluff stayed in the cage at night, out of reach of any predator. When I was at home, I opened the cage door and let the owlet wander around, unrestrained. When it was about six weeks old, I left it outside, uncaged and untethered. I wasn't worried about it wandering away. I was its provider, and it knew that.

Calling the owlet "it" was awkward, but I couldn't tell its gender. As is common with raptors, the female great horned owl is about one third larger than the males. Since my owlet was growing up in unnatural conditions, I couldn't be sure if its size was normal. Then again, I never weighed the bird. I just used the generic "him." That made it easier to call him the cool name I chose.

When I was a child, I sat entranced in front of the television on Saturdays when *Sky King* ruled the airwaves. Sky King was a rancher who saved lost children and an occasional wild mustang by flying his Cessna over the remote western skies with his niece Penny. Maybe that excitement subconsciously contributed to my becoming a pilot decades later. The show's tagline, "Out of the clear blue of the western [Massachusetts] sky comes . . . Sky King!" seemed appropriate for this situation, too. Playing on a common nickname for great horned owls—"king of the night skies"—I named my ward Sky King.

Sky King the Owl grew strong on day-old chicks that I procured from a hatchery. Because I had to feed a bevy of carnivores at Laughing Brook, I needed dozens of dead chicks daily. Every few months, I drove a pickup truck to a hatchery in Boston or somewhere where chickens or ring-necked pheasants were raised. The hatchery folks culled most of the male chicks (which they could tell by the shape of the comb on a chick's head) because males could never lay eggs. A few were occasionally needed to fertilize the eggs, so that more hens could be hatched to replace aging ones. The morts (biologist-speak for dead bodies) they donated to us.

When I returned to the nature center with a haul of chicks, the Young Volunteers (as the high-schoolers were called) and I gathered around the animal center for a boisterous afternoon of repackaging the morts into smaller bags for freezing. Although we were all in the business of protecting wildlife, the Young Volunteers understood that the food web is an integral part of keeping the balance of Nature. Some animals die so that others may live.

I fed chicks to most of the carnivores at the nature center—coyotes, red foxes, raccoons, snakes, eagles, owls, and even the snapping turtles. I had a steady supply of food for Sky King, but if I wanted to train him to be self-sufficient in the wild, dead chicks wouldn't work.

Thus, once Sky King was old enough to start hopping onto the railing, I brought him live baby rabbits and squirrels. Luckily, I worked in a place where they, too, were easy to obtain. Early spring had arrived, and all I had to do was to hang around the nature center. Sooner or later, someone would bring in a supposedly orphaned rabbit or squirrel and beg me to take care of it. Whereas the previous year I would have said, "Take it back to where you found it, because it probably isn't orphaned," now I said coolly, "Sure, I'll take care of it." My definition of "taking care of it" was a little different from theirs.

I brought the hyperactive little mammals home and let Sky King figure out how to catch them. First, I released one on the dirt driveway, where he could clearly see it. He had to learn to fly so he could pounce on it. After a few days, he mastered that. Then I started moving the furry babes farther away toward the field. Eventually, I released a little rabbit or squirrel in the tall grasses, where he could hear but not see it. He caught on quickly. Every few days, I placed the prey farther and farther away. He always found the prey.

After a few weeks, I started releasing the quarry at night. By this time in the season, the rabbits and squirrels were older and fast sprinters, so it became more of a challenge for Sky King. Nonetheless, he never went hungry.

Unlike most of my surrogate-mothering episodes, I had to wear leather welder's gloves when handling this baby. Sky King's talons grew strong as he perched on branches at night. The automatic locking of the muscles controlling the toes is common in many birds so that they can sleep on a branch without falling off. The difference is that great horned owls have such massive talons that they can puncture a human cranium and certainly a human arm without trying. The leather would help only under normal perching conditions. If something spooked Sky King, heavy leather wouldn't save my flesh.

When I thought Sky King understood how to hunt, I pared back his food, skipping days at a time. During the daytime, he roosted in the sugar maples in our side yard. At night, he would vanish into the woods. He recognized the crinkling sound of a plastic bag (the type that the chicks came in) as an invitation to dinner. I would stand in the yard after dark, and with just one bout of crinkling, he would appear in minutes.

Eventually, my dinner invitations tapered off to once every few weeks, and Sky King disappeared in the interim. I never knew if he was surviving. Whenever he returned, he would stand on the porch roof outside my bedroom window, clacking his bill as a form of communication. What he was saying, I'll never know. Clack, clack, clack, clack, clack. I would wake up, see him through the window, and go back to bed.

Summer turned into fall, and he seemed to be able to take care of himself. Then he disappeared, and I had to keep faith that he was alive. I wondered how he would fare in the winter.

During the time Sky King was gone, I cared for many other animals. The following spring, someone brought in an ailing American kestrel, the smallest falcon in the United States. These birds average about 10 inches long with a 23-inch wingspan, and they weigh about four ounces—about what a peach weighs. Kestrels are also known as sparrow hawks because they resemble a bird by the same name in Europe. Our disabled bird may have recently returned from its wintering grounds, possibly as far south as Panama.

Our kestrel exhibited signs of poisoning or electric shock because it was partially paralyzed but well-muscled, and it showed no obvious wounds. Electric shock more commonly happens to larger birds, such as eagles and California condors, when they perch on power lines. The wings would have to span from one wire to the other. A bird that is perched on a wire will not be electrocuted if it is touching only that wire. That is why power companies are now required to keep the parallel wires a certain minimum distance apart.

The odds were good that this kestrel was poisoned, probably accidentally by eating poisoned insects. Chemicals used in modern agriculture and lawn maintenance are rampant in the environment. In the spring, kestrels eat grasshoppers and other insects, the primary targets of pesticides. Untold thousands or millions of other birds probably die each year from poisons applied to lawns and crops.

My plan was to feed the kestrel "clean" (uncontaminated) food, such as mice we raised. I would also give it physical therapy. Its wings and legs would require assisted exercise to prevent the muscles from atrophying.

For a few weeks, the Young Volunteers and I set the bird on its back several times a day and wiggled its little legs in and out, as if it were riding an imaginary bicycle. We flapped its wings as if we were teaching a child to wave good-bye. Gradually, the appendages began to move without our help, encouraging us to continue. After several weeks, I brought the bird to our palatial slum and let it flit around a spare room.

When I was sure it could fly strongly, I brought the kestrel out to the yard on a sunny, warm afternoon. Our haunted house was set in a rural area with an ample population of small birds, rodents, and insects for a hungry kestrel. We used no pesticides.

Gently, I opened my hands to allow the little falcon to take off on its own. After shaking its feathers, the kestrel launched itself into the air and flew to a nearby oak tree. I watched it for a few minutes, beaming at my success. It needed to get its bearings, so I expected it to sit there quietly for a while.

Sipping from the well of reward, I imagined the joy of the scared bird finding itself free, independently mobile, and back in the familiar protection of the foliage. Just as I was about to walk away and leave it in peace, a motion caught the corner of my eye.

What happened next was a blur. Out of nowhere came the beating of wings, raucous squawking, and a frantic rustling of leaves. When the commotion stopped, there sat Sky King, perched on the branch in the oak tree, with the kestrel hanging limply from his talons.

Spellbound, I didn't know whether to cry or clap. I had painstakingly saved the kestrel's life for a brief flash of freedom. I had also tried to teach the owl to hunt, and I was never sure I had succeeded. Now I knew.

In the end, I was relieved to see that Sky King had survived the winter on his own. He visited me periodically over the next few years. I always knew him, because he would sit on the porch roof outside my bedroom window in the wee hours of the night and clack his bill. Clack, clack, clack, clack. I would hear it in my sleep, wake up, and go to the window, where I would confirm it wasn't a dream. His silhouette would be visible in the same place. I would watch him for a few minutes, go back to bed, and find him gone in the morning. With its very own owl, our haunted house was complete.

Sky King, the great horned owl, calls outside my bedroom window in the evening.

Chapter 2.
Sleeping with Rattlesnakes

Beauty may be only skin deep, but sound penetrates to your brain. The rattling sound is intended to stir action. If you don't heed the rattlesnake's warning, you'll be sorry. So, why did I teach myself to ignore it?

Two of the permanent residents of the Laughing Brook Audubon Sanctuary exhibit collection were a timber rattlesnake and a northern copperhead, the only two venomous snakes native to Massachusetts. I don't recall the story of how the daunting duo came into our care. They had arrived many years before I did. The copperhead had resided there for about twenty years, and if we had known how old it was when it arrived, it might have set a longevity record for the species. Thousands of people, mostly families and school groups, passed through our doors to learn about snakes in the outdoors around them.

The rattling sound theoretically evolved as an alarm to large hoofed animals that once roamed commonly across the Americas (bison, deer, elk, moose, and pronghorns) to prevent the rattlesnakes from being trampled. It means "watch where you step." Despite the utilitarian audible warning, the snakes are reluctant to expose themselves to threats unless absolutely necessary. Generally, they slither away silently at the vibration of heavy footsteps The rattling occurs when the segments of the "buttons" on the snake's tail knock against each other as the snake whips its tail back and forth rapidly. The hollow segments amplify the sound, acting as a resonator.

Rattlesnakes and copperheads are members of the pit viper family, so called because they have pits (holes) on both sides of their heads between the eyes and the nostrils. These pits sense heat and aid the snakes in detecting and aiming at warm-blooded prey. Snakes can't hear sounds through the air, but their long bodies hugging the ground can feel the vibrations from nearby footsteps.

Some species of venomous snakes, such as copperheads, lack rattles. To confuse the forest interloper, copperheads and a few nonvenomous snakes may whip their tails against dry leaves to mimic a rattle and thus scare away enemies.

Another intriguing aspect of pit viper biology is their method of reproduction. While most mammal offspring are born alive, most birds, fish, reptiles, and amphibians lay eggs. However, there are exceptions. Some mammals lay eggs (the duck-billed platypus of Australia comes to mind), and some reptiles do not. Rattlesnakes and copperheads are among the latter. They are ovoviviparous, which is a hundred-dollar term meaning they have eggs but do not lay them. Their eggs are merely membranes without shells, and the embryos develop in the membranes inside the mother. When the membrane-covered babies are born, they open the membranes with an "egg tooth"—a tiny projection on the tip of the snout—and emerge wriggling, complete with fangs and venom, ready to hunt.

Rattlesnake and copperhead populations have suffered serious declines since the 1700s. Not only have people destroyed their habitat, but they also deliberately slay the snakes for fear of being bitten or the desire for showy boots and purses. Their wild brethren are an integral part of the ecosystem.

Compounding the habitat loss, rattlesnakes have a low reproductive rate. Males mature in about five years and females in seven to eleven years. The females reproduce only every three to five years and bear four to fourteen young. This makes their population decline even more dramatic.

In the northeast United States, rattlers and copperheads are active from late April to mid-October. Rattlers hibernate in rocky dens with dozens of other rattlesnakes but are loners the rest of their lives. Copperheads may share hibernaculums with other snakes or may rest solo.

The rattler and copperhead in our nature center were difficult to keep in captivity because, like their free-roaming brethren, they ate live prey. Common prey items for rattlesnakes are chipmunks and other small rodents. Copperheads eat mice, lizards, frogs, and other small animals. In this way, they help keep the populations of rodents and other small animals under control and thus help maintain the ecological balance. These snakes locate their prey by the potential victim's body heat, its breath, and its movement. Thus, a dead animal might just as well be another rock to slither around.

Snakes are poikilothermic or so-called cold-blooded animals. "Cold-blooded" is a misnomer because their body temperature can closely match cool air temperatures. During the winter in the wild, rattlers and copperheads hibernate because their body temperatures dip too low for them to remain active.

Under normal conditions in the wild and when snakes are healthy and strong, a chipmunk will be no match for a rattler, nor a deer mouse for a copperhead. When our captive snakes slowed down in winter, however, you would be surprised how effectively a terrified house mouse could attack a venomous snake. Put one adult mouse in a tank with a sluggish copperhead, and you may sacrifice your copperhead. Ditto with a lab rat versus a rattlesnake.

The solution is to feed baby rodents to the sluggish snakes. Thus, we would raise house mice and Norway rats (both non-native species and commonly used in laboratories) in a back room of the nature center and remove the babies from their mothers before they grew fur. At this stage, their bare skins are pink and they are defenseless. However, they are warm and mobile, motivating the snakes to catch them. Biologists and laboratory workers know these small rodents as "pinkies."

At our nature center, we fed pinky rats to the rattler, the larger of the two snakes, and pinky mice to the copperhead. In the warm months, they gobbled them up. Every winter I put the pinky mice and rats in their cages. Snakes slowed down but wouldn't hibernate because it was too warm. Thus, they burned calories but didn't feel like eating (an overweight person's dream). I worried that they would lose too much weight over the winter. In the frosty season, the snakes simply ignored the luscious treats. I concluded that I should force-feed them a few times over the winter.

Force-feeding is common in veterinary care and wildlife rehabilitation. Sick or injured dogs, cats, and baby birds get personal care and no one thinks twice about it. However, force-feeding a rattlesnake was new territory for our veterinarians and me. I was on my own.

Planning the procedure in advance ensured I had the right helpers. I depended on a bevy of volunteers to assist me with all aspects of our animals' care. However, only the most elite volunteers earned the coveted job of being a venomous-snake holder. They had to prove they were totally unflappable under adverse conditions, not prone to shrieking, giggling, or fleeing at the slightest reptilian wiggle or twitch. Most of my volunteers were teens, and despite their youth, never disappointed me with their composure.

One of my most dependable and talented volunteers was Richard Haley. He burst into the volunteer scene around the age of seventeen, already effervescent and full of energy, humor, wit, and amazing maturity. He desperately tried to hide that maturity, but it slipped through often. There was never a dull moment when Richard was around. He would anticipate a slow day, usually on a winter weekend, because school groups came only on weekdays. On those monotonous days, he would arrive with a wacky story or a song, and whoever was present would sit around the Burgess house after chores while Richard entertained us.

Richard went on to Cornell and the Yale School of Forestry and became a distinguished environmental educator and conservationist. He directed several nature centers and then became the director of education for the Audubon New York. Richard eventually married Eileen, my haunted-house housemate, certainly a perfect match of incorrigible humor and dedication to conservation. Many years later, as 43-year-young Richard was driving alone on a remote road near the Grand Canyon, his brilliant life ended in a tumbling car.

But that is a sad digression. Teen-aged Richard loved helping with the snakes and often held the six-foot-long black rat snake for children to touch. For him, holding the rattler and copperhead were simply a matter of paying a little extra heed.

Many people who have never touched a snake believe that a snake's skin must be slimy, probably because the skin is shiny and appears wet. I have held many types of snakes, and although they feel cool to the touch, they are all clean and dry. In fact, some species have a skin so smooth and dry that it holds fingerprints.

Some women flock to dermatologists to get expensive facial peels for that young and vibrant look, while snakes get body peels for free every few months. As their bodies grow, the outer skin doesn't, and the snake rubs it off against a tree or rock. We humans shed our skins naturally, too, but we do it a few unnoticeable cells at a time, unless we suffer a blistering sunburn.

Handling these snakes was, as you can guess, a risky task. Copperheads and rattlers have venom that they inject through hollow fangs. The venom attacks the circulatory system of its victims. In comparison, the venom of coral snakes is a neurotoxin. Coral snakes live in Florida and Arizona and eat snakes, lizards, and amphibians. The neurotoxin attacks the prey's nervous system, which works better than a circulatory toxin would on cold-blooded prey. Few people are bitten by venomous snakes in the United States, and even fewer of those bitten will die. Nevertheless, fingers and toes have suffered some mortality.

Note that I refer to these snakes as venomous, not poisonous. The semantic difference is that poisonous creatures contain a substance in their bodies that poisons you if *you* bite or touch *it*, such as those fugu (puffer) fish the Japanese are fond of eating, or poison arrow frogs, whose skin contains a deadly poison used in blow darts by traditional South American hunters. A venomous animal has to deliver the irritant by *it* stinging or biting *you*. The ray that caused the death of Steve Irwin, Australia's famed Crocodile Hunter, had venom in its tail barb.

When I force-fed the snakes, all I had to do was to keep them from biting me. I never used gloves, because I could get a better grip with bare hands. First, I would catch the snake by pressing a stick against the back of its neck and grabbing around the neck with one hand. Once I had the head secured, the volunteers would deftly grab the body. Because the rattlesnake was about four feet long, I wanted two volunteers to hold the body. The copperhead was about two and a half feet long and required only one body-grabber.

Next, I "milked" the venom by gently coercing the snake's mouth open and pressing its fangs onto a cloth stretched across an open jar. The venom oozed out. Did I get every drop? I was never sure. I washed the venom down the drain. Milking is a common practice for researchers who collect venom and make snakebite antitoxin from it. Snake handlers like me, however, milk the snakes in case we get bitten.

After the milking, I would push a pinky rat or mouse into the snake's mouth and into its throat. My hand on the snake's neck was the crucial safety factor. I had to hold the neck with a delicate balance—loosely enough to allow room for the pinky to slip down, but tightly enough so the snake couldn't slither through or turn its head backwards and strike my hand.

Once the food was in the snake's throat, we snake handlers moved in unison and set the snake back in the cage. The volunteers released their grip first and then I released the head. I made sure the cage was warm enough for the food to digest. Otherwise, it would literally rot in the snake's stomach. I am not sure how much the force-feeding helped, but the snakes did survive from winter to winter.

I must caution readers here that this procedure was risky, and I must deliver that oft-used cliché, "Don't do this at home" or anywhere else, for that matter.

When our nature center building was scheduled for remodeling, I needed a safe place to keep the two snakes for a few weeks. It had to be a place where they could be cared for by an experienced person, where they would not disturb anyone, and where they could be fed live food. The best alternative seemed to be my house.

I brought the cages home and put them in the living room. They were glass tanks with lockable wire screen tops. The snakes' tongues were flicking constantly, trying to decipher the new scents. Snakes smell with their tongues, which pick up particles in the air that are then deciphered by an organ in their mouths.

The rattler sensed that it was in a new location and registered its agitation by rattling at every movement we made. During the night, the dog would pace around the living room, and the snake would rattle at this strange new animal smell.

The cages were always locked except during feeding, and they were quite secure, but the rattling sound was still unnerving. After a few weeks, I adapted to the sound, and the rattling served to lull me to sleep, like leaves in the wind or a babbling stream.

After the remodeling was complete, I brought the cages back to the nature center. It seemed strangely quiet at home. I missed the rhythmic music.

Several years later, when I was a graduate student at the University of Connecticut, our ecology class went on an overnight field trip. The Sharon Audubon Center in northwestern Connecticut offered us a free place to sleep. The staff allowed us to lay our sleeping bags on any vacant floor space in the nature center.

Most students chose the open space of the classroom in the basement and packed themselves across the floor like a logjam on a river. Others scattered into the exhibit rooms with the live mice, salamanders, turtles, and fish tanks.

I didn't think I would be able to sleep with a bunch of snoring semi-strangers, so I sought a space devoid of other humans. I found it in the live rattlesnake display room. No one else dared to sleep there. I laid my sleeping bag down and rested peacefully, lulled asleep by the rattling of a snake that sensed something new was in the room.

Chapter 3.

Wildcats, Peccaries, and Drunken Grouse

Sky King, the baby great horned owl I raised, was one of a long parade of needy creatures that passed through our haunted doors on South Road. Two of the more memorable were babies with fur.

Laughing Brook Wildlife Sanctuary had permanent exhibits of native Massachusetts animals, including the male bobcat Yowler and the female Priscilla. Priscilla had been found raiding garbage cans in the Cambridge section of Boston and probably had been a dumped pet. I don't remember Yowler's origin, but he clearly behaved like a former housecat gone incorrigible. Neither could survive properly in the wild. I was in charge of their care.

Yowler was named for a Thornton Burgess character, probably after a wildcat that Burgess heard while living by the Laughing Brook. I don't know how Priscilla acquired her moniker.

Bobcats are native to Massachusetts and not uncommon in rural areas, so it wasn't surprising to find that local people had acquired them. In fact, other than in the Midwest, bobcats are found across most of North America, from southern Canada to Mexico and coast to coast. They are among the most versatile animals on the continent, able to live in deserts, wetlands, mountains, prairies, and woodlands.

The range of vocalizations these cats make is astounding. Yowling is certainly one of them. However, unlike the big cats of the Old World, roaring is not part of their repertoire. I have heard bobcats at night while I was camping and could have sworn the sound was coming from an animal the size of a mountain lion. However, the spotted wildcats are barely larger than large domestic cats. Female bobcats weigh about ten to thirty pounds and males weigh about fifteen to fifty pounds. The short or bobbed tails, for which the cats are named, are usually four inches long but may reach eight inches.

Our two cats had lived for many years in an outdoor chain-link pen about thirty feet long, ten feet wide, and eight feet high. The pen had two sections that could be partitioned to separate the inmates or to put them both on one side while repairs were made to the other.

While making the water bucket rounds one day, young Beth saw something in one of the pens that was so strange it sent her running to find me.

"There's a kitten in the bobcat cage, and Yowler's trying to kill it!" she exclaimed.

Beth didn't know what to make of it and neither did I. Beth was always energetic and excitable, so it could have been something simple. Did some local tabby give birth nearby in the quiet woods and her kit wander into the pen through the gap in the chain-link door? I dashed out to the pen, and sure enough, there was Yowler, batting a kitten around like a ball of yarn. Nearby, Priscilla was guarding another kitten that Beth hadn't seen.

But the kittens didn't crawl into the pen—they started life there. Those little spotted furballs were not housecats. There was no time to be embarrassed that I hadn't noticed Priscilla was pregnant. Appalled at the battering the bobkitten was enduring, we enticed Yowler to release it and lured him into the other side of the pen with his favorite food.

Once Yowler was sequestered, we coaxed Priscilla away from the other kitten, retrieved both babes, and made sure there weren't any more. Bobcats in the wild usually have litters of two to four kittens.

I took the bobkittens to veterinarian Don Crouser, who normally treated common household pets. Every year, when he came to the sanctuary to examine our coyotes and fox, he also vaccinated the bobcats against rabies and distemper. Mostly, however, we transported our needy animals to his animal hospital.

Don treated the wounded kitten and examined the other, which seemed weak but unharmed. Like me, he had never seen a wildcat kitten before. They were about the same size as housecat newborns.

After scrutinizing them closely, he proclaimed, "They're just like domestic kittens—except their teeth and claws are a lot longer!"

Don advised against putting the unharmed kitten back with its mother because of the chance that she would reject it. I brought both kittens home and fed them pet formula every few hours as he had instructed. The wounded one died soon. The other died a few days later, possibly from distemper. The mood at the sanctuary was somber.

The next year, not wanting a repeat failure, I was prepared. For several months before the date the kittens had been born the previous year, I scrutinized the bobcats' behavior closely. When it got close to that date, it did seem that Priscilla's belly was hanging a little low. To be safe, I separated Yowler into the other side of the pen. Soon I was rewarded by the sight of two more bobkittens, this time resting peacefully with their mother.

Priscilla, the bobcat, poses at Laughing Brook
Wildlife Sanctuary.

Priscilla seemed to have motherhood under control, now that the mischievous influence of her mate was absent. This time, Don advised me to let the kittens nurse for at least three days to acquire the colostrum from the mother. Colostrum is the milk produced by all mammals, including humans, during the first few days after parturition. This milk is exceptionally nutritious and contains high concentrations of antibodies to help the newborn fight disease. After about three days, the composition of the mother's milk changes to fit the growth of the newborn. Most likely, the lack of colostrum the previous year had caused the unwounded kitten to acquire a disease it couldn't fight off.

I did as Don suggested and left the feline family in peace. During this time, I agonized over what to do next. My instinct urged me to leave the kittens alone and let the mother raise them. I could keep Yowler in the other pen for a few months. But, we didn't have room to keep four bobcats permanently. We could never release the two captive-born wildcats. It's against all wildlife management morals. The mother couldn't teach the youngsters how to hunt and protect themselves. The desperate kits would end up raiding chicken coops or glued to a road. I would need to find another zoo-type home for them, and that could happen only if the young were semi-tame.

On the fourth day, I removed the kittens from the cage. I had an inkling of what was in store for me, after my three-day feline mothering experience the year before. But a few days did not prepare me for several weeks of round-the-clock bottle feeding, biting, scratching, and pooping.

I don't know what I would have done without Eileen to share the nursing duties. She willingly split the task with me down the middle and relished the opportunity. We set up a schedule to feed the kittens every three hours, day and night, and prepared a warm place to keep them in our house.

As with bottle-feeding humans, we first had to heat the formula. Then, we had to feed both kittens—no serene task. Following that, we cleaned and sterilized the bottle. Last, we had to rub under their tails with a damp cotton ball to stimulate their digestive tract on the outgoing end. This action mimics the mother's tongue, and she would have done that naturally if she had been there. After a few weeks, the kittens started defecating on their own.

The observations by the veterinarian a year earlier about the longer teeth and claws played a memorable role when we became surrogate mothers. No matter what we did to thwart the kittens, they scratched Eileen's and my hands and arms until they looked like they had been through a meat grinder. The older the kittens grew, the stronger they became, and the longer their claws grew. Every attempt we made at wearing gloves resulted in clumsy failure.

After about four weeks, we started weaning the kittens. They were strong, healthy, and relentlessly squirmy. Just hanging on to them was a challenge. I brought them to Laughing Brook and set them up in a small indoor pen. They grew robust on homegrown mice. After a few months, I found them permanent homes. One went to another Massachusetts Audubon nature center (Blue Hills Trailside Museum in eastern Massachusetts), and one went to The Children's Museum in West Hartford.

I thought I was done with bobcats after I left Laughing Brook and started graduate school. I had been accepted into the master's degree program at the Northeastern Research Center for Wildlife Diseases at the University of Connecticut, the only student they matriculated that year. The program had an excellent reputation. In addition, it was the only such program in all the surrounding states, so I considered myself fortunate to be a part of it. I even had a research subject already selected.

Every spring, the neighborhood's Good Samaritans flooded our rehabilitation center with paralyzed American robins and yellow-shafted flickers that eventually died. I tried all my tricks to save them.

I strongly suspected that the birds were poisoned by insecticides applied to lawns by lawn-care companies. Robins and flickers in particular appeared on lawns in early spring and ate the ants, grubs, worms, and other invertebrates that were targeted by the common insecticides Diazinon and Dursban. Since both are organophosphates, as is DDT, the poisons would accumulate in the birds' bodies until they died of the effects. I had read technical papers about geese dying after eating Diazinon-treated grass on golf courses. Although I was personally convinced of the cause and effect between the application of lawn-care chemicals and the deaths of birds, I needed proof.

To get that proof, I started my wildlife pathobiology classroom work under the tutelage of the Research Center's longtime director, Dr. Svend Nielsen. Dr. Nielsen was near retirement and had built a reputation as one of the leading wildlife pathologists in the country. He recommended I take such courses as histology, virology, and wildlife diseases.

After reviewing the curriculum for the rest of my program, I asked Dr. Nielsen, "When do I take field classes?"

Nielsen answered confidently, "We do all our work in the lab. Fieldwork isn't necessary."

Miffed and bewildered, I formed my own conclusion about the curriculum within a few weeks of matriculating. One day in late September, I walked into the office of a master of science-degree candidate I'll call Ted, who had already been there for several years as a wildlife pathobiology major. On his desk, sprawled on top of a plastic bag, was a dead ruffed grouse.

Ruffed grouse, also called partridge, resemble small chickens and were common in the Connecticut woodlands at that time. In a good year, you could walk across the woods on the backs of grouse, so to speak. During their breeding season in spring, I saw them frequently and heard the males' classic "drumming" echo through the woods.

Drumming is the term for a sound a male grouse makes with its wings, which the bird performs to attract a female mate. The male usually stands on a log or a stump as an elevated stage and starts to flap its wings. At first, the rhythm is slow, but the beat increases to a drum-roll crescendo. The final wing beats are so quick that they create a miniature sonic boom that can be heard for hundreds of yards. One round of drumming lasts about eight seconds.

Wordlessly, I picked up the bird from Ted's desk and examined it—no obvious wounds and no broken bones.

"It flew into my fence," Ted explained.

That was all I needed to know. "Oh, it's September. In the fall, they eat fermented berries and fly into things in a drunken daze." I noted the break in the bird's black tail band and added, "It's a female."

Hearing that, Ted asked, "Gee, if you know so much about it, maybe you could tell me what it is. Is it some kind of quail or something?"

Silently, I choked on his words. I hadn't mentioned the name because I thought it was obvious. That this wildlife disease student didn't know what kind of bird it was or what its habits were never occurred to me. This is what happens when all the work is done in a laboratory. I lectured him politely on ruffed grouse ecology. He had planned to necropsy the bird to determine what caused it to fly into the fence. I hoped it was evident that a little field knowledge could save him a lot of lab work.

After that incident, rumors spread through the department that I knew something about wildlife. When the veterinarian in charge of mammal necropsies asked me to tell him whether a rabbit he was autopsying was domestic or wild, I knew I had to leave. If he didn't know the difference between a wild and a domestic rabbit, something was wrong with the department. At least it was wrong for me. Flopsy looks nothing like Peter Cottontail.

I completed my classes that semester and then transferred out of the Wildlife Disease Research Center and into the Systematics and Evolutionary Biology program, which included zoology. The zoology program employed the esteemed mammalogist Dr. Ralph Wetzel, who specialized in researching sloths, anteaters, armadillos, and peccaries. Peccaries are piglike animals, such as the javelina (collared peccary) of Texas and Arizona. Scientists thought one peccary species had been extinct for two million years. Then in 1975, Ralph, assisted by his graduate students, rediscovered the Chacoan peccary in the Chaco region of western Paraguay. This was the only large species of mammal that anyone had discovered worldwide since 1901, and it earned Ralph international recognition.

I was the last graduate student that Ralph accepted before he retired. "I'll take you on if you promise not to dawdle," he insisted.

Dawdling happened occasionally to graduate students. A few of Ralph's graduate students were approaching the decade mark, still working on their dissertations, and he was afraid they would never graduate if he retired. Safe and enlightening, staying in graduate school seemed preferable to the real world of getting a job. However, being the impatient and independent type, I assured him, "Don't worry. The sooner I get out, the better!"

When I entered the mammalogy program, my research focus shifted away from my original plan. I never proved my theory about the correlation between insecticides and the deaths of birds. But someone else did. Twenty years later, the U.S. Environmental Protection Agency phased out Diazinon for indoor use (2001) and lawn use (2003), citing the risks to humans and birds. The agency removed Dursban from the home-use market in 2001. Sometimes I wonder if my research plan, had I stuck with it, would have resulted in a speedier ban, thus saving incalculable numbers of birds.

However, I don't regret the switch. After leaving the lop-sided wildlife pathobiology program, I was welcomed by a group of down-to-earth, let's-get-muddy field biologists. Whether you are studying wildlife in the Chaco of Paraguay or in Connecticut, learning about wildlife means you have to go outside, and they knew that. Ralph's graduate students often did their research in Central or South America. In fact, most of the students in the biology program went somewhere that required a passport. That made me an anomaly.

In my first semester there, word reached me that the Connecticut Department of Environmental Protection (DEP) was looking for someone to commence a study on bobcats. They needed to know how much bobcat habitat existed in the state and if it could support a bobcat harvest (hunting or trapping). Bobcats, you say? I know a little about them.

Thus, while many of my graduate-student colleagues were in Panama or Paraguay, I was stomping through the wilds of Litchfield County, northwest of Hartford. I barely had to leave home. The whole state is only fifty by one hundred miles.

As I started my investigation, I discovered that no one had ever published a major study on bobcats in Connecticut. Since bobcats were never extirpated from the state, and since they are one of the largest wild animals found there, I was amazed that the first research specifically on this mammal began with me in 1980. So many other researchers from the state university had gone to the exotic places to do pure science (research to learn more about something without a specific need) that the local applied science (research with a defined need) was yet undone. The least-explored place was our own backyard.

Little information on bobcats exists in state records, partly because the felines often were categorized as "wildcats," which included feral housecats, Canada lynxes, and mountain lions. The local government paid a set price (a bounty) for every dead cat someone turned in. However, towns were not required to keep records of the type of cat for which they paid a bounty. Housecats probably accounted for most of the bounties paid. The bounty law was repealed in 1971, only nine years before I started my research.

In 1974, bobcats became totally protected by the state. At least, intentional killing was prohibited, although motor vehicle bumpers went on murdering bobcats legally. Population numbers barely inched upward.

When I started the project, a DEP biologist told me that hunters were pressuring the agency to open a hunting season on bobcats because the hunters wanted to use their dogs that were trained to chase bears up trees. Bear hunting was prohibited in Connecticut, and the hunters didn't want to drive to other states or pay out-of-state hunting fees. I don't doubt that, but there was another motive for opening a season in the state that DEP neglected to tell me.

From the 1950s to the 1970s, bobcat pelt prices brought five to ten dollars apiece. By the early 1980s, prices were skyrocketing. Pelts were fetching a staggering three hundred to four hundred dollars each, sometimes even six hundred dollars. I read between the lines why hunters were pressuring DEP to open a season.

But what caused the sudden jump in value? In 1975, the Convention for International Trade in Endangered Species of Wild Fauna and Flora (CITES) entered into force. This pact of eighty countries (including the United States) listed the jaguar, ocelot, cheetah, and other spotted cats under its Appendix 1, which generally prohibits international trade. These cats were the main species trapped for the spotted fur trade. When it became illegal to sell these furs, the industry turned to the next closest substitute— any cat with spots that was legal to hunt. In the United States, that was the bobcat. Suddenly, bobcats, which attracted little notice before, became star targets. Never mind that bobcat fur is of poor quality because it is brittle and sheds easily. As long as it has spots, naïve people will pay exorbitant prices for it.

The harvest pressure caused CITES to list the bobcat in 1977 under Appendix II, which regulates trade. Thus began the controversy that resulted in the U.S. federal courts prohibiting the foreign export of bobcat pelts from all states after July 1981. Any state wanting to open a season subsequently had to provide the federal court with evidence documenting that its population could be sustained with the harvest.

That's where I came in, commencing a two-year study of bobcat habitat and population status in Connecticut. I reviewed reports of bobcat sightings that DEP had been collecting from eyewitnesses. I interviewed many people, and whether they had seen a real bobcat or some other feline remained for me to determine. Usually, the other creature was a spotted housecat that had lost part of its tail to a car tire.

As I investigated each report, I prompted the eyewitness, "Tell me about the bobcat you saw." Occasionally, he or she would answer, "Oh, *that*. You don't want to hear about *that*. Let me tell you about the mountain lion I saw!"

This would always perk my ears, but in a wary sort of way. Eastern mountain lions are known colloquially as cougars, panthers, pumas, and catamounts, but they are all the same species (*Felis concolor,* which means "cat of one color"). Wild ones weren't supposed to be anywhere near Connecticut. Once upon a time, until the early 1800s, yes, they populated Connecticut. However, they were exterminated under the wildcat bounty sometime in the nineteenth or early twentieth centuries.

What were these people seeing? Canada lynxes have larger paws (hence, larger tracks) than mountain lions, the better to walk on deep snow in the far north. Lynxes were not supposed to be as far south as Connecticut, so either lynxes or mountain lions in Connecticut would be a feline jackpot.

But, here is the catch. In Connecticut at that time, the laws regulating possession of wild animals in captivity were quite lax. A person could legally purchase a mountain lion from South America (also *Felis concolor*) through an animal dealer and keep it at home. It wouldn't surprise me if some of these cats escaped or were kicked out after they became too bothersome to keep. If a subspecies from somewhere else in the western hemisphere was roaming around Connecticut, no one could tell from the appearance or the tracks. I suspected the believable reports of mountain lions were the escaped or banished pets from South America.

I sampled habitats all over the state where I had reliable sightings of bobcats or where I had seen them myself. I compiled the information and found the most common types of habitats where bobcats were found. These were wooded, rocky areas with the least human disturbance. In those days before computerized GIS (Geographical Information Systems), I mapped what I found by hand. Using giant sheets of Mylar plastic over the geologic, topographic, and vegetation maps of the state, I outlined the areas that had the most bobcat habitat.

Ultimately, I concluded that there were approximately 220 to 380 bobcats in the state, mostly in the northwest and northeast corners. However, their current ranges were too small and fragmented to support a harvest. The good habitat was in pieces, separated by impassable obstacles—major interstates and rail corridors, wide river valleys that were heavily developed, and major urban centers. If a population decreased in one area, another could not repopulate it, and decades could pass until it increased on its own.

Based on my findings, DEP was not able to support a harvest season. More than 25 years later, because I chose my own backyard to do applied science and left the exotic adventures to others, these graceful felines are still protected in the State of Connecticut. Maybe that will make up for the robins and flickers I failed.

Chapter 4.
They's Dangerous

Wood storks started permeating my life in 1984, just after the official announcement from the U.S. Fish and Wildlife Service that they had added the species to the federal Endangered Species List. How else would you describe their effect on me when, among my seemingly odd behaviors, I disguised myself in black pants and a white shirt and waded slowly through a swamp, my body hunched over and swaying back and forth, my arm dragging through the water like a long bill, just so I could get close to a foraging stork? Whether out of nearsightedness or the stork's curiosity, it worked.

At the time the storks were considered endangered, the 310-square-mile Savannah River Plant, operated by the U.S. Department of Energy in southwestern South Carolina, had wood storks feeding on the property. The Savannah River Plant was officially "a nuclear industrial facility." That's a euphemism for producing the plutonium and tritium used in hydrogen bombs.

The Department of Energy was planning to restart an off-line nuclear reactor and dump the outflowing cooling water into the swamp where the wood storks fed. The water would be used to cool the reactor, so the outflow would be warmer than the normal swamp water and the water level would rise. The Savannah River Plant already had several operating reactors that dumped heated water into other parts of the swamp.

The Endangered Species Act, which was passed in 1973, states that any federal agency that has a threatened or endangered species on its property has to ensure that none of the agency's activities will contribute to the extinction of that species. After all, how foolish would it be to have one arm of the federal government bending over backwards to save a species while another was killing it off? The process of federal agencies consulting together to find a plan that allows them to mutually accomplish their missions is a fundamental part of the Endangered Species Act.

Thus, the listing of the wood stork as an endangered species prompted the Department of Energy to engage in scientific studies of the storks that fed at the Savannah River Plant. There just happened be the high-caliber Savannah River Ecology Laboratory, operated by the University of Georgia, on the Savannah River Plant property.

The lab needed biologists to study the storks. I arrived with Larry Bryan, Lisa Huff, Bill Lee, and Lynne McAllister, as well as the project leader, Malcolm Coulter, to find out if the heated water would harm the storks.

Did I have trepidations about working on a nuclear power facility only five years after the memorable meltdown at Three Mile Island? Did I hate to leave cool, rugged New England for the steamy, flat South? The choice was vexing. I was living in Maine, but my job with Maine Audubon had terminated for the season. I had heard about the stork job from friends who worked at the ecology lab, and I accepted it only after they explained that the stork study site was across the Savannah River in Georgia, where the storks nested, and not at the Savannah River Plant. Research jobs weren't beating a path to my door, and the idea of studying the secretive, charismatic wood storks drew me like a salamander to a pond on a rainy spring night.

For two years, I lived, breathed, slept, and nearly ate wood storks. Had the birds not been federally protected, I guarantee that I would have tasted one of the unfortunate morts. It's rite of passage among field biologists that we should sample our research subject's culinary attributes to truly understand the species.

The wood stork (*Mycteria americana*) is the only true stork native to the United States. It is related to the white stork of European rooftop fame and baby-bringing legends. Another stork, the jabiru, lives in Mexico and Central and South America, but occasionally wanders into southern Texas. At one time, the wood stork flourished from South Carolina to Florida, west to Texas, and south through Mexico.

During the infamous plume-hunting bird slaughter period from the late 1800s to the early 1900s, the wood stork population plummeted from an estimated sixty thousand birds to only a few thousand, eventually causing the stork to become listed as a federally endangered species. The dingy plumes of storks were not especially sought, but the birds shared nesting sites with the divinely plumed egrets and were caught in the crossfire, literally and figuratively.

Wood storks suffer from an identity crisis. Wood ibis. Pond gannet. Gourdhead. Flinthead. Iron-head. Spanish buzzard. Preacher. These are all colloquial names the storks have acquired.

In shape, the stork resembles its smaller cousin, the white ibis, hence the most common nickname of wood ibis. The adjective "wood" becomes obvious when you watch storks foraging in densely treed swamps. A pelagic (sea-going) bird called the northern gannet has a white body with black wing tips and a large bill, so someone might guess that a stork could be the pond-dwelling version of a gannet. One could also see how the featherless head of a wood stork would prompt a person to liken it to a gourd. The dark, shiny skin of the head and neck resembles flint or maybe iron. As for the buzzard part, the naked head is reminiscent of that of a vulture (commonly known as a buzzard), which also has a featherless head. The bird's formal attire (black and white garb) could remind one of a preacher's vestment.

Colloquial, or common, names are flighty things, rather like the birds they describe, but equally flighty for mammals, reptiles, plants, and other types of life. In the United States, many common names have been standardized by scientific organizations, such as the American Ornithologists Union (AOU), which has done so for birds. Mexico has so many regional languages and dialects that it can't standardize the common names. One species may have dozens of names, none of which stand out as the main one. Thus, the Mexican endangered species lists of plants and animals use only scientific names.

In 1983, the AOU changed the name of the wood ibis to wood stork, since the bird in question is a true stork. In deep pockets of the rural Southeast, people still often call it pond gannet or gourdhead, and especially wood ibis. Not knowing which term was in usage on a particular property, we biologists were accustomed to describing the bird when we addressed local landowners.

"Hey, there. We're looking for pond gannets, er, gourd-heads, er, well, they are birds this tall [gesturing] and mostly white with black heads." The landowner would perk up in recognition at some point.

At more than three feet tall with a five-foot wingspan, the stork is an imposing figure by size alone. But it stands out even more by its stark coloration—white body with black head, legs, tail, and wing edges. Its stiltlike legs and long neck reveal its membership in the wading-bird guild—those spindly masses of feathers and limbs that poke around the shallow marshes and ponds searching for anything aquatic that moves, only to end that movement with a swift sweep of their long, specialized bills. The storks' favorite fare includes fish, frogs, tadpoles, crayfish, baby alligators, amphiumas, and sirens. Sirens are eel-like, aquatic salamanders with large, external gills; two nearly vestigial front legs, and no hind legs. A full-grown siren would be a challenge to a stork—sirens can reach three feet in length. Amphiumas are also aquatic salamanders, but with no external gills and four puny legs. Two-toed amphiumas, found in the Southeast, can reach almost four feet in length.

The wood stork's shape is designed to take advantage of the thick, murky waters that the birds wade through while foraging. Storks wade slowly through soupy waters, brown with tannins from the oaks and tupelos, probing with their bills in the muddy bottoms for anything that wriggles. Since the water is so dark, the birds can't hunt by sight, so they feel with their bills to locate prey. Thus, they need a high density of prey to increase the chances that their bills will bump into something edible.

This tactile locating ability is possible because the stork's long, stout, downward-curved bill is ultra-sensitive to pressure. Yes, that big graceless bill that seems to weigh the bird's head down is actually a sensitive appendage. As the stork swings its bill, slightly agape, from side to side, hoping to bump into some live critter, the bill is ready with lightning-fast reflexes. On contact with potential food, the bill snaps shut on the prey with what may be the fastest voluntary reflex in the animal kingdom. Voluntary, in this case, refers to the reflexes that the bird can control, such as moving wings and legs. Involuntary muscles are the ones that work automatically, such as the heart and digestive muscles. Because storks don't need to see their prey, they also forage at night. That the storks can feed so efficiently in dark waters makes them invaluable in keeping aquatic populations in balance.

To find a stork, go to the deepest, darkest, spookiest swamp you can find in summer, anywhere from southern South Carolina to Texas. The best bets are Florida and Georgia. In their heyday, storks were secretive dwellers of the deep swamps, bayous, and glades, far from civilization. Cypresses, tupelos, water oaks, and willows cloaked their movements.

If you can't (or won't) traipse into a mire, you can spy a stork in a roadside ditch, a stormwater runoff pond, or even a golf course water trap. Now that civilization is almost everywhere, necessity has made the storks depend on rock quarries, golf courses, resorts, and other people-populated places. The birds have lost much of their anxiety over humans. Wherever there is shallow fresh water with small, live critters, you may find storks.

That is not to say that wood storks are common. They remain federally endangered, although they are making a comeback. Finding storks depends on the season, too, because the storks spread out in summer to all the southeastern states but concentrate only in Florida in the winter. Even storks from Georgia make the short migration to Florida.

Another way to locate storks is to find a thermal (a mass of hot air rising over a flat patch of land) that has a flock of birds circling in it. Study the shape of the birds. Some undoubtedly will be vultures, but some may be storks. Storks can soar high, then glide far on their broad wings, allowing them to travel great distances on little energy. In flight, storks can often be identified by their silhouette because they fly with their long necks extended. Vultures have short necks. Most other waders fly with their necks curved in an "s" shape.

Larry, Lisa, Bill, Lynne, and I were the five field biologists at the Savannah River Ecology Lab who were tasked with studying every aspect of the storks' lives during their March to September nesting season. Our colony was the northernmost-known nesting colony of wood storks in North America. The storks would arrive in March from points south and gather in the cypress swamp about thirty miles southwest of the Savannah River Plant.

After checking each other out, the storks pair up and start building nests up to three feet in diameter made with sticks, usually in the highest trees around. In most of the southeastern United States, those trees would likely be baldcypresses (*Taxodium distichum*). Around one hundred pairs of storks would nest each year.

Baldcypress trees are not true cypresses. They are more closely related to redwoods than to true cypresses. They are known in the Southeast as cypresses, and thus hereafter on these pages. Cypresses are extolled for their resistance to decay and insect pests. However, they are so slow-growing that regeneration hasn't kept pace with logging.

The adjective "bald" refers to the tree's pattern of shedding its needles in the winter, like a broad-leaved tree, although it is a conifer. The most distinctive feature of cypress trees is their unique "knees"—woody projections that rise from the roots above the water surface. The knees help the roots with gas exchange and provide support for the trunk in the unstable, soft, muddy bottom. Cypresses that are planted on dry land won't grow knees.

Cypresses can grow to 150 feet high, although that is rare. They grow naturally from southern Maryland to Florida and Texas, and up the Mississippi River basin to southern Illinois and Indiana.

The swamp that the Savannah River Plant storks call home is known locally as Big Duke's Pond. It is located in Millen, Georgia, just across the Savannah River from the nuclear facility.

Big Duke's Pond is an oval depression in the land that holds water all or most of the year. Ecologists refer to this type of swamp as a Carolina bay. Carolina bays exist from New Jersey to Florida, but they reach their greatest concentration in North and South Carolina, hence the name. "Bay" refers to the abundance of bay trees (sweet, loblolly, and red bays) found in such wetlands. A rim of sand holds water in during the wet season. Only about ten percent of Carolina bays remain, the rest having fallen victim to logging and development, as well as draining for the sake of draining.

Carolina bays are generally oriented northwest–southeast. They range in size from two hundred feet to seven miles long, but most are about a quarter-mile long. Depths can reach to fifty feet, but most are three to ten feet. Big Duke's is about twelve hundred acres, and the depth where we waded was about three feet. At least I didn't have to swim.

The landscape around Millen is dotted with Carolina bays of various sizes. The presence of these wetlands is one of the main attractions of storks to this area. When seen from a stork's-eye view, they must act as roads on a map would to humans.

The rest of the land in east-central Georgia could have been plucked straight out of *Gone With The Wind*. Giant live oaks, laden with pendulous Spanish moss, shade the yards and streets. Fields of cotton, onions, and peanuts stretch to the horizon. Lazy rivers and creeks with wide, cypress-studded floodplains complete the landscape.

During the fall and winter, our crew worked at the Savannah River Ecology Lab in Aiken, South Carolina, where we compiled and analyzed the season's data. During the spring and summer field season, Larry, Lisa, Bill, Lynne, and I lived in Millen to be close to the nesting birds.

Our rented abode was in a hamlet of Millen called Birdsville. The cottage on the Andrew plantation had four bedrooms and a recreation room with a ping-pong table. That meant five biologists were stuffed into a four-bedroom house. Always marching to a different drummer, I chose to sleep in the ping-pong room.

I don't remember how long I lived in Birdsville, assuming that it was named for the spectacular colony of storks that nested there. I do remember my surprise when our landlords, the Andrews, who were longtime residents of Birdsville, explained the history.

In the early days of the United States Postal Service, small villages were often served by postal carriers who delivered mail to plantations along their routes. The plantation owners would then ensure that their neighbors received their mail. In 1813, a post office was established on a plantation along the Savannah–Louisville route (the old Ogeechee Road), and the villagers were asked to name it. They named it after the postmaster. His name was Samuel Bird.

The attraction for choosing this particular cottage, other than the short drive to Big Duke's Pond and the lack of five-bedroom homes for rent in Millen, was that it had its own airstrip. Private airstrips are usually the prerogatives of exclusive communities, and downscale Millen hardly qualified as exclusive.

The Andrews' teen-aged son Franklin counted among his weekly chores the mowing of the field behind our house into a grass runway suitable only for the smallest of planes. A windsock on a pole stuck in the ground at one end and a couple of 55-gallon drums of aviation gas we brought in by pickup truck completed our airport. We were rich.

The airstrip was invaluable to us, since much of our work was aerial and the nearest real airport was in Augusta, about a 45-minute drive north. An hour and a half of driving every day would bite into our work time, so we had the pilot fly down and pick us up. He would announce his arrival the traditional aviator's way—by buzzing the house. When we heard the familiar engine, we would exclaim "De plane! De plane!" in *Fantasy Island* style. Then one of us would rush out to the grass airstrip, squeeze into the Super Cub, and take off to spend the morning chasing birds in a sardine can with wings.

Of course, we were not really chasing them. We were following them. The plane we used most frequently was a Piper Super Cub, a two-seat tail-dragger. What it possessed in maneuverability, it lacked in other features. Our only contact with the ground was with two-way, handheld radios. The plane biologist had one and so did the ground crews. The plane had no radio of its own.

The aerial work required one pilot and one biologist. The biologist would sit in the back seat and watch the storks, as the pilot circled tightly around the colony. When a stork left the colony, the biologist would yell to the pilot over the engine's din, "Follow that one!" The biologist would keep a constant eye on the bird so that the pilot could—oh, so briefly—glance away occasionally to check the skies for obstacles to our flight. He would dodge the circling vultures and cut sharp turns until the stork landed in a watery feeding area.

Then the plane biologist would direct a ground crew by radio to that feeding area. With one biologist in the plane and another in the observation blind, that left two or three people to go to the foraging site. Before going onto the site, the ground crew would need permission from the landowner, assuming the stork was on private land, which it usually was. Figuring out where the landowner lived was the task of the aerial guy or gal, who flew over the surrounding area and compared the houses.

From the air, you needed only to look for the closest immaculately kept, upper-class house, and you would find the landowner or farm manager. An in-ground swimming pool was a tip-off. Laundry hanging in the backyard and a junked car in the front were clues that a field hand lived there. After a few flyovers, we could proclaim with some confidence where the landowner lived. Then, the ground crew would drive the pickup truck to the landowner's house and ask permission to sample on the property.

Giving directions from above to a ground crew sounds easy, because flyers can see much more than crawlers. But the stork's-eye perspective has its flaws, especially when it comes to judging distances. Here is a typical radio communication:

Plane: "Oh, this one is going to be easy. Just turn right at the next dirt road and you'll be at the house in a few minutes."

Truck: "Where's the dirt road? I don't see anything but swamp."

Plane: "Keep driving. You're almost there."

Truck (five minutes later): "Oh, I think we're coming to it now. Just turn right?"

Plane: "Yup. Easy as could be."

Truck: "We're about to turn. What do you suggest we do about the chain across the road with the sign that says, 'Absolutely no trespassing—violators will be shot'?"

Plane (long silence): "Don't turn."

Once, we were perplexed when our usual aerial search for the landowner failed to find a stylish house, but inquiries by the ground crew led to a small shack. The ground crew who went to talk with the landowners this time consisted of me and Andy Comer, a graduate student from the University of Georgia, who was assisting with the radio telemetry segment of the project as part of his master's degree research.

Andy was tall and strong, with wavy blonde hair and a natural smile that could melt a snowdrift. He was a Georgia native and connected comfortably with the local people. I was a northerner whose previous contact with the Peach State had been zipping by on Interstate 95 while heading south to the Everglades for a winter vacation.

Andy and I knocked on the front door. An elderly black couple appeared.

"Hey, there. How ya'll doin'?" Andy inquired in his laid-back Southern drawl. "We're from the University of Georgia. Is that your pond over there?" he asked, as he pointed behind the house.

"Why, yes, suh," replied the man.

"We're studying some birds that we saw at your pond from an airplane and we'd like permission to go on your property to study them better," Andy explained. "They're called wood storks. They're white and black and about this tall [gesturing]. Have you seen them here?"

"Why, yes, suh, we see 'em here all the time," the man answered and the woman echoed. The couple welcomed us inside graciously. "Wha' dya want with 'em?"

I let Andy do the talking because I figured the couple would warm to a local more easily. "We're studying them because they are an endangered species," he explained.

The old man gasped. "They's dangerous? If they's dangerous, you cain't go near 'em. No, suh, you cain't go near 'em."

Suspecting the man was hard of hearing, Andy reworded his explanation, and emphasized, "No, they're an *endangered species*. There aren't many left. We're trying to help them. They're not dangerous. Really!"

The old man repeated, "Unh, unh, you cain't go near 'em. They's dangerous."

I appreciated that the man was trying to protect us from harm. Nothing Andy said made a difference. I tried in my own Yankee way, but the damage was done. The man kept mumbling, "No, suh, if they's dangerous, you cain't go near."

That was it for that site. We never did sample it. A little miscommunication goes a long way.

The five of us biologists, plus occasionally Andy, rotated fieldwork tasks, so each of us did everything equally. For the aerial work, the person flying had a relatively easy job—sitting and observing—but it was dangerous, cramped, and hot. Super Cubs are Lilliputian planes. Even at my diminutive size, I had no squirm room. The metal cabin sizzled like a tin can over a Sterno stove. After all, if it didn't have a radio, it certainly didn't have air-conditioning. We're talking Georgia in the summer. Add to that the fumes from the aviation gas. By sitting so close to the engine, breathing them was unavoidable. As someone with a strong stomach for flying, those fumes were the only thing that set my innards to trembling. I had to fly with a window open for fresh air.

The pilots we hired usually maintained a tight-lipped policy regarding their passengers' weaknesses. If anyone regurgitated, the pilots kept mum. Once one of them slipped up, which provided the power of suggestion to set me off on the same track hours later. Among the many items equipped as standard in commercial planes but lacking in ours was a barf bag. On the other hand, at least we could open a window.

The potential hazards of flying low in a Super Cub included flying into the storks and other birds. A four-pound stork hitting a three-foot wide windshield would have caused quite an irreparable mess. Although it didn't happen, it was an any-minute-now worry. Even watching a stork or vulture whiz past your plane with only yards to spare makes your heart go ka-*boom*. We flew barely above the cypress trees, usually with tight turns, to follow the flying storks. Then there were the thunderstorms that popped up regularly during the summer field season, causing the plane to bounce like a yo-yo. Not insignificant were the crop-dusters competing with us for low-level airspace. Finally, landing a small plane on a backyard grass strip surrounded by huge live oaks makes for blood-draining suspense.

The ground crew had a tough job physically with hazards of its own. Rarely did the storks respect us by choosing a foraging site next to a road. Often we had to bushwhack through catbriers and other thorny vines, following a compass reading or useless, albeit well-intentioned, directions from the plane. Hours could be wasted bumbling through dense brush, following a compass bearing, because the Super Cub that led the ground crew there couldn't hover until the crew found the site. Long after the plane left, the ground crew had to find its way back to the truck.

We lugged all of our equipment by hand, including the 25-pound fish-sampling trap. The trap was constructed with a one-meter wide by one-meter deep by half-meter high frame of metal pipes. Small-meshed netting was strung around the sides of the frame (not the top and bottom). When the trap was thrown into a shallow part of the pond, it formed an area of one-square meter, so that we could calculate how many fish per square meter were in that pond.

I remember that fish trap every day, even twenty years later. Every time I bend forward or backward, that familiar stabbing pain in my lower back reminds me of the time I threw that trap at the cow-pie pond. That particular pond was a favorite cooling-off area for a small herd of cows. The trampling hooves churned the pond bottom into two-foot-deep muck and manure. I volunteered first to throw the trap, so I waded up to my knees in the muck. I lifted the trap over my head and tossed it the required eight feet from me, so that it hit a place where we had not walked. Two colleagues scooped through the mud with nets to sort out fish, crayfish, tadpoles, or any other living creatures that a stork might eat. After they finished scooping, they lugged the trap back to me so that I could toss it again in another direction. With muck clinging to the frame, the trap now weighed significantly more than 25 pounds. Not accounting for the increased weight and the fact that my legs were stuck in place, I tried to turn my body to face another direction while holding the heavy trap over my head. But I could only twist at the waist. Manured mud was dripping onto my hair. I hurled the trap. Snap! That was my back. I thank my guardian spirit for my gymnastics days, which gave my torso disproportionate strength than my size warranted. Thus, my injury wasn't severe. However, it was permanent.

Other hazards faced the ground crews. Timber and pigmy rattlesnakes could pop up anywhere. We had to wade into murky water, replete with alligators and cottonmouth snakes (also called water moccasins). If the fire ants didn't get us, the poison ivy would. Or perhaps the lightning, so common in the southern summers, ready to strike while we were standing in water holding the metal probe of the water-quality meter. Just the heat and humidity could zap our strength, but this was compounded by carrying the cumbersome measuring gear through the woods, climbing over logs, ducking branches, and so on, while wearing long sleeves to keep from getting scratched by thorns and bitten by insects, and heavy pants to keep the snakes from finding flesh.

Then there was the matter of the water purity. We didn't worry about the swamp water, because Nature kept that relatively germ-free. The farm ponds were the putrid ones. Sometimes we measured the water variables with a hydrology meter while the cows stood next to us, pouring streams of urine at our immersed feet. Cow pies lined the shore. If the storks ate fish from that water, we had to sample.

No, we did not wear rubber hip waders. They were too heavy to carry with our other gear, and too hot and bulky to wear through the thick brush while clambering over fallen logs. We waded into the water in canvas boots and army-surplus field pants. I wore pants with drawstring cuffs to keep the leeches from sucking my legs.

Despite the potential showstoppers, the worst fates we suffered were sprained backs, wasp stings, scrapes and bruises, overheating, upchucking, and other minor maladies.

To gain additional insight into the natural feeding behavior of our storks, I devised a time-lapse video camera setup that filmed a foraging pond while we were absent. With a five-gallon bucket as a waterproof housing, I set the camera on a tripod wherever there was an obliging landowner. I needed a location where the camera was secure, so I wouldn't stress about it walking off, so to speak.

One such landowner was a Mennonite family, part of a small enclave that had moved from Pennsylvania when land there became too expensive. They farmed the land with respect, joy, and rarely seen stewardship.

The family welcomed me and my camera with enthusiastic support. They were insatiably curious about the storks. The younger children would follow me quietly while I set up the camera in their stock pond. It was a perfect situation, except that the cows kept knocking over the tripod. A little extra work on my part of placing the camera in a nearby tree solved that problem.

Besides the aerial and water-sampling tasks, we also had to observe the storks from an observation blind in the nesting colony at Big Duke's Pond. This involved one person driving a pickup truck about a mile along a sandy road, normally used only by hunters, to the edge of the swamp. He or she would park the truck and hoof it from there, carrying lunch, water, a clipboard, and a two-way radio through the swamp to the blind.

Once, I was driving along the sandy road on the way to the blind for my shift when a nine-foot alligator, lying on the single-track road, necessitated an unplanned stop. The reptile had chosen a sunny spot and was probably digesting its recent meal. What should a gal in a hurry to get to work do?

I sat for a while and tried to think like an alligator. What would coax me to leave? If I were a larger-than-human, leathery-skinned, toothy predator lying in the sun and digesting my latest meal, nothing would. There was no other way to the blind, but I couldn't just sit there. I could be waiting until dark.

Honking the horn would make almost anything jump, I figured. So, I sat there tooting the horn to the wind for a few minutes, without seeing so much as a blink of the nictitating membrane (the semi-transparent third eyelid) from the big reptile.

What was Plan B? Maybe if I could slowly sneak past it—there was just enough room off the road for the truck to fit between the animal's snout and the nearest tree. It was worth a try. Slowly, I started rolling the truck along, almost imperceptibly.

Maybe it wouldn't notice me. I had seen gators move this slowly, sneaking up on their prey. I would become a sheet-metal alligator. The wheels inched forward at glacial speed. When the truck was directly alongside the gator, I held my breath. Gently, gently . . . so near, so good! The gator seemed oblivious. Apparently, it was content to let me pass. The animal's head was only a few feet from my toes, separated by a couple of thin layers of metal. When its snout was even with the driver's side door, it rose up on its feet and took a step back. *Whew! It's retreating!* I thought.

Apparently, alligator behavior was not my forte. The gator did not have surrendering on its grape-sized mind. Instead, it puffed itself up to larger-than-life size, let out a hiss that curdled my blood, and lunged headlong at the truck. Its snout smacked the door with a hollow *thump*. The reptile recoiled, readying itself for another lunge. Fearing not for a dented door but for a wounded quadruped, I flattened the gas pedal, spun out on the sand, and barely managed to roll the whirling wheels out of reach of the next attack. Thirty feet past, I stopped and looked back to see what fate befell the alligator.

The mass wasn't moving. A concussion? A corpse? I strained for any sign of life. A four-legged kamikaze? I prayed that I had not harmed it, but administering first aid, or even examining its wounds seemed like a career-ending move. Lacking a better idea, I continued on my way to the blind, driving along the sandy edge of the swamp. On my return, the gator was gone. Apparently, the battering-ram impersonation didn't faze it. I can only surmise that the full-body punch to my truck left only a bruised snout or ego.

The sandy soil rimmed the Carolina bay, but the swamp was unmistakenly mud. Our normal routine was to park the truck at the swamp's edge and continue on foot. The swamp segment of the trip involved ten to fifteen minutes of wading through waist-deep water, while following our trail of hot-pink flagging that hugged the trees. Along the way, felled logs created a nasty obstacle course for each of us. The swamp had been logged for its valuable cypress trees decades earlier, with many prone trunks and stumps left submerged. This alone was a hindrance, but mixed with the notorious black water of the swamp, it created a treacherous journey into the hinterlands. The inky tint resulted from the tannins in the leaves of such trees as the black tupelo soaking in the water, brewing a swamp tea. We couldn't possibly see more than a few inches into the water.

After smashing my shins to pulp on the almost-daily trips, I eventually learned to carry a small branch as a walking staff each time I entered the swamp and to probe the opaque water before each footstep. Poke, poke, step. Poke, poke, step. It became a dance—a swamp waltz that everyone on our crew independently engaged in, secretly at first. The phenomenon resembled convergent evolution, as when two unrelated organisms evolve separately but end up sharing a similar trait because of similar conditions. Even the probing staff wasn't enough for me sometimes, and when my shins couldn't take any more abuse, I wore my shin pads from tae kwon do class in the water.

While I couldn't ignore the woody impediments, I could pay lesser heed to the alligators and cottonmouth snakes. They hid cleverly, but I knew they lurked there. These potentially dangerous animals preferred to avoid humans. Provided I didn't step on them, I was safe. Thus, the swamp stick served another purpose, that of warning the critters to scoot out of the way.

I danced my way to the depths of the swamp to where the observation blind was. Then the fun began. No room for acrophobia here! The blind platform was sixty-five feet up, atop a scaffold frame that our crew had assembled by hand. The frame featured a lower storage platform at fifty feet. Metal rungs spaced about eighteen inches apart allowed us to climb to either level. A canvas cover above the top platform provided shade and camouflage.

On a typical day, only one person at a time went to the blind, one in the morning and one in the afternoon. When we arrived at the blind, we had to climb the sixty-five feet, while carrying a daypack containing food, water, two-way radio, and other gear. We hauled ourselves, hand over hand over hand, like climbing a ladder, until we reached the blind platform.

Once on the platform, the biologist would settle down for the long shift, usually around seven hours. He or she counted the number of chicks in each nest, how many times an adult came to feed its young, and recorded notes about other useful information, including the weather.

The Georgia sun would beat through the spindly needles of the cypress canopy and onto the canvas tarp. Without a breeze, the shade wasn't always enough. One afternoon on my blind shift,

I read the air temperature thermometer—114 degrees. When the time came for me to descend, the rungs of the scaffolding were hot enough to burn my hands. I was grateful that the only eyes watching me were those of the alligators and the birds. I had no gloves. To descend the height of a six-story building, I had to take off my T-shirt, my only upper garment, and wrap it around my hands like a potholder. Do you think the animals are still talking about the show?

While sitting in the tree canopy, I could peer down into the black water and see the snouts of the alligators hovering around the bases of the nest trees, waiting for some unlucky stork chick to lose its balance and tumble—*kerplunk*—into the water. The gators had an additional opportunity to munch, since the storks' nesting attracted other birds to the water. Little blue herons and great egrets foraged around the bases of the stork nesting trees, scrounging for fish that fell out of the stork nests when the adults returned to feed their chicks. If something disturbed the stork chicks, they regurgitated the fish they had just eaten, and these would fall to the water below. Thus, occasionally, an unwary heron or egret feeding on the free handouts could become table fare for an alligator.

The gators can tell when a splash from a fallen object signals something living or something inedible. They hone in on the live fare. A young bird that tumbles into the water will flail around, creating ripples that the gators can sense. To amuse myself, sometimes I would drop a peach pit into the water from the safety of my high perch and watch the gators paddle toward it, only to stop abruptly when the ripples ceased.

Other wading birds—such as great blue herons, green herons, and white ibises—nested or roosted among the storks. Together with the frogs, snakes, turtles, and fish, the swamp was a lively place.

Hanging out in a wading bird colony is not for the squeamish or swank. The swamp reeks of bird droppings that whitewash the branches and cloud the water. Rotting fish regurgitated by nestlings lie on the branches or rain into the water. After a while, I adjusted to the stench. Much as soft classical music becomes "white noise" at your desk, regurge stench eventually became a "white smell" in the swamp.

The cacophony, from chicks so ravenous they wailed for food, was easier to handle. When the parents return to the colony with crops full of fish, they listen for the calls from their nestlings. Most birds in large colonies identify family members by voice. How they can isolate one baby's voice among hundreds or thousands baffles scientists.

Observing the nests was just part of the work in the nesting colony. When the chicks were old enough, we banded them for later identification. That meant putting permanent, aluminum U.S. Fish and Wildlife Service "bracelets" with unique numbers on the birds' legs so that we could some day track their individual movements and their fates. Engraved on each metal band is a number traceable to that bird alone, plus a telephone number toll-free from the United States, Canada, Mexico, and most of the Caribbean, to report the band if someone finds it.

The aluminum bands from U.S. Fish and Wildlife Service are made in 28 band sizes to fit the legs of birds from humming-birds to trumpeter swans. Colored bands are also approved for use on birds, although for shorter-term observations. With the aluminum band, it is nearly impossible to read the number while the bird is not in hand. To identify a live individual stork from a distance, therefore, we needed colored bands.

Banding can only be useful if people find the band and report it to the Bird Banding Lab in Patuxent, Maryland. Only a small percentage of the bands are ever recovered, but even those few give us valuable information without the cost, risk, and time investment of radio-tagging (attaching radio-tracking devices). Most band returns come from birds that can be legally hunted, such as ducks and geese, because the dead birds are retrieved by the hunters. Otherwise, people rarely encounter dead birds.

People who find and report bands are rewarded by the Bird Banding Lab with information about where and when the bird was banded. Considering the distances birds fly and the ages they live to, people who report bands may be shocked at what they learn. A white-throated sparrow, for example, flew 418 miles in one day. A wood duck banded in New York was shot 1,111 miles away in Florida three days later. Neither example is an extreme record. The longest-lived bird in the wild, documented by banding, was a Laysan albatross that lived to fifty years and eight months.

The Bird Banding Lab, which compiles reports from re-searchers all over the country, has been keeping records for a hundred years.[3] Since 1902, researchers have banded more than 63 million birds of nine hundred species and subspecies. However, from 1908 to 1999, only 3,273,319 bands were recovered or reported. That is a mere 5.5 percent. From 1914 to 2004, 3,279 wood storks were banded, and only 53 bands were recovered or reported, a paltry 1.6 percent. Thus, much work goes into the effort for a little, albeit invaluable, information. We can predict the spread of such diseases as West Nile Virus and avian flu by the migration patterns determined by banding returns.

Before we could band the chicks, we had to reach them in their nests. As if climbing the 65-foot observation tower wasn't challenging enough, we had to scale the cypress trees to the nests, grab the chicks without being attacked by the defending parents, lower the chicks safely to the ground crew, and later raise them back safely to their nests.

For that process, let me start by explaining how we climbed the trees. My colleagues and I all claimed some tree-climbing experience, later revealed as somewhat exaggerated. The cypress trees had no branches up to thirty or forty feet above the ground. Merely reaching the first branch required the use of ladders, which didn't exist in the swamp until we hand-carried them in.

As a group, we agreed to practice setting up the ladders outside of the wood stork colony where we wouldn't disturb the birds. Then we would be quick and smooth when it counted. A local landowner gave us access to a stand of tall pines near our house in Birdsville. The climbing method we used involved a set of aluminum sectional ladders. We knew them as "Swedish climbing ladders," and they came in identical ten-foot sections, each with a chain at the top and points at the feet.

We agreed that each person should set up the ladders on a tree with minimal assistance from the others. We would practice as if we were in the stork swamp, each of us taking a turn. The cypress trees grew in water and we were practicing on dry land, but we figured getting the ladders up would work the same way.

Larry went first. He leaned the first ladder section against a pine tree, made sure the pointed feet were securely pushed into the ground, then climbed to the top of the ladder, where the chain was. He wrapped the chain around the trunk and secured the loose end to the other side of the ladder to prevent it from falling. Then he descended partway, low enough for someone to hand him another ladder section. Clutching that, he climbed to the top of the first section, muscled the second one up, and set the points of the feet into the holes at the top of the first section.

"This is a snap!" mocked Larry.

Once Larry had centered the second section, he climbed that section, as yet unsecured at the top. As a safety measure, Larry wore a tree-climbing belt that was loosely wrapped around the tree trunk. He could fall, but probably not to the ground. When he reached the top of the second section, he wrapped that section's upper chain around the trunk, as he had done with the first section. This he would repeat until he had four sections of ladder secured and had climbed almost forty feet.

Larry was doing an exemplary job, smoothly lifting the sections up and fitting them into place. All was going well until, hanging on to the third section, he erupted in a frenzy of arm-waving and leg-kicking, simultaneously shouting a few choice words. Baffled, the four of us stood on the ground spellbound by this bizarre behavior. Finally, through clenched teeth, the normally unflappable Larry managed a curt, "Fire ants!"

That's when we looked at the base of the tree and noticed that we had selected a practice tree with a fire ant mound strategically guarding it. Encumbered by the safety belt, Larry managed to squiggle to the ground, whereupon he shook off the rest of the little rascals.

The critter I am talking about is the red imported fire ant (*Solenopsis invicta*), whose ancestors allegedly hitched a ride on a freighter from South America that docked in Mobile, Alabama, in the 1930s. Since then, the insects have spread to most of the southern tier of states and have damaged crops and farm equipment and even killed livestock.

If you haven't experienced a fire ant's bite, consider yourself fortunate. Actually, fire ants don't bite, they sting and inject venom. The immediate effect is intense sharp pain, a burning sensation to which the pests owe their name. After it dissipates in an hour or so, the itchy pustule remains for up to a few weeks. One sting is a nuisance, but nothing more, unless you're allergic. Multiple stings are undeniably miserable. At least eighty people have died of allergic reactions.

After Larry's excruciating experience, a reasonable person would assume that we moved the ladders to a safer practice tree. But, no, we were stalwart, dedicated biologists. What if we encountered fire ants in the colony? Or a wasp nest? Or any other pestilence that could come our way? How could we be sure we would succeed in our mission if we became flustered over this? We wanted to be prepared for anything.

A round of "one for all and all for one" glances was sufficient. Esprit de corps prevailed. Back went Larry up the ladder. One more section and dozens of bites later, he descended to Earth, smugly victorious.

"Next?" he chided. One by one, Lynne, Bill, Lisa, and I repeated his steps, including the flailing arms, kicking legs, and choice words. Gradually, the convulsions would pass as each person steeled himself or herself against the pain, returning to Earth with the same stoic grin. Nothing would deter us—not heat, wasps, rain, wind, angry storks, and certainly not fire ants.

Climbing the ladders was the easy part. The next step was to carry the ladder sections to the colony through the blackwater swamp, one person at each end. The obstacle course of submerged cypress logs tried to thwart us at every step. It wasn't possible to coordinate the swamp dance as a twosome. Walking was exasperating enough.

Our dry-land practice session paid off. Even in two or three feet of water, with the fat buttresses and knees of cypress trees, we could handle the ladders smoothly. However, once we erected the ladders, we still had to get to the nests.

Four sections of ladder (forty feet) were the most we could use, because above that the branches blocked the way. Many nests were fifty, sixty, or seventy feet high. That meant we had to free-climb (climb without ladders) the rest of the way. This we did not practice, because we all claimed tree-climbing experience.

Each person chose a cypress tree to climb. Sometimes it helps to be tall or long-limbed, especially when reaching for branches. I was neither. I had never climbed more than ten feet up a tree. But I had powers from my high school and college gymnastics days that allowed me to stretch my legs higher than other people and gave good balance, the upper-body strength to hoist myself to higher branches, and no fear of heights. Furthermore, I could climb on limbs that heavier people would snap.

So, you would think I would scurry up the first tree, and in fact, I did enthusiastically volunteer. The whole crew gathered around the tree that first day. Just as I had practiced, minus the fire ants, I assembled four sections of ladder against the tree up to the first branches. All was going according to plan.

When I started my eagerly anticipated free-climb, I flung my leg up to reach a branch. To my dismay, it stopped far short of its goal. I strained and strained, but I could not hoist my leg high enough. Our practice session on dry land had not prepared me for this. Wet pants cling. Especially tight, wet pants. I had chosen the wrong wardrobe that morning.

Should I tell them my pants are too tight? I wondered. I stretched and stretched, still in vain. Embarrassed, I meekly called down below, "Uh, guys, I gotta problem."

I descended to the ooze, explained the situation, and resolved to wear my baggiest pants from then on. Never mind that my slim figure would be lost in a potato-sack garment. After the snickers diminished, my reputation besmirched, someone else uneventfully ascended my tree.

The next day, after doing some aquatic stretches, I scaled my first tree in loose bloomers. Climbing into a tree canopy with your own hands and feet is a "high" all its own. Looking down on the little dolls standing in the muck made me feel taller than anyone. It reminded me of my days in college, when I would hike to the top of Mount Mansfield, the highest peak in Vermont. Standing on the geodetic marker at the summit, I would shoo my fellow hikers back down the trail or make them kneel.

"Please," I would beg, "just for a minute, I want to be the tallest person in Vermont." They obliged.

At nest level, I could see into the lives of birds and imagine how it feels to live on a slender branch—precarious, crowded, dusty, noisy, and smelly. I don't think they noticed the latter. Except for flightless species and scavenging vultures, most birds have no appreciable sense of smell. Smelling wouldn't do them much good in the sky, where scents swirl around on the wind and it is impossible to know where they came from. Scents need something to cling to, like soil or trees, to be of any use. Furthermore, adding the biological features necessary to make a usable sense of smell would make the birds' heads too heavy to balance in flight.

Larry Bryan, left, assists as I prepare the ladders to climb a cypress tree in Big Duke's Pond.

Once I was up in the branches, I still had to reach out to a nest and grab a chick. This may sound easy, but the chicks already weighed about four pounds and had stout bills that they weren't afraid to use. A flapping, flailing chick could not only hurt me, it could hurt itself, something we strived to prevent at all costs with this endangered species.

Besides the two climbing belts I wore to keep me from falling, I also wore safety goggles. This worked well for keeping a frantic bill from poking my eyes out, but most of the time, the lenses were so foggy from chronic humidity and my body steam that I could barely see. So, off they would come. Long sleeves and pants and leather gloves protected my skin from rough bark, sharp bills, and claws. Canvas boots with lug soles gave me traction on the bark, wet from my pants still dripping with swamp water. In the ninety-degree heat and ninety-percent humidity, my skin was covered from face to toes. Between the soggy clothing and the climbing belts, I didn't feel so free when I climbed.

Reaching out cautiously to the end of a branch to grab a chick, I would gently guide it toward me until I could grab it. Hanging by a climbing belt freed my hands to tuck the feisty bird gingerly into a pillowcase. Using a rope that was dangling from my belt, I lowered the squirming pillowcase, weaving it carefully through the branches, so it didn't snag or bump its occupant. Its destination was the ground crew below, waiting waist-deep in the swamp water.

The ground crew deftly weighed the chick, measured its wings and legs, and attached leg bands (two on each leg) with an individual identification number and color combination. When the crew was done, they stuffed the chick back into the pillowcase and up I pulled—ten . . . twenty . . . thirty . . . forty . . . fifty feet—into my waiting hands. Finally, I would set the chick back in its nest.

Although we all worked with steady speed, the process was time-consuming. Once I spent three hours in a tree just to get four chicks banded.

After someone had climbed a certain tree, it became his or her tree. We formed this unspoken pact for efficiency, because the climber knew the route through the branches and could scale it faster and with more confidence than someone who had not climbed that tree.

Research is full of surprises, and we had our share. One year, we noticed that some chicks had holes in the skin of their necks, a dreadful sight to see, but one that the chicks seemed to ignore. These dermal lesions appeared to be caused by an ectoparasite, a tiny organism that lives off a larger organism. In this case, it was an insect known as a dermestid. Dermestid beetle larvae feed on dead bodies. I had never heard of them feeding on living animals, as we were witnessing.

I collected some of the larvae from the nests and sent them to Northern Arizona University, where dermestid expert Dr. R.S. Beal identified them as *Dermestes nidum*. The species had not previously been recorded in Georgia, so my proof was the first.[4] This dermestid had been found, however, in wood storks and great blue herons in Florida. Later, I also found it on a little blue heron in Florida.

Some of the chicks survived their ectoparasitic infections, but others disappeared from their nests. We can only assume that they died of their wounds or a parent "helped" them out of the nests as undesirable weaklings.

When biologists work closely with a species, we begin to believe we can predict their behavior. Thus, you can understand how baffled we were when one of us flew over Big Duke's Pond one day in early spring and found that most of the birds were suddenly gone, the eggs in their nests abandoned and exposed. Within a few days, all the nests were abandoned. We searched for signs of predators, human disturbance, or any clue why the parents would leave so abruptly. Where did they go and why?

One reason for leaving would be if the water under the nest trees was disappearing. Dry ground would cause the alligators to leave, because they need water. This would open a safe passage for raccoons, opossums, snakes, and other terrestrial predators to walk or slither in, climb the trees, and prey on the chicks. However, we saw no indication that the water level was dropping.

Thanks to the Piper Super Cub, we found the birds easily after undertaking a short aerial search. They had settled in Little Duke's Pond, a mere one air-mile away. To us, it seemed that the smaller swamp was a poor choice, since there were fewer trees to buffer the nests from the outside world. No explanation for the move could satisfy us—that is, until a month later.

Imperceptibly to us, the water level *was* slowly dropping in Big Duke's Pond. In a month's time, and at the peak of nesting activity, the water under the nest trees in the big swamp was gone. Strangely, the water in Little Duke's stayed deep throughout the nesting season. How the storks knew that one swamp would shrink and the other wouldn't baffles me to this day. The birds returned to Big Duke's Pond to nest the next year.

Eventually, the chicks were old enough for us to attach radio transmitters (tracking devices) to their bodies. We planned to apply a technique used successfully on another endangered gliding and soaring bird, the California condor.

Malcolm, our project leader, was new at the job when we commenced this phase. He assumed the responsibility from the man who developed the wood stork project and who had planned the radio telemetry methods based on the condor project. Thus, we proceeded to put the same type of solar-powered radio transmitters on the storks as the condors wore.

Stork chicks remain in the nest for about fifty days, after which they practice flying around the nest trees. Just before our chicks were old enough to fly was the time we chose to put the transmitters on. If we waited any later than that, we wouldn't be able to catch them.

We set out for the swamp and chose a nest tree. One of us climbed it and retrieved a chick, choosing the largest chick within reach.

The transmitter was a patagial one, meaning it was placed on the patagium of the wing, a membranous area without muscles or bones. To attach a transmitter to the wing, we cut a hole in the skin, placed the transmitter's photovoltaic face on top with a post through the wing, and secured the other end of the post with a nut. I don't know if this hurt the bird, but it seemed to be the only way to get the information we needed.

The transmitter's solar cells would face the sun when the bird was flying and would absorb energy, so that we could receive the transmitter's signal from a great distance. The solar cells allowed the transmitter to be lighter than a battery-powered one because batteries are heavy.

Our crew attached two more transmitters that day and checked on the birds daily. Within days, it was obvious that there was trouble. The transmitters were so heavy that the chicks couldn't lift their wings. They were dragging their bangled bones so badly that their feathers became scraggly. These birds were too young to have developed their flight muscles.

By then, Malcolm was traveling out-of-state and incommunicado. We were on our own to decide what to do. We did not make any decisions lightly. We recalled the uproar when an endangered California condor chick died at the hands of a biologist who was trying to save the species. We did not want to be responsible for killing another endangered bird.

We believed that leaving the transmitters on would surely condemn the hosts. But removing them was risky, too, since they would leave holes in the wings and the wings were already badly weakened. Nevertheless, gathering our collective sagacity, we decided that removing the transmitters would give the birds a better chance for survival.

One bird disappeared from its nest about four days after we accessorized its wing. We searched around the cypress trees in vain.

Two days later, Lisa radioed from the blind that a chick had torn its pierced wing. Since the nest was in my tree, Larry and I rushed to the swamp in slow motion (remember the loose-sand road and the blackwater obstacle course?). I set up the ladders, climbed the tree, and brought the weakened bird down. We unscrewed the transmitter and carried the bird out of the swamp in a pillowcase. We took the bird to a veterinarian, who cut away some dead tissue. I returned the chick to its lofty nest just as the sun was setting. Bats, owls, and other crepuscular creatures were emerging when Lisa, Larry, and I felt our way out of the darkening swamp. Poke, poke, step. Poke, poke, step. Poke, poke, *ouch!* Poke, poke, limp.

Two days after that, Andy radioed from the blind, "I'm watching a chick that fell out of its nest. That blasted electronic bracelet threw it off balance. Someone has to come out and take care of it."

Lisa and I went back to the colony. After we removed the contraption from the bedraggled bird's wing, Lisa climbed to the nest and returned the downtrodden chick.

Later, we removed the transmitter from yet another bird, which fared better, but its prognosis for a normal life was still doubtful. We had already unanimously agreed that we would boycott putting more patagial transmitters on storks. Fortunately, when Malcolm returned, he gave no argument.

One of our challenges became finding a safer method for attaching transmitters to the birds. After consulting with stork researchers in Florida, we settled on placing the solar transmitters on the backs of adult storks, using a backpack harness that involved no permanent alteration to the stork's body.

The other challenge was catching the adult storks. Even the Chutes-and-Ladders game of getting the chicks seemed easier than catching the adults. The chicks were a captive audience. Furthermore, we believed that the chicks were less stressed by capture than the adults were. Nevertheless, we had little choice.

We switched to a scary-sounding capture method called rocket-netting. Rocket-netting isn't as high-tech as it sounds, although it does involve small projectiles. First, we had to scout out an area where storks were likely to feed—a shallow shoreline uncluttered by vegetation. The birds might cluster near that shoreline. Then we had to stretch a net about twenty feet long, folded accordion-style into a strip, along the water's edge. We would stake one edge to the ground, and the opposite edge would be attached to the rockets—six-inch metal canisters stuffed with a propellant. We would hide nearby in a blind, and when the storks wandered into the area where the net would cover, we would fire the rockets with a remote detonator. In a flash, the net would fly over the birds, trapping them underneath. We would rush in, untangle them—preferably before they drowned in the shallow water—and place the transmitters on as quickly as possible.

The method worked. We injured no birds. Placing a transmitter on a bird's back turned out to be preferable to using its wing because it balanced the bird better. Unfortunately, by this point, we missed collecting data from a whole segment of the birds' lives—what they did when they left the nest. We would have gotten that if we had transmitters on the chicks.

The transmitters gave us information that we weren't learning any other way. In the winter, the storks left Georgia, but no one knew where they went until we placed the transmitters on them. Around December or January, when there was no fieldwork to do, I flew to Florida in a Cessna 152 that I outfitted with telemetry antennas on the wing struts. I was able to locate the birds in various places across the state.

The intense banding efforts also proved valuable. Two years after I left the stork project, I was studying herons for the National Audubon Society in the Florida Keys. One day in December, one of our biologists heard about a faunal feeding frenzy at Mrazek Pond. Mrazek is a popular birding stop in Everglades National Park on the road to the village of Flamingo. During the dry winter season, the water level often drops in the pond and the aquatic creatures become concentrated into a small area and stressed. This makes them easy prey for piscivorous (fish-eating) birds, as well as otters, alligators, snakes, and turtles. The predators gather so numerously to enjoy the banquet and so near the road that the location offers phenomenal wildlife sights.

Three of us were working in our Audubon office when the phone call came that the spectacle was in progress. A quick glance among us—another one-for-all and all-for-one—and we were grabbing spotting scopes and binoculars and skipping out the door. It was a two-hour drive in the middle of a workday, but we decided we could do some wading bird foraging studies while we were there (wink, wink). Resourcefulness is a great ally.

When we arrived at Mrazek Pond, a crowd of people was gathered on the bank, rows of spotting scopes ringing the edge of the water. The proverbial little birdies had done their job of telling local birders and tourists of the avian party.

The pond was packed with life. At one time we tallied 96 snowy egrets, 75 great egrets, at least 55 white pelicans, 19 wood storks, 9 white ibises, 5 great blue herons, 4 roseate spoonbills, 3 tricolored herons, 2 black-crowned night herons, and 2 anhingas. It was impossible to count the alligators and other less brightly colored animals.

For all the pastel grace and beauty of spoonbills, the ballet of the dainty egrets, and the incongruous size of the pelicans, it was the wood storks that caught my eye. Anyone who has ever banded birds will always be watching for one of his or her birds. Forget looking at the heads first. We look at their legs.

As I scanned the stilts of each stork, my eyes fell on a pair wearing familiar bracelets. The bird appeared to be a second-year bird. I could tell because its fuzzy head was a medium-to-dark color and its bill was dark yellow, nearly black. Adults have completely featherless heads, showing a shiny black pate. Stork bills are yellow when they are chicks and turn darker with age. The heads are fuzzy and yellow on chicks, turning darker and balder as they approach adulthood at four years.

I scribbled down the four band colors: right leg = aluminum over orange, left leg = orange over white. The U.S. Fish and Wildlife Service band number was too small to read from that distance.

I knew there were several stork-banding projects around, but they used different styles of colored bands than did my former project. I recognized the ones I saw as Savannah River Ecology Lab bands, the same ones I'd put on storks a few years earlier. If I was wrong about the age, it could have been one of my birds. Did I hold this bird in my hands 550 miles away?

As soon as I returned to the office, I called Larry Bryan, who was still watching over the storks in Birdsville, and gave him the color combination.

"Great find!" he exclaimed. "I'll look it up and get back to you."

Shortly thereafter, Larry called back with the answer. "You're right. It's from Birdsville. We banded it two years ago on 'E' tree."

Larry had the exact nest and date. Since I had left the project in March, and banding didn't start until mid-May, it wasn't one of my birds. Nevertheless, the thrill of finding a banded bird from "my" colony was, in simple words, what biologists live for. I knew that our tampering was not harming the bird because it had found its way to this wintering paradise for storks, and I confirmed that saving the Everglades was just as important to the Birdsville colony as saving Big Duke's Pond.

Our wood stork project did more than just study the birds. We assisted the National Audubon Society with the creation of a foraging pond for the storks. Audubon provided the site at their Silver Bluff Plantation's Kathwood Lake, and we provided the technical expertise to allow them to partition the pond into segments to raise fish of different sizes. The project was labor-intensive but provided a replacement feeding area for the wetlands that were expected to be impacted by the restart of the nuclear L-Reactor.

A wood stork guards its chick at Big Duke's Pond.

Stork populations are making a gradual recovery. A species that doesn't start nesting until it is about four years old and raises only two or three offspring a year cannot have a speedy population recovery even in good times. The artificial wetlands, such as at Kathwood Lake, help to bolster the population.

In 1984, biologists counted 6,040 stork nests in South Carolina, Georgia, and Florida. In 2006, they counted more than 10,000 nesting pairs. In 2007, a severe drought year, there were around 5,000 pairs. Although the numbers fluctuate dramatically from year to year due to weather, the Fish and Wildlife Service now thinks it's ready to reclassify wood storks as threatened. But for now, "they's endangered."

Chapter 5.
Who Says It's the Size that Counts?

Tae kwon do instructors in sleepy Aiken, South Carolina, were few and far between. Finding a good one in a large city was tough enough. I visited several dojos (Japanese for studios) and settled on the one that seemed the best, although I longed for the old days with Mr. Choi.

Grandmaster Seung Choi came from Korea in 1976, handpicked by the U.S. Army to train our troops because he possessed the rare quality of being not only a master of the Korean martial art, but also an excellent teacher. After Mr. Choi retired from teaching the Army, he opened his own dojo in Portland, Maine. Shortly after I moved to Portland to work for the Maine Audubon Society, I discovered Mr. Choi's dojo. I had been wanting to learn a self-defense art and could not afford the lessons until then.

Typical of his east Asian heritage, Mr. Choi was sparely built. He taught all shapes and sizes of students with equal ease, and he could teach each of us how to use our peculiar physiques to our advantage. To me, he would explain in pidgin English, "You are small. You must get in close and fast, like mosquito. Always close and fast, just like mosquito!" He should know. He was barely a dragonfly himself.

So skillful at judging people's strengths was Mr. Choi that he taught an unusual student with casual ease. A woman in my class, maybe in her late twenties, had lost a leg as a child when a tree fell on her. Toni ambulated with crutches and couldn't do the kicks and punches as the rest of us could. However, she was determined to fool any human predator who assumed she was helpless. Each time Mr. Choi showed the class a new traditional move, he would turn to Toni and show her a similar move using a crutch instead of an arm or leg. These he invented on the spot. Toni became as adept at self-defense as the rest of the class. That Mr. Choi could instantly adapt to new circumstances made him the epitome of a good sensei (Japanese for teacher).

In graduate school, I spent a lot of time alone in the boon-docks—hiking, camping, snowshoeing, birding, or whatever else drew me into the woods. I had known my career would take me away from civilization. Actually, I was probably safer forest-bound than on city streets, where I also walked alone. Keeping a gun for protection was out of the question, because I have always despised guns. The only one I have ever fired was an animal-tranquilizer gun. At my size, learning self-defense seemed prudent.

Size, or lack thereof, is a recurring theme in my life, although I would like to prove that it shouldn't be. I learned shortly after college that what most people perceive as gender discrimination is actually a bias against small-sized people, who usually happen to be women. After years of simple observations, I see the correlation. Small women have the most difficult time obtaining almost any type of job, but certainly in physically and intellectually challenging ones. Even small men suffer that fate. Taller people, regardless of gender, generally hold higher-level positions and obtain them more easily. Line up the staff of any large company by rank and see for yourself if the taller people are lumped at the upper management end and the shorter ones at the lower-income end.

Here is how the hierarchy appears to me: Tall men have the easiest time obtaining high-level and high-paying positions. Next are medium-height men and tall women (about equal), followed by medium-height women and short men (about equal). Last are the short women.

Guess where I fit in? At barely five feet, I was on the bottom rung of the ladder when I started my career. After proving myself over and over, but losing job after job to taller people, I finally inched up a few rungs.

Many times I felt I had lost out on a job after a face-to-face interview, or face-to-chest in my case. Telephone interviews landed me the jobs, however. We're all of equal height on the phone.

Once, I had a close call. After an in-person interview for a physically demanding job, I was hired. Later, Liz, who volunteered at my new place of employment, confided to me what had transpired. We already knew each other because we had just worked together at very strenuous summer jobs as Youth

Conservation Corps crew leaders. We cleared woods for a trail and fields for planting wildlife foods.

The male director who interviewed me found out that Liz knew me and asked her, "Can Su handle the physical work?"

Liz answered, "Absolutely. She worked as well as anyone." If that situation hadn't existed, I doubt I would have been hired.

My lack of mass has often inspired me to find creative ways to overcome my "handicap." At Thanksgiving one year, I flew home to New Jersey to visit my family. My mother, who is about my height, picked me up at the airport the day before the holiday. This is generally the most heavily traveled day of the year, and the airport in Newark is one of the busiest in the country. As expected, throngs of noisy people crammed the concourse when I arrived. I couldn't see past the overcoats in front of me. How would I ever find my mother? Spotting an empty chair, I stood on it. My mother found me in minutes.

Then there was the time I was doing a snail kite survey by airboat in the Everglades. My colleague Fred, six-feet three-inches tall, shared the driving with me. I had inferred from his actions to date that Fred had been raised to view a woman's role as that of staying home to raise children. I suspect it was hard for him to accept a woman he dwarfed doing the same work as he.

On this particular trip, Fred and I expected our survey in the marsh to last the entire day. We brought an extra gas can because we knew the gas tank would run dry partway through the day. When the motor sputtered and died at midday, Fred jumped into action to reach the gas can before I did. He emptied it into the gas tank, and we continued our survey.

Just as we approached the boat ramp at the end of a long day, the motor sputtered and died again. This time we were out of fuel—no more gas cans. Immediately and wordlessly, Fred jumped into the shallow water and started towing the boat toward the ramp, à la Humphrey Bogart in *The African Queen*. Between us and the ramp, however, was one very deep, very alligator-packed canal.

"Hey, Fred," I asked, "what are you going to do when we get to the canal?"

Knowing he couldn't pull the boat while swimming, he mumbled, "I don't know."

I slipped down from my seat, picked up the gas can, and shook it. Hmmm. Something was sloshing. As Fred watched with one eye, I shook the last drops from the can into the gas tank and turned the starter. There was just enough. The engine roared to life.

"Fred, get in quickly!" I yelled over the din. He jumped into the boat and, seconds later, we were at the boat ramp.

For every disadvantage to being short, there is an opposite but equal advantage. Aside from heightened cranial resourcefulness, we lightweights can climb onto stork nesting branches that heavier biologists would snap. Our air tanks last longer when we scuba dive. We can reach into puffin burrows that would wedge a heftier person. We can walk across the famous Everglades floating peat islands that leave others crawling in slow motion. Whom do you want in your canoe when it is heavily loaded? And, in a single-engine airplane, when every pound adds to the risk, do you want a petite pilot or a Paul Bunyan?

Respect for others is frequently based on what you learned as a child. Thus, successful women are often touted as role models for girls. This is fine, but it only covers the aspect of gender and only for girls. Boys also need women as role models to see that women can be capable leaders. Here is an example that happened to me, and I hope this type of situation is never repeated.

When I was the senior biologist at Arthur R. Marshall Loxahatchee National Wildlife Refuge (hereafter referred to slightly more succinctly as Loxahatchee National Wildlife Refuge or just Loxahatchee) in Florida, the refuge manager asked me to guide a high-ranking Water Management District administrator on an airboat tour of the refuge. The man, who shall go unnamed, had requested the tour. We frequently gave tours to office-bound water managers so they could understand the Everglades' problems better. The administrator showed up—all six-feet six-inches (my estimate)—with his ten- or eleven-year-old son (also my estimate). The refuge manager approved the child's presence for educational reasons, so I gave the duo the standard airboat safety spiel, fitted them with floatation vests, and across the marsh we zoomed.

Periodically, I stopped the boat to point out a plant, a bird, a tree island, a floating peat mat. As I explained their significance to the ecosystem, the man would interrupt and finish my sentences, directing them toward his son. After a while, he didn't even wait for me to start speaking. As soon as the boat stopped, he commenced lecturing to his son about what we were seeing. The man was obviously quite knowledgeable.

Why did he want a tour when he already knows everything? I wondered.

Gradually, a disturbing thought dawned on me. Were we being used? The man seemed to want to impress his son. Whether it was the father's intention or not, the boy would see that his dad could figuratively snap his fingers and get a free airboat ride. Then Dad could flaunt his expertise. I was reduced to the menial task of airboat driver. Inadvertently, what the son saw was the leadership of a tall man. What he should have seen was that the small woman could do the same thing—more, actually, because I could also drive the airboat. I felt sorry for the child and more so for any woman who someday became his boss.

Tae kwon do was a good choice of a martial art for a small person because it uses kicks as often as hand strikes, and my legs are longer and stronger than my arms. Tae kwon do is an ancient Korean defensive art characterized by fast, high kicks and spinning kicks. The style was influenced by Japanese karate during the Japanese occupation of Korea, which is why Japanese terms are often used. It develops strength, flexibility, speed, coordination, balance, and self-control.

The physical stature of my instructor, Wayne Herring, in Aiken, South Carolina, was the opposite of Mr. Choi's. Wayne could scare away an opponent with just a scowl. He never got the hang of teaching a petite gal how to use her resourcefulness instead of her missing brawn. I suffered through his classes, punching and kicking the air, as I mimicked his every move.

One day in 1985, Wayne told the class that he wanted us to enter a tournament in Columbia, about an hour's drive from Aiken. I wasn't sure if he was giving us a choice, but I wasn't interested in getting kicked and punched by total strangers.

I replied, "No thanks." Wayne spewed forth a lecture about team spirit and how it could prepare me for a real situation, since I would be sparring with total strangers. After some weak rebuttals and continued prodding by Wayne, I surrendered.

Our class arrived at the big high-school gymnasium in Columbia, ready to spar (fight in matches) and do forms (individual choreographed routines) for the First Annual YWCA Tae Kwon Do Karate Championship. It was only the second tournament I had ever competed in or even attended. I was a green belt, a common level, so there were many competitors in my arena. Some belt levels were combined for this tournament, as there were too many levels to justify separate events, and belt levels vary from dojo to dojo. Most often, white is for the beginners, yellow and orange are the next levels, blue and green are higher, and brown and black are the highest belts.

Each corner of the gym floor held an event, and there were two events in the middle. At any one time, six different events could be occurring, like a six-ring circus. Among them were the kata (forms), the kumite (sparring), and the weapons (such as the bo, a six-foot-long hardwood staff) for men, women, and children, and for all belt levels. The competition lasted all day to accommodate the large number of events.

The only event that stood alone was the men's black belt kumite. This was considered the highlight of the tournament and culminated with the awarding of the "Grand Champion of the Tournament" trophy. These final fights commenced only when all other events had ended.

I watched the blue–green belt rings and awaited my turn. I entered kumite and kata events, winning a second and a third place. I have the trophies to prove it, but it was a budget event, and they aren't marked which was for sparring and which was for forms. I don't remember. I didn't want to be there.

During the tournament, I heard an announcement on the public address system. "Is there a woman with a blue or green belt who is willing to spar with a brown-belt woman? There is only one registered competitor for the brown–black belt level, and we'll have to award her first place by default if she doesn't compete. She came here to compete, so we'll take someone from the next lower belt level."

I pondered it briefly. The sparring competitors wore padding to prevent serious injuries. Nevertheless, the sport is intense and injuries can happen to lax competitors. I figured that I would rather give her a chance to earn her trophy. I must have been crazy. I wasn't prepared to fight a brown belt, and I was volunteering for something I could get clobbered at. Heck, I didn't even want to be there in the first place.

I was the only woman who answered the announcement, so the referee waved me into the ring. I don't remember much about it, except that I fought better than I did against my own belt level. I guess I was learning. I have no recollection if I scored any points. I do believe that the woman had a decent match, and she earned her trophy. To my surprise, I walked off with the second place brown–black belt trophy.

After all of the six-ring events ended, everyone crowded around the men's black-belt ring. The competition was arranged with three weight classes: lightweight, middleweight, and heavyweight. I guess the heavyweights were considered the main attraction, because they went last, the position of honor. There it is again—biggest is best.

As the lightweights went through their rounds, men were eliminated, one by one. Eventually, one was left and he raised his trophy to the crowd. The jockey-sized winner had displayed excellent technique and clearly deserved the award. He executed every move exactly as designed—fast, straight, and smooth—with no need for massive size or strength.

Technique is what a good sensei, like Mr. Choi, tries to teach his students. But most students cheat because they're tall or strong and too lazy to practice properly. They can usually get away with that.

We watched the middleweights next. Again, one by one, men were eliminated, until one was left. He was a beanpole. He flailed his mile-long arms and legs constantly. No one could get close to him.

Last were the heavyweights. It was a brutal competition among a pack of testosterone-laden oxen. One by one, they yielded to a mountain, burly and powerful. How could anyone hope to defeat him? After he dispensed with the competition, he sat down to rest, winded, while the grand champion battle began.

The three weight-class winners had to vie for the Grand Champion of the Tournament distinction. First, the lightweight had to spar the middleweight, and that winner battled the heavyweight. Whoever won that match would be the Grand Champion.

The first contest was riveting. The lightweight faced the mile-long arms and legs fearlessly. Strike after strike, he used his superior technique to outdo his opponent. Close and fast. Like a mosquito. The endless arms were too long for perfectly executed moves. The Mosquito dodged and weaved, drove in hard with blurry jabs and kicks. Daddy Long Legs telegraphed his moves, and the Mosquito saw them coming.

Finally, after an edge-of-your-seat match, the referee raised the Mosquito's hand in victory. But, the contender wasn't done yet.

While he was sparring what may have been the most intense fight of his life, his next opponent was resting. No rest for the Mosquito. On cue, the heavyweight jumped up and entered the ring, facing an opponent half his size. *This is going to be easy*, I could hear Jumbo thinking.

The match started. I imagined the blood would soon flow, because the Mosquito would put everything into this fight. Jumbo tried all his usual moves, which had vanquished his previous opponents. But the Mosquito was too quick. Out flashed that superior technique. Long arms, long legs, big muscles—none was a match for the Mosquito's technique. Point after point went to the lightweight. He tried a combination move—punch-kick-punch. Point. He tried it again. Punch-kick-punch. Point! No one gets away with the same move twice unless his opponent is tired or inexperienced. More kicks, more points.

Finally, the bell rang. Match over. The referee raised the Mosquito's hand and presented him with a six-foot-tall trophy. It towered over the winner. I still remember him heading out the door, dragging the trophy behind him.

Throughout the match, it was clear that the lightweight's impeccable technique beat every move thrown at him. Not only did he fight someone much larger, but he had fought one tough match while the big guy was resting.

I thought about that on the drive home, and I still think about it. No more cursing my pitiful size. I can defend myself against anyone, as long as I practice my technique and maintain my composure. Brute strength bows to resourcefulness.

But the lesson doesn't stop there. In all walks of life, the better technique will triumph, no matter what your handicap is. If you want to succeed, you have to strive to improve your own abilities. Now, instead of saying, "I don't get mad, I just get even," I say, "I don't get even, I just get better."

Chapter 6.
We Get Paid for This?

The M.V.B.

"Is it dead?" The three of us leaned over the cardboard box and peered in, each one chiming our opinions. "It looks dead." "It's not breathing." "Rest in peace."

I picked up the limp slate-blue, maroon, and white bird. I drew its walnut-sized head to my ear, closed my eyes, and concentrated for any tiny puffs of air. "It's not breathing," I mumbled again.

Using a method usually guaranteed to get a reaction from a live body, I touched its open eye with my finger. Nothing happened. I felt through the feathers for a heartbeat. Nothing.

Bill, a volunteer, tried next to find a sign of life, also in vain. Bill had come to us for reasons I did not know, but we were grateful for his help. All I knew was that he came from a privileged family and he didn't need a job. He was somewhere in his early twenties, I'm guessing, and had materialized with his own BMW and the keys to a condominium on the adjacent Florida Keys island of Islamorada. But, for someone who didn't need to work, he labored as hard as anyone. Mud, heat, mosquitoes, and long hours did not dissuade him. Maybe it was a yearning to do something adventurous, or maybe it was a search for the meaning of life that brought him to our dock. It didn't matter. We needed another set of hands or sometimes just a buddy to accompany a lone biologist into the field. He was there for us.

Also searching for signs of life was Dr. Tom Bancroft, the head of our project. Tom was the consummate project leader. He was an expert on wading birds and the Everglades, and he led us to be independent in our work. He could find a joke in the smallest of cues, but this was an exception. Tom poked and prodded, listened for vital signs, and finally gave a resolute sigh.

I placed the lifeless tricolored heron (*Egretta tricolor*) gently back in the cardboard box, prayed silently for its eternal peace, and left the box on the coffee table. There was nothing we could do. We would deal with the body in the morning, probably by returning it to the colony where it came from, to disintegrate into the swampy earth, nibbled to the bone by crabs and fish.

Our rented cottage held an air of somberness that evening, as the three of us realized we had caused the heron's death. We were supposed to be helping these birds, yet here we had overdosed the third one of our research subjects. The herons had suffered enough as a hunted and pestered population.

The cottage was in Flamingo, halfway between our office on Plantation Key in the Florida Keys and our wading bird research colony in the Everglades. We had rented it for a few days to save us the long boat ride across Florida Bay during an intensive fieldwork phase.

That night, I lay on the couch next to the box on the coffee table and agonized about our bungle. One bird, even three, would not affect the population. But, if we wanted to help these birds, we needed to know more, and we couldn't do it the way we had planned.

The story of this particular bird had begun for us earlier that day in a remote mangrove swamp in the backcountry of Everglades National Park. The swamp was near the Lane River, one of about a half-dozen tidal rivers that drain Shark River Slough into Whitewater Bay in southwestern Florida. These mangroves were home to a colony of three hundred pairs of wading birds, including great egrets, snowy egrets, tricolored herons, little blue herons, and white ibises.

Our mission was to study the wading birds in the southwestern Everglades for the National Audubon Society. Specifically, our National Audubon research team was working under a grant from the South Florida Water Management District from 1986 to 1990 to measure the effects on the birds from hydrological changes in the Everglades. The Water Management District was responsible for much of the surface-water manipulation in South Florida.

We were studying how the water flows, water levels, and the timing of those flows affected the food the birds preyed on and, ultimately, the birds' nesting success. Our data would be useful for determining how to restore the health of the Everglades.

To accomplish our mission, we had to capture breeding egrets and herons, fit them with radio transmitters, follow them wherever they roamed in the Everglades, and, at the same time, monitor their nests. I was in charge of the field operations.

The colonies we studied were in remote areas of Everglades National Park, accessible only by boat. Our office, National Audubon's research headquarters, was on Plantation Key, adjacent to the famed Key Largo.

It may seem strange to have a headquarters office in the Florida Keys, but only until you remember that National Audubon got its start protecting wading birds from the murderous plume hunters in South Florida a hundred years earlier. Since then, biologists from Audubon have been intensely studying the birds and looking for ways to restore their populations. Research on other species across the country came later.

That day, our trio had arrived as usual at the cramped observation blind via a long circuitous water route. As we did twice a week from March through June, we departed our dock on Plantation Key around 4:30 in the morning. We crossed Florida Bay in the dark in a seventeen-foot Mako, the *Ibis*. Its open deck allowed us to work from the boat, and its small size helped us to navigate the bay's tricky shallow waters and carpet of submerged seagrasses.

The sun was just rising 25 miles later, as we arrived in Flamingo, a midway interlude in our voyage. We had to pause there to get our boat from the bay into the Buttonwood Canal.

We took the Buttonwood Canal to avoid the open ocean during windy days. The canal had been dredged in 1957 to connect Florida Bay to Coot Bay. Coot Bay connected to Whitewater Bay, and thus the canal created a continuous interior nautical path for the Intra-Coastal Waterway. However, the connection had the grievous effect of allowing salt water to flow with the tides up the canal and to the fresh-to-brackish water in Coot Bay. So, in 1982, the National Park Service installed a concrete wall across the Buttonwood Canal to fix the blunder—to plug the saltwater intrusion that was destroying Coot Bay.

Thus, we had to have our boat hoisted over the wall and into the Buttonwood Canal in a giant motorized sling. Since we had to disembark to lighten the load, we helped the hoist operator place the two wide straps under the hull of the *Ibis*, one in front of the center and one near the stern. Then the operator started the motor that raised the slings out of the water, boat and all. When the boat was high enough to clear the wall, the hoist carried the boat across to the other side, and the operator gently lowered it to the canal. On our return, we would do the same process in the other direction.

The *Ibis* is hoisted over the plug at Flamingo, laden with our cargo of a johnboat and a ten-foot tower section.

After cruising up the Buttonwood Canal, we continued to Coot Bay and then to Whitewater Bay along the Wilderness Waterway. The Wilderness Waterway is a 99-mile-long marked water trail along the mangrove islands and the coast of western Everglades National Park between Everglades City and Flamingo. The National Park Service has created small, primitive campsites along the way. The route is popular with canoeists and motorboaters.

Partway up Whitewater Bay, we veered east onto the Lane River, heading into ever-narrowing waterways, leaving all markers and any trace of humans behind. From there, it took a practiced eye to recognize individual mangrove trees that marked the turns.

We idled slowly upstream to where the mangroves became too thick to navigate. There, we tied the boat, clambered over mangrove roots to our secretly stashed canoe, and paddled the rest of the way to the colony.

We transported all of our blinds, tower scaffolding, canoes, johnboats, and equipment in the seventeen-foot Mako from

Tavernier to as far into the mangroves as we could. From there, we lugged by canoe and by hand through the tangled roots and mucky water. We would carry the johnboat (a wider, flat-bottomed boat) from the Mako, drag it across the red mangrove roots, and launch it in the shallow water near the nesting colony. Then we would carry the blinds, observation towers (in ten-foot sections), and so on, to the johnboat, pile them into the boat, and tow the johnboat with a hand-paddled canoe. Of course, this required many trips by canoe to tow the laden johnboat at the start and finish of every field season.

Audubon staff tow the johnboat with the tower section to the bird colony.

Handpower reigned supreme, and we used no power tools in the colony. We erected the twenty-foot towers (topped by a metal platform) by hand, using ropes, pulleys, and a lot of muscle. If we had to cut down some mangroves, we did it with handsaws. I still remember the glorious feeling of falling into bed after one of those sixteen-hour days of old-fashioned hard labor.

From Tavernier to the colony was about forty miles and another world away. The trip took three hours by boat. We would have only a few hours to do our work, since our presence frightened the parent birds from their nests, exposing the eggs and chicks to scorching late-morning sun. Then we would wait until mid-afternoon to resume. We spent the interim observing flight patterns from a distance.

We had selected the Lane River colony to study for three reasons. First, it was located where the effects of the changes in Everglades hydrology would show. Second, we needed a colony that we could expect to appear each year in the same place for the duration of our four-year project. Colonies in the sawgrass area of Everglades National Park tended to be ephemeral. They would appear on one tree island one year and on another the next, depending on the water flows. How could we set up our blinds or map a colony if it kept shifting locations?

The mangrove colonies stayed put, probably because they were located on the transition between freshwater and saltwater habitats. Here, the birds had short flying distances to a variety of feeding habitats, providing a choice for almost any water condition. And the third reason we selected this site? Believe it or not, it was the easiest to access.

Marjory Stoneman Douglas dubbed the Everglades the "river of grass" in her 1947 book *The Everglades: River of Grass* because the water flows in a broad, shallow sheet from north to south. Historically, the largest wading-bird colonies were located in the headwaters of the rivers, such as the Lane, East, Shark, and Watson, along the mangrove fringe on the western side of what is now Everglades National Park. The peak nesting occurred between March and May each year.

During the early part of the nesting season, which coincided with the end of South Florida's dry season, the "river of grass" would slowly dry, offering wading birds a moving edge of shallow water and concentrated aquatic prey. In wet years, the birds could forage in the mangrove estuaries of Whitewater and Rogers River Bays, instead of the flooded sawgrass marshes. The different water depths along the drying edge and the estuaries allowed wading birds of varying leg lengths to forage efficiently and provide for hungry chicks.

Wading birds have been a barometer of the environmental health of South Florida, particularly the Everglades, for a century. Before the end of the nineteenth century, when few white people lived in South Florida, wading birds were so abundant—very roughly estimated at two and a half million birds of seventeen species—that they came to symbolize the Everglades. The number and variety of wading birds were greater there than anywhere else in the country.

In the late 1800s, fashionable women wore hats with long, soft plumes from great egrets, snowy egrets, reddish egrets, tricolored herons, roseate spoonbills, and other species. The women believed (because the milliners told them) that the living birds shed the plumes and were not harmed by the collecting.

While it is possible to collect fallen feathers, that is not what happened. The birds were killed when their plumes were the showiest—during the breeding season. And, of course, the easiest place to kill large numbers of plumed birds is around their nesting colonies. If one member of a nesting pair is killed, the mate will abandon the nest because it cannot care for the young alone, thus causing the death of the next generation. Plumes could bring up to 32 dollars an ounce, even more than gold. It was a big business, causing the deaths of hundreds of thousands of birds and stirring such a massive disturbance in the colonies that reproduction by the surviving pairs plummeted.

In 1901, the State of Florida banned plume hunting, a first but insufficient step because the demand continued. The next year, the National Association of Audubon Societies (the precursor to the National Audubon Society) hired Guy Bradley, a young resident of the fledgling settlement of Flamingo, as warden to protect the birds. After three years of making arrests and trying to educate people about the effects of plume hunting, Bradley was shot to death in his boat by a neighbor who was illegally harvesting plumed birds.

The news of Bradley's heroic action and tragic demise spread to the fashion industry, and women in distant cities began to comprehend the deadly price of their vanity. Many stopped buying plumed apparel. New York State banned the sale of plumes in 1910. When the demand dropped, so did the price of feathers, and eventually so did the poaching.

During the next few decades, wading bird populations began to rebound, and by the 1930s, their numbers had reached an estimated 180,000 to 245,000. Just as most species were recovering, other threats appeared.

Over the succeeding decades, the slow torture of the Everglades accelerated. Dredging for canals intensified, causing marshes to ebb into farmland. Earthen levees, some as long as seventy miles, sprang up like a network of giant mole tunnels and blocked the vital sheet flow throughout the remaining marshes. Development mushroomed along the east coast. Water was diverted from the Everglades to quench the irrigation and municipal needs of the new tenants. The sullied water was pumped back in, loaded with pesticides, fertilizers, mercury, and other heavy metals.

The environmental tampering caused chain reactions of many types, including a rapid expansion of nuisance plants, such as cattails, that disrupted the food chain for all Everglades creatures. By the 1970s, the population of wading birds in the Everglades had crashed again. Everglades biologist John C. Ogden estimated that, from 1934 to 1976, the wading bird population in the central-southern Everglades declined by 75 to 80 percent. It has declined further since then.

This concise history lesson should explain our *raison d'être*. We needed to know how the manmade shift in hydrology patterns was affecting the success of the colony.

The main challenge for the radio-transmitter aspect of our study was to catch the adult birds safely on their nests while still incubating their eggs, so that we could correlate their movements with the stage in their nesting cycle. For example, did the adults feed in one area when they were incubating their eggs, then switch to another when the eggs hatched? Our three main research subjects—tricolored herons, little blue herons, and snowy egrets—all are significantly smaller than wood storks and nest lower in the trees.

To capture the adult birds, we had to lull them to sleep. Not knowing any heron lullabies, we resorted to a method used by a French biologist. We would fill a gelatin capsule with a measured amount of a sleep-inducing drug and stuff the "sleeping pill" inside a small fish that we placed on a nest. Oddly, although herons and egrets normally catch fish alive in shallow water, they will recognize a dead fish on the nest as food. When the bird fell asleep, usually within an hour, I would radio to my colleagues, who were waiting out of sight in the canoe, and they would paddle to the nest and retrieve it. Then they would paddle to the blind, and we would weigh the bird, band it, and attach the radio transmitter. The bird would nap through the entire ordeal and be returned to the nest, oblivious to human meddling.

The French biologist had accomplished this technique on little egrets (*Egretta garzetta*, a similar European species) in France with great success. However, that project used a sophisticated weighing system with a scale he placed under the nest. When the bird returned to the nest, the scale recorded the extra weight. That was important because, as with many drugs, the dosage depended on the body weight of the patient.

Our low-budget operation didn't include a scale, so we had to guess the bird's weight. We had an approximate idea of what a tricolored heron weighs (just under one pound), based on previous research. However, the weights of individual birds can vary up to thirty percent, so we had to guess each bird's weight. Too much of the drug would be fatal, but too little could cause it to stagger from the nest and injure itself.

Without a scale, our attempts were fizzling. The first two herons slipped past deep comas into the final act. By the time we were ready to drug our third heron, and anxious to prevent another disaster, we reduced the dosage.

As I peered from a slit in the blind on this sweltering day, 25 feet from a nest on a red mangrove branch, I saw a parent tricolored heron pick up and swallow the spiked fish. Although the genders look alike, and both parents incubate the eggs, I will call the bird a male. It was 3:13 on an early May afternoon. Twenty-one minutes later, the now-wobbly heron tried to shift one of the three eggs around in the nest, but instead knocked it into the water. He had gotten so groggy! As I watched, he teetered too far and tumbled into the water.

No time to call for the canoe! Frantically, I jumped out of the blind and pushed through the chest-deep murky water toward the floating heron, ignoring the omnipresent gators. Alligators love to hang out in wading bird colonies. What could be more inviting than an easy meal of an occasional chick falling out of a nest and into your waiting maw? I had to beat the waiting gators to the booty. Running in slow motion through the water, I reached the splash point and scooped up the limp body.

The heron had fallen into such a deep sleep that Tom, Bill, and I were certain then that we had fatally overdosed him. We brought our comatose patient back to the cottage in Flamingo. That's when we poked and prodded and sadly proclaimed him our third fatality.

Depressed, I drifted asleep on the couch in the living room, near the cardboard coffin on the coffee table. Sometime during the night, I awoke to the sounds of weak scratching coming from the direction of the coffee table. Puzzled, I turned on a lamp and peered into the box. There, to my astonishment and joy, sat the heron, hunched on its legs but upright, staring at me with wide, dark eyes.

My excitement was hard to stifle. I wanted to shout, "Hooray!" and wake Tom and Bill. But our day had been arduous, and the next was promising to be the same. I left the bird and the men, undisturbed, and tried to return to sleep. The feeble scratching from the box made that difficult.

At dawn, the heron was perky and pecky. When Tom and Bill arose, I pulled them over to the box.

"Look!" I shrieked. "He's alive!"

The men responded with gasps of delight and relief, and we all danced around the box. This was one tough bird, so we decided to proceed with our plans. With our spirits lifted, we fitted the heron with a half-ounce, solar-powered radio transmitter. When we weighed him, we realized that his large size had helped to save him.

We attached the radio to a backpack harness that I designed, based on my experience with the wood storks, to allow the bird complete freedom for flight and all other activities. The signal was an individually identifiable frequency solely for that bird, which was very helpful, since I subsequently caught and radio-tagged seven other birds in that colony.

I steadfastly refused to drug another bird. Tom voiced his agreement by saying simply, "Okay, but you'll have to find another way to catch them." After investigating other projects, I built a wire cage-trap that sat on top of the nest and had a pull string for me to close the door from the blind. It worked safely, although the birds didn't sleep through the capture trauma.

Radio-telemetry, also known as radio-tagging, has been used for decades to track the movements of animals. On large, ground-dwelling mammals, such as wolves, bears, and panthers, the weight and placement of the transmitter isn't as critical as it is with birds. Birds must be balanced in flight and cannot fly with too much extra weight. The size and placement of our transmitters were significant. We bought solar-powered ones for the adults because they could last for years and transmit strong signals, plus they weighed less than radios with batteries. Eventually, we also radio-tagged younger birds using smaller, battery-operated transmitters that I built.

I learned how to build the tiny transmitters from scratch while working for National Audubon. Few biologists go to this length to obtain transmitters. Most will scrounge up the money to buy ready-made ones. However, we needed many transmitters and the cost was more than our grant provided. This financial consideration prompted us to strike a deal with a biologist at Tall Timbers Research Center in Tallahassee. The biologist was an expert at designing and building transmitters for bobwhite quail. He agreed to teach me how to design and build them myself for the birds in our studies. I spent a few days at Tall Timbers learning about basic electronics and building a transmitter from scratch.

Once back at my office, I bought the materials—sheets of copper board and piles of components—at electronics stores such as Radio Shack, and set to work designing something for my respective study subjects.

I cut the copper board into inch-long rectangles and etched non-conductive gaps with acid. Then I soldered the components to the board. The capacitors, resistors, transistors, crystal, battery, and antenna all had their places. That sounds relatively easy, but I spent days of testing to determine the right-sized components. Which transistor was right? Which resistor? Which capacitor? And then they had to be tried in different combinations—endless combinations to see what worked the best. I could vary the other components to get the desired characteristics for the signal.

I had no choice with the crystals, however. I ordered them from a company that cut them to resonate at the frequency I requested. The Federal Communications Commission assigns to scientists a certain bandwidth of frequencies that will not interfere with other radio transmissions. I chose a range within that band that wasn't being used by other local radio-trackers.

After soldering the transistors, resistors, capacitors, and crystal to the board, I attached the battery and whip antenna. The antenna protruded about ten inches from the back of the radio package, like a delicate, hairless rat's tail. It was called a whip antenna because it was so flexible that it resembled a whip. I could cut the antenna to varying lengths to find the best one—the shortest length that would still send a signal. When all the components were attached, I encased the radio in epoxy to make it waterproof and able to take winged abuse.

I would have barely squeaked by, making pathetically cumbersome transmitters, if not for the excellent mentoring of a friend and electronics guru, David Feder. We had met in a tae kwon do class in Key Largo, where he eventually earned his black belt, and I, my brown belt. He was a jack of many trades—he could repair anything electronic or mechanical and was a talented musician and songwriter as well. His enthusiasm for creating electronic widgets was infectious. David lent me an oscilloscope and other sophisticated equipment with which to test my creations, and I dived in wholeheartedly.

Between the fieldwork and building the transmitters, I worked about one hundred hours a week that summer—sixteen hours a day during the week and ten hours each day on weekends. Overtime pay was not part of the grant. Luckily, I lived a few blocks from the office, and I could pedal my bicycle there in two or three minutes.

The beauty of building my own transmitters was that I could design them to suit our needs. If we needed transmitters to last a long time, I could shorten the duration of the signal. A constant beep would drain the battery too quickly. Having it beep only half the time would double the battery's lifespan. Besides adjusting the length of the beep, I could adjust the length of time between the beeps and the strength of the signal just by switching components. I could even produce *Outer Limits* music, loon calls, and a variety of fascinating but useless tunes.

All this noise was silent to the human ear without a receiver. Only by using my little blue Telonics receiver could I hear the signal. It's a good thing that the herons couldn't hear the beeps emanating from their backs. Or could they? I had always assumed they couldn't hear it, but what if they could hear more than we knew, and we forced an electronic beeping torture on them that lasted for years?

My handmade transmitters were for later use, when the chicks were old enough. With our resurrected heron, we used a commercially purchased transmitter. We called the heron "151" after the frequency of his radio signal and released him near his nest at the Lane River colony. Unfortunately, during his absence, fish crows had consumed the two remaining eggs. We weren't too worried, because other researchers had documented herons and egrets laying replacement clutches in the same nests when the first clutch was destroyed. Unexpectedly, 151 took the egg loss seriously and disappeared from our search area in southwestern Everglades National Park.

I spent about fifteen hours a week in a Cessna 172, learning which feeding areas were important to the Lane River colony, as I tracked the other radio-tagged birds and searched for 151. We had to track by airplane, due to the lack of roads through the Everglades, the maze of unnavigable waterways, and frequency-absorbing mangroves; these radio signals worked by line-of-sight. Even leaves on the trees could block or weaken a signal.

I studied the radio-tagged birds so intensively that I discovered how their habits varied, even between individuals of the same species. For example, I almost always found one tricolored heron foraging alone in the mangrove region, while another regularly foraged in open marshes with a mixed flock of wading bird species. I couldn't make many generalizations about the herons' or egrets' collective movements. They each had their own preferences. Day after day, I kept searching for 151.

Three weeks after catching and releasing 151, I expanded my search northward to Everglades City. One day, with the receiver tuned to the 151-megahertz frequency, I heard a faint signal. "Keep heading north," I instructed my pilot, Chuck Leverich. "It's getting stronger!"

I bounced up and down in my seat with excitement, as much as one can do in such a diminutive plane. After such a long disappearance, I was afraid something dreadful had happened to this bird, and I would have felt responsible. As it turned out, 151 was a bird with a cat's lives.

I found the signal coming from a colony on a small island in Fakahatchee Strand State Preserve, fifty heron-miles north of the Lane River. The next morning, I drove two-and-a-half hours from the Keys to the preserve, launched my sixteen-foot canoe, and paddled over to the mangrove island. To my relief, I found 151 on a nest with eggs.

Apparently, the drugging had caused no permanent harm—at least, if he had brain damage, he hid it well. I also found another missing heron at the same time. Although I'm relating this calmly, the truth is, I had to sit perfectly still in the canoe while my insides were jumping with excitement.

Previously, biologists didn't know whether tricolored herons were loyal to one colony, declining to nest if local conditions were unfavorable, or if they would seek alternate colonies. This incident marked the first time anyone had documented that tricolored herons do change colonies, even if their original one is still thriving. The birds' nesting flexibility was great news for conservation.

Heron 151 surprised me again by appearing in April of the next year at a colony on Frank Key near Flamingo in Florida Bay, about fifteen miles south of the Lane River colony. Frank Key was a much larger colony than either Lane River or Fakahatchee Strand colonies, with several thousand pairs of herons (great blue, great white, tricolored, little blue), egrets (great, snowy, reddish), brown pelicans, and double-crested cormorants. Here, it was inappropriate for me to locate 151's nest, since my search would disrupt too many nesting birds. I left him alone.

I kept track of 151 by airplane and by using an automated receiver setup on the island. The latter was a nifty gizmo that I built to keep track of 151's comings and goings all day, as well as those of other birds carrying our transmitters. Here's how it worked: I built a wooden box to protect the equipment from the elements. Inside, I placed a receiver, like the one we used in the plane or on a boat, and set it to "scan" mode. On this setting, the receiver would run through a series of pre-set frequencies and stay on each one for a few minutes. If a bird was present, the receiver would send a signal to a stylus that made marks on a roll of paper just as an electrocardiogram machine (for monitoring a heartbeat) or a seismograph (for monitoring earthquakes) would. By reading the marks on the paper, we could tell when the birds arrived, how long they stayed, and when they left. Wouldn't all parents want one of these for their teens?

It was a marvelous contraption. But you wouldn't say that if you had to hand-carry the twenty-pound, twelve-volt, deep-cycle battery about three hundred yards over spider-legged red mangrove roots, around spiny cacti, and through muck, all in a heat index of one hundred five degrees. (Heat index is a measure of how hot the air feels when accounting for humidity along with air temperature. It often felt more than one hundred degrees on our field days.) Deep-cycle batteries are similar to car batteries, complete with acid that can leak or explode. Periodically, the battery needed to be exchanged, and I had to carry the spent one back to the boat. Isn't it lamentable that batteries aren't any lighter when they are spent?

In a few weeks, 151 amazed me further by leaving his apparently good nesting situation for the mangrove colony in Rogers River Bay, located between Lane River and Everglades City. I don't know what prompted his departure, but at least I couldn't blame myself. There, he stayed for the rest of the season with a new mate and two chicks. For a third time, I could document a tricolored heron switching colonies.

The second winter left me guessing: Of the four colonies that 151 had visited in the past two years, where would he choose to set up housekeeping next? My National Audubon colleagues were equally curious. To ease the subtropical doldrums, we set up a pool of wagers around the office, all betting a restaurant dinner on which colony 151 would choose that spring. Our office included some of Florida's most experienced wading bird biologists, but no one guessed right. Wouldn't you know that 151 would make fools of us all?

During the third May, Tricolored Heron 151 appeared in a fifth colony, a cypress swamp along the Tamiami Trail near Forty-Mile Bend, about thirty miles northeast of Lane River, and well inland. Almost two thousand great egrets, snowy egrets, and tricolored herons had already established their nests there. Luckily, I was able to locate 151's nest relatively easily, and I visited him periodically by canoe to watch him raise two more chicks. However, the radio that 151 carried gradually lost signal strength, and I was not able to track him after that year.

During four years of radio-tracking 33 adults and many juvenile birds, I documented six tricolored herons and two little blue herons changing colonies. But 151 was my favorite. None was so transient, so reproductively active, or had such a long-lived radio as 151. Thus, he became our "most valuable bird."

The significance of our discovery—that tricoloreds and little blues may change colonies even if the original colony still thrives—had both a good side and a bad one. On the positive side, if a colony suffers from human disturbance, the birds may find another place to nest and still reproduce that year. Wildlife managers may even be able to lure wading birds to a new colony site, using decoys and other attractants. On the negative side, the seemingly haphazard wanderings of some birds during the nesting season may mean that surveys of nesting wading birds are not accurate. If surveys are conducted periodically through the nesting season, such as the ones that National Audubon and the National Park Service have done, there is potential for counting some birds twice, thus inadvertently inflating the numbers.

It's a relief to know, however, that wading birds can be adaptable. They will respond to our attempts to heal the Everglades. And, they will be part of the healing, for they have a function, too. They keep the small aquatic life in balance and move nutrients around the ecosystem. Without wading birds, the Everglades would be an unbalanced and critically ill place. If we can restore the water flows and water quality in at least some parts of the Everglades, the wading birds will return. Maybe this time they will stay.

Bull's-Eye

"What's that white thing floating in the water?" I asked, as I steered the boat toward the nesting colony.

"It looks like a plastic bag. I'll get it," answered assistant biologist Rick Sawicki.

We were at the Rodger's River Bay colony on the west side of Everglades National Park to do our usual nest checks, including our "Most Valuable Bird"—Tricolored Heron 151 and its two chicks. Out in the pristine wilderness, litter was not something we tolerated.

I steered the seventeen-foot Mako toward the floater. As we got closer, the bag took on an ominous shape. Not a bag at all, it was a white ibis, as lifeless as a plastic bag. Rick scooped it up.

"There's another white blob!" he exclaimed.

We puttered over to it, and Rick scooped up yet another white ibis. In the slightly choppy water, we scanned around and all the plastic bags became dead birds. What the heck had happened?

As Rick and Paul Cavanaugh, another assistant biologist, scooped them up, a new type of trash appeared, red and so much smaller than the bird corpses that we almost didn't see it. Experienced at rounding up litter from moving boats like a form of pick-up polo, Rick and Paul gathered shotgun shell after shotgun shell. We had part of our answer for the fate of the ibises. But who did the shooting and when? Hunting is not allowed in national parks, and ibises are federally protected from hunting anywhere.

The birds on the island were more agitated than usual at our approach. As we drifted closer, we noticed ibises running around on the ground. That was out of ibis character.

We drifted the boat quietly up to the island and tied it to a mangrove tree. As we climbed awkwardly around the spindly roots of the trees, the reason for the pedestrian birds became obvious. They, too, had been shot—except they had survived. All they could do was scramble around and flap their injured wings in a futile attempt to return to their egg-laden nests. That some of them still had so much energy set me wondering. When did this awful plunder happen?

We were there in early morning. If my hunch was right, some hooligans from Chokoloskee or Everglades City had cruised south along the Wilderness Waterway to target practice while the birds were heading to their nests for the evening (that would have been the night before) or leaving to find food (that would have been that morning). Assuming the worst seemed sage. That would mean that those whackos, who didn't care about the law, could still be nearby with shotguns.

Less than one hundred years after the first Audubon warden was fatally shot in his boat while protecting wading birds in the Everglades, there we were, driving a boat with a big, red circular Audubon logo on its side. We had always jokingly called it the Audubon bull's-eye. Now we weren't laughing. We were thirty miles by water from the nearest law-enforcement office.

Rick, Paul, and I proceeded despondently. We gathered as many dead ibises as we could find—27 in all. The live ones we left to their fates. Even if we could have caught them in those dense mangroves, we couldn't treat their wounds. We also collected the six-gauge shotgun shells as evidence in case the snipers were ever caught.

But, the birds weren't the only victims. Another lifeless mass appeared floating near the island, big and dark and scaly. An alligator! The three of us heaved and hefted and eventually hoisted it onto the bow of the boat. A bullet hole through the skull was its death knell, not a shotgun pellet. What was it? A handgun? A rifle?

The alligator measured eight feet from nose to tail. That the tail was still there was revealing. Most poachers would remove the tail to eat or sell. But these barbarians seemed to be interested only in live target practice, unless we scared them off before they had finished. . . .

Could they still be around? Out of radio range with the park rangers, thirty miles from the nearest ranger station, with only a pokey workboat and no defenses, our nerves were on edge and our senses heightened. All we could do was to wait for our rented research plane to fly over on its daily telemetry mission. As part of our routine, one of our crew would fly over the boat to check on the boat people for safety and to exchange information about the birds.

Dr. Wayne Hoffman was the biologist on board the plane that day, and as standard practice, he carried a handheld marine radio. It may seem odd that the airplane would carry a marine radio, but it was the only way the boat people could communicate with the plane people.

We were relieved when we heard the whine of the plane's engine growing louder in early morning.

"Wayne," I called on the radio, "you've got to get a message to the rangers. We've got some poaching here!"

Wayne knew what that entailed. He would have to yell my message to the pilot sitting inches from him in the noisy cockpit. The pilot would have to radio to his home base dispatcher at the airport. That dispatcher would have to telephone the dispatcher at Everglades National Park Headquarters, and the park dispatcher would have to radio the message to a ranger station. Then a ranger would have to radio a message to a ranger who was on a boat patrolling nearest to our location. Then that ranger would have to find us in the mangroves.

Our message was, "Send a ranger to Rodger's River Bay!" Remember the game of "Operator" you played when you were a child? You whispered a sentence to the person sitting next to you, and, by the time it was repeated around the circle of people, the entire sentence had changed. Grownups can't do it any better.

All day we waited, nervously continuing our work, listening for the thrumming engine of a boat, which could be either friend or foe. Luckily, tricolored heron 151 and his two chicks were safe, and we put a transmitter on one of the chicks.

Another typical task we performed that day was a strange type of fishing expedition. Like the storks I studied in Georgia, the parent herons and egrets regurgitated their latest meals to feed their offspring. Regurgitation is a ten-dollar word for vomiting.

The panicked chicks also regurgitated their latest meals, involuntarily we believed, when the parents were flushed from their nests at our arrival. The theory is that, since a baby bird can't defend itself, the only hope the chick has of avoiding predation is to divert the predator's attention away from itself. The fish falling into the water distract the predator and may even cause the predator to change its mind and nibble on an easy fish snack instead.

The falling fish is a bonanza for wading bird biologists. We collected the "regurge" in plastic bags and put them in a cooler for later examination in our lab. If we want to know what our study subjects eat, what better way than by having their stomach contents land practically in our hands? Well, okay, it would have been better had they not reeked, as rotting fish are prone to do.

Had the regurge actually looked like the animals they were would have also been nice. I was the privileged biologist who had to identify the species of each of those blobs by sight. After several hours in the digestive system of a bird, the acids start to break down the prey's softest tissue. With fish, the fins dissolve first, then the scales, and then the skin. Occasionally, the herons ate other small creatures. With insects and crayfish, the legs and wings disappear first, and with amphibians, the skin disappears quickly. Often, all that remains for a biologist to study is a colorless, amorphous blob.

When the field season was over, outdoor work turned indoors, and I spent days on end identifying the regurge by using field guides and taxonomic keys. My eyes would be glued to the dissecting microscope as I strained for any remaining shapes or markings. The most excitement I would have would be when I found a fish I had not seen before.

The largest fish we ever caught, so to speak, were around four or five inches long. Mostly, they were one or two inches—that is, when they were in their original lively state. Eventually, I became adept at identifying finless, scaleless, colorless carcasses. In fact, I could identify them better than the live ones, which I almost never saw. I recall the first time I saw a live golden topminnow, one of the more common species in the birds' diets. I blurted out, "So that's what they're supposed to look like!"

As we collected regurge that anxious day for later identification, we found more dead ibises. For some reason unknown to us, the white ibises seemed to be the only victims. We left the dead birds on the deck of the boat because we hoped a ranger would appear at any minute. The birds didn't require much room, but the alligator was different. We had no more room on the deck, so we carried the reptile on the bow of our small boat for all of eight hours—the Everglades version of a Viking ship's figurehead. Luckily, no fishermen or other park visitors cruised by that day to witness the bizarre sight.

When the motor was off, we could hear hissing sounds emanating from the reptile's head. No, it wasn't a reflexive defense. The hissing came from the brains oozing out of the bullet hole. In the heat of the April Everglades day, decomposition had set in quickly.

We tote a shot alligator on the bow of the *Ibis*.

While I have encountered other cases of poaching, this was the worst I had seen. In the old days before bird protection and local law enforcement, people from the small town of Chokoloskee, near Everglades City, about thirty miles north of Rodgers River Bay, hunted the wading birds for food. So plentiful were the white ibises, and so easy to shoot, that they were dubbed "Chokoloskee chickens." I could believe that people still shot and ate them, although they have been protected even outside the park since 1918 by the Migratory Bird Treaty Act. That seemed to explain why only the ibises were shot.

With the sun slipping low in the sky, our hopes also faded that a ranger would arrive to search for the perpetrators. We dumped the alligator on an island where a ranger could find it another day. On our way back through Flamingo at day's end, we dropped the birds and shotgun shells off at the ranger station as evidence for an unlikely criminal case. We would have heard if there was indeed an active case. The bang-happy poachers are still out there.

The Gulf of No Return

As I walked in my front door, the phone rang. Nine o'clock on a Wednesday night, and I had just arrived home from work in the Everglades, salivating at the thought of eating leftovers from the refrigerator. My friend Karen from Massachusetts had been trying to call all evening to chat.

"Hi, Su. How was your day?" Karen asked. She had been one of my most revered volunteers at Laughing Brook Audubon Sanctuary, with inexhaustible energy and sunny charm. Her dedication to protecting wildlife provided the bond that made us fast friends.

"Oh, just another boring day in paradise," I sighed, quoting a cliché we were fond of saying in the Florida Keys. Stifling a yawn and hunger pangs, I recapitulated the last sixteen hours.

Before sunrise on that summer day in 1988, I had set out for fieldwork in a twenty-foot Aquasport with my two assistants, Allison Brody and Rick Sawicki. The boat, named the *Minnow* after one ill-fated tour boat known to television viewers of the 1960s, had been transferred to us from another National Audubon Society project in Texas.

One of our tasks was to count wading bird chicks in their nests, band the chicks, and put radio transmitters on the older chicks and adults. Later, we would follow the marked birds by small airplane. We concentrated on tricolored herons, little blue herons, and snowy egrets—all small, dainty wading birds that were declining in population in the Everglades.

I had snagged this esteemed job after earning my bachelor's and master's degrees in wildlife biology in New England. I loved New England, but wildlife jobs there were almost as scarce as heath hen's teeth—and heath hens are extinct. After all, we were living under the Reagan Administration, and conservation was not the president's priority. Most of the fulltime jobs available seemed to be in the South, I assumed because the field season is so short in the North. After spending two years in Georgia and South Carolina spying on storks, I had the chance to join a new project in the Keys. If I had to live in the South, the neatest place would be in the Keys, and the neatest place to work would be in the Everglades—many a biologist's dream.

The logistics of doing fieldwork in the Everglades were knotty. To transport ourselves to the study colonies, the fastest way from our office on Plantation Key (one island down from Key Largo), we had to go entirely by water. Crossing Florida Bay by boat was a zigzaggy 25 miles over shallow, island-studded seagrass beds. Then, depending on which colony we went to, it could be another 35 miles up the west coast of Everglades National Park. That's 120 miles round-trip, in case your mental calculator is hibernating.

We kept a fleet of vessels of varying sizes for different projects. Since our office was small, we couldn't afford to keep a boat mechanic on staff. Thus, a colleague and I took three-month turns overseeing the upkeep of the boats. We were responsible for ensuring that the boats ran well and were equipped for safety. Usually, we trailered them to a marina for servicing. I learned to undertake some of the routine maintenance on my own to save the office's coffers. Besides, our study sites were remote, and the more I knew about fixing simple motor and propeller problems, the sooner we would return home if something went awry.

To my amusement, I was labeled a boating expert after unintentionally proving my mettle with the smallest of achievements. My new bailiwick started evolving one day when I noticed that the end of a boat's bowline was frayed. Too embarrassed to go to a boat shop for such a measly repair, I took the rope home, unshelved my U.S. Coast Guard Auxiliary's *Boating Skills and Seamanship* manual, and looked up "splicing." All the how-to diagrams were carefully sketched. I followed the instructions and produced a functioning, albeit lumpy, eye splice. The next day, everyone marveled at my feat of seamanship and assumed I possessed hidden mariner talent. Thereafter, if a boat in our fleet had a problem, the solution was "Ask Su." I let that status cultivate a life of its own.

Due to the remoteness of the colonies and the three hours it took to boat there, our field team (me and one or two assistants) often camped overnight to allow more time for fieldwork. The best time of the day to labor in the colonies was in early morning or late afternoon. Until we arrived, the parent birds would take turns protecting and shading the young with their bodies. At our arrival, the parents would temporarily spook and fly away, leaving the chicks exposed to the baking sun.

Camping involved pitching a free-standing tent on a "chickee," the Seminole word for house. A chickee is a wooden platform a few feet above the water that is sized to fit a few tents. The chickees were built by the National Park Service and stood in the water surrounded by islands of mangrove trees. Chickees were placed every few miles along the Wilderness Waterway so that paddlers and other boaters could always be near a place to camp. If not for the chickees, there would be almost nowhere dry or out of alligator reach to lay a sleeping bag down.

The wooden slats that comprised the platform had half-inch gaps, which we called cracks, to allow the copious rain to drain through. The cracks allowed us to wrap our tent lines around the slats to keep the tents from blowing into the water while we were working offsite. For all the good the cracks did, they also became our nemesis. If we weren't careful, our forks would fall through the cracks. Or our toothbrushes. Or our pocketknives. Set something slender down on the platform and it was sure to disappear. Eventually, we stopped blaming each other when we couldn't find something smaller than a breadbox.

"Hey, where's that pen for marking the eggshells?" someone would ask.

"Don't know. Guess it fell through the crack," would be the answer, and the subject was dropped. We meant it literally.

Campers and picnickers could pull their boats up to the chickees, leaving the alligators and cottonmouths in lonely frustration. That fewer mosquitoes hung out over the water was insignificant—if you could still punch the air and hit ten of them, what did it matter?

Mosquitoes are a ubiquitous distraction in South Florida. During the rainy season in summer, most tourist places are ghost towns because of the curse of the little insects. The worst location is in the mangroves, where the salt marsh mosquito lives—the mangroves, as in where we worked. Alaskans brag that the mosquito is their state bird, as if to say the bigger the mosquito, the worse it is. I can testify that Alaskan mosquitoes are so large and slow that they are easy targets and not the nuisance that the smaller, annoyingly evasive salt marsh mosquitoes are. On the positive side, salt marsh mosquitoes don't carry human diseases. Furthermore, like all mosquitoes, they pollinate the wetland flowers as bees do in the uplands. The female mosquitoes only bite animals when they need protein to lay their eggs. They have an indispensable role in keeping the ecosystem healthy by being a food source themselves and by pollinating plants.

That said, we still didn't want to provide protein for more mosquitoes. Some of our staff used insect repellent. I rarely put DEET repellent on my skin after I read medical articles about it absorbing through the skin, appearing in the urine, and causing convulsions that led to death. I used insect repellent on a special net jacket that I put over my long-sleeved shirt. The netting absorbed the repellent and kept the insects away. I always wore long sleeves and pants, no matter how hot the air was. At the chickees, I wore a head net while cooking or writing notes at night. Eating was a tricky venture, and we generally turned off the flashlights, so we couldn't see exactly what had fallen lucklessly into our chow.

If we didn't camp, we left the dock in the still before dawn, worked all day, and pulled up dockside in Tavernier around eight o'clock in the evening. A fifteen-hour day, 120 miles of boating, crawling across mangrove roots in 100-degree heat index left me winking, blinking, and nodding as I drove the boat home— and I was standing.

The Wilderness Waterway owes its distinctive charm to the mangroves that line the water's edge along the entire trail. Mangroves are trees of many species that live in the fuzzy boundary between land and sea on tropical shores around the world. Florida has three species: red, black, and white. Red mangroves grow closest to the water; white mangroves grow farthest inland, and black mangroves grow in between. Red mangroves may attain heights of eighty feet. Whites and blacks may grow to sixty-five feet. Mostly, however, the trunks are beaten down to a fraction of their potential height by the occasional tropical gale.

Mangroves live along shallow shorelines, where the waves are gentle and the stiltlike roots can trap and hold nutrient-laden sediments. The nutrients are bits of detritus and provide food for small marine organisms, such as fish, crabs, shrimp, oysters, and spiny lobsters. These and other organisms spend part of their lives around the mangrove roots. Some of the most important nursery grounds for seafood are the waters around the mangroves. Without these trees, many types of seafood for our tables would be seriously depleted or nonexistent. Over many years, the gradual trapping of sediments extends the shoreline—that is, unless global warming causes the sea to rise faster than the land is formed. Mangroves are at a tremendous risk from any rise in sea level.

Isn't it odd that trees can grow in salt water? Indubitably, but mangrove trees have their own desalinization "plants," so to speak. The cells of the roots screen out salt, allowing only fresh water to flow into the tree.

On this day, we were going to carry out a typical marathon field day—leave before dawn, boat across Florida Bay in the dark, arrive at the colony by eight o'clock in the morning, work during the cooler hours of early morning and late afternoon, and return to our dock at dusk.

Just as we were about to cast off from our dock, I remembered, *Darn, I didn't buy that big anchor!* It was my turn to oversee the boat upkeep. The two anchors that came with this boat worked well in the Texas bay waters, but they were too small to hold in a strong ocean wind or current. We seldom had to anchor because we typically tied the boat to mangrove trees. The wind was usually calm in the bird colony, so in the few months that I had been running the boat in the Everglades, I rarely needed even one small anchor.

Ignoring a gnawing feeling in my gut, I postponed the purchase again. Our mission was waiting. We needed to get to the colony early to live-trap some herons and put radio transmitters on them. Expediency weighed heavy on my mind. If we delayed, the sun would be too hot to disturb the birds.

The sweat was already beading on my skin at sunrise, despite the steady, easterly breeze. Humidity in the Keys never takes a vacation. We had sixty miles to go, so Allison, Rick, and I alternated driving the boat across Florida Bay and up the Gulf Coast along a remote part of Everglades National Park. As biologists for the National Audubon Society, we had permission from the National Park Service to study the wading birds within the park boundaries.

When we emerged from Whitewater Bay into the Gulf of Mexico, I noted gratefully that the wind wasn't blowing from the west. A west wind coming off the ocean whips the water into a froth and makes for a bone-jarring trip. An east wind sheltered by the mainland means a placid, paradisiacal ride.

On days like this, gliding along the mangrove beaches, when the air was warm and the water glassy, with dolphins racing beside our boat, we would gleefully exclaim, "We get paid for this!"

But just past Ponce de Leon Bay, 45 minutes from our destination, the motor wheezed, grinded, sputtered, and finally died. Coolly, I removed the cowling from the motor and checked a few basic parts. I could feel Allison's and Rick's eyes watching from behind.

"Well?" they piped in unison. "Can you fix it?"

With a sinking feeling that grows as you realize your packed day of fieldwork is rapidly becoming a fantasy, I sheepishly admitted the problem was beyond my skills to repair with duct tape or chewing gum.

"Let's set an anchor while we figure out what to do," I suggested.

We set the larger of the two Danforth anchors while we pondered a course of action. The best chance seemed to be to enlist our marine band VHF transceiver and try to contact the ranger station. Failing that, we might reach a fishing boat that could relay a message. We were too far from our office for the signal to reach there and too far from any marina or other civilization.

We radioed to the Flamingo Ranger Station, about thirty miles away. At that time, unlike only a few years later, the rangers were permitted to assist hapless researchers if they had cooperative Park Service agreements. That was because the results we garnered would be useful to the park managers. Fortunately, the atmospheric environment was also benevolent, and our radio waves connected with a ranger. The voice in the speaker informed us he would send a ranger to tow us, but it could take hours. We settled down to wait.

The breeze kept us cool in spite of the blazing South Florida summer sun. How nice to have that cooling air! The wind gently rocked the boat. Oh, yes, we would have a pleasant wait. Allison, Rick, and I settled down for a relaxing break.

Our trips to the nesting colonies normally were uneventful. To me, they were routine—simply part of my job. As I waited for the floating cavalry, I recalled an earlier trip. A local newspaper reporter from Homestead wrote a column called "A Day in the Life of _____ (fill in the blank)." He would select a person from the community with an interesting occupation and request to follow that person around for a day. On someone's suggestion, he asked to accompany me to a bird colony. I agreed and carried out my normal routine, as he tagged along. During that day, I asked him what his most boring story had been. He quickly responded that it was the Dunkin' Donuts baker. The reporter had asked the baker, "Is it true that you rise at five o'clock every morning to bake the donuts?" The baker answered curtly, "Yes." Every question the reporter asked was answered monosyllabically. Eventually, the reporter discovered that the baker hardly spoke English.

That day with the reporter was uneventful, unless you consider a torrential rainsquall while we were cruising in our open boat on the way home to be an event. We didn't. The invisibility of the channel markers and the pelting raindrops were common during the summer. When the interview concluded, I asked the reporter how his trip with me ranked. I wasn't surprised to find that he placed my "average" day as his most interesting experience.

A gust of wind jarred me back to reality. My complacency was misguided. That steady east wind—that same gentle one for which I was always grateful, that offshore wind that made the waves smooth and the trip speedy—was now blowing our boat out to sea!

The puny anchor wasn't holding in the muddy bottom. Quickly, we tossed the smaller anchor out, setting the two into the wind at right angles to each other and letting out all the scope (length of rope) in the most effective pattern. Silently, I cursed myself for procrastinating on buying a larger anchor and hoped no one remembered my oversight.

The water was barely six feet deep, so we could set the anchors at a small angle far from the boat. The smaller the angle between the rope and the sea bottom, the more likely the blades of the anchor would grab the bottom.

We could also use the eighteen-foot push pole, which we normally only used to thrust the boat through water too shallow or weedy for the motor. We jammed the pole into the muddy bottom a few feet off the bow and tied the boat to it. With two undersized anchors and the pole, the boat barely held in place. One strong gust and we would be watching the mangroves shrink on the eastern horizon as we drifted off into the Gulf of Mexico, never to be heard from again.

But the shore was so close! Or so it looked. We could swim to it. In fact, that water seemed so shallow we could almost walk to it. So tantalizing was the thought that Rick had to try. We pulled the anchors, and he jumped into the water, but it was too deep to walk. Gallantly, Rick tried to swim while towing the boat. I pushed off with the pole. Allison worked furiously with a canoe paddle, which we kept for just such emergencies. We cheered Rick on until it was obvious that we were making no progress. All our efforts did was to tire us. Rick climbed back in the boat. We set the anchors and pole again and settled down to wait for help.

With every gust of wind, the boat dragged a few inches seaward, and my heart skipped a beat. Would we find our own Gilligan's Island?

Allison declared she wasn't worried. "I've never been to New Orleans, and it looks like we'll get a free trip."

Of all the days to lack our camping gear, we had to pick this one. That extra food could come in handy. And the self-standing tents for cover from the sun and rain? We could only hope we wouldn't need them.

Hour after hour we waited, mentally measuring our progress toward Louisiana or Texas each time the anchors dragged and the push pole bent. The inches seemed like miles. As long as the anchors reached the muddy bottom and the shoreline was visible, we should be okay.

What was it that we often said to each other? "We get paid for this!" When you've peeled down to your bathing suit, and you're cruising along a palm-studded, tranquil bay, with fun-loving colleagues beside you, and food in the cooler, it's easy to forget the rest of the story.

The flip side reads something like this: Fifteen-hour field days. Humidity that drenches you day and night. Heat that could drive a camel to whine. Daily thunderstorms for the entire field season when you're in an open boat or wading in water. Rain so intense it stings your skin like BB pellets when you're cruising in a boat. Winds that bat your boat around like a rubber duck in a rambunctious kid's bath. Alligators everywhere you step. Rattlesnakes and cottonmouths, too. Slogging through shoe-sucking muck to get to the nest trees. Climbing over mangrove roots till your legs feel like lead. Bumping into those same roots until your shins are solid hematomas. Brushing against the poison ivy, the more poisonous poisonwood, and the most poisonous manchineel. Getting showered with vomited fish, compliments of baby birds that are reflexively defending themselves. Getting pecked and scratched by birds with daggerlike bills that don't know you are trying to save them. Picking your way through a cloud of mosquitoes, some of which settle on your back like a shawl. Scratching off the tiny no-see-ums that can penetrate the smallest break in your insect armor. Fire ants that sting so sharply they could make a sumo wrestler leap in pain. Your Cessna's control panel catching afire a thousand feet over the Everglades. Carrying a twenty-pound battery a third of a mile across cacti and ankle-tripping mangrove roots. Boats breaking down in the middle of nowhere. This and more, we didn't get paid for.

As we waited for a ranger to ride to our rescue on a white boat, we fretted about the wind. To distract ourselves, we played a kind of three-dimensional tick-tack-toe in two dimensions on the back of a data sheet. I'm not sure, but I may have invented that version of the game based on a three-dimensional chess game I saw on *Star Trek*. I drew a tick-tack-toe pattern with nine blocks. Then I drew two identical patterns next to the first. The object was to imagine the three patterns horizontally as layers on top of each other and make three marks in a row in any direction. With one person tending the anchors, the other two played 3-D tick-tack-toe, or should I say tick-tack-*tow*, as we hoped it would become.

The wind held constantly, and hours later, the cavalry came in the form of Ranger Donna Emery. Our anxious wait was over, and we jumped into motion to prepare the boat for towing. We fashioned a "bridle" (a rope strung between two metal cleats on the stern of the towboat) for Donna's boat, and tied one end of the towrope to the bridle and the other through our boat's bow ring. After I lashed our steering wheel to keep the rudder straight, we set off toward Ponce de Leon Bay with the crippled *Minnow* in tow. Rick, Allison, and I were aboard the patrol boat with Donna. The small towboat had quite a load, so we chugged along at no-wake speed, just a few miles per hour.

Taking the inland waterway to avoid the wind and choppy water, Donna headed toward Flamingo. Between Ponce de Leon Bay and Whitewater Bay is a maze of mangrove islands. We had passed there numerous times and knew the way from memory. Donna also knew the way—when she was paying attention. As I was now on her boat, I was no longer captain, and I spent my time facing aft, nervously watching my helpless boat fighting its long leash. Donna had to watch our boat, too, because she was responsible for it now. While she was looking back, she took a wrong turn.

Well, mangrove islands are confounding things. When viewed from a certain direction by a practiced eye, they can be distinctive and look comfortably recognizable. When viewed from any other angle, they might as well be in the Mekong Delta. Despite the presence of nautical charts and four nautical minds, it took us an hour to emerge into familiar territory.

We arrived safely at Flamingo about six o'clock in the evening. Bill, the Audubon volunteer, was waiting at the marina with the Suburban truck and a boat trailer, summoned by a ranger at our request. During the two-hour drive through the Everglades, across the bridges and causeways, and back to Plantation Key, I contemplated changing the name of the boat and wrote myself a note to buy a really big anchor. I would have to use another boat the next day.

After parking the disabled vessel, I returned home sixteen hours after I had left, having not done a lick of fieldwork. That's when Karen called, and I recounted my ordinary day at work.

"You be careful out in the field tomorrow," she scolded. "And don't get stuck in the Gulf of No Return!"

It's Just a Short Walk

The Everglades were parched. The vast sheet of shallow water was reduced to a film of moisture with scattered alligator holes clinging to useful existence. In April of 1989, our carefully planned fieldwork in the wading bird colonies along the western fringe of Everglades National Park had disintegrated because none of the colonies had formed.

Six months earlier, the Everglades and surrounding towns were flooded. While airborne over the eastern Everglades, I saw watery wakes forming as cars drove along flooded roads where people had built houses on land that wasn't zoned as residential. We biologists never expected that the marsh could dry out so quickly. However, it had barely rained since then.

Scrounging for colonies that we could access to study, we found a distant one in Water Conservation Area 3A. WCA 3A was north of Everglades National Park, in part of the Everglades that was managed by the state's wildlife agency and the South Florida Water Management District. The colony was inland and surrounded by a sawgrass marsh. Our motorboats were useless there. In a good year, with oodles of water, the vegetation precluded the use of motorboats anyway. Now there wasn't even enough water for an airboat, even if we had one. We certainly didn't have the money to rent a helicopter. No matter. We would walk.

I measured the distance on a map as about one and a half miles from the nearest levee. My plan was to drive about three hours on paved roads from our office in the Keys to Tamiami Trail (Highway 41), then drive north on Levee 67-A until we were straight across from the colony. The levees are unpaved access roads that are off-limits to the public. I obtained the gate key from the South Florida Water Management District. Because we would be on the opposite side of the canal, we would have to cross about thirty feet of water. That's why we would bring a canoe. In a few strokes, we could ferry people across to the other bank. Then the fun would begin.

A mile and a half of walking doesn't sound strenuous, but the Everglades is a tough place. The April sun is brutal in the treeless marsh, with an air temperature often in the eighties and feeling like the nineties. Just carrying several quarts of drinking water per person adds more than two pounds per quart to your load. The muck grabs your feet and sometimes sucks your shoes off. Making progress can be almost literally at a snail's pace. There is nowhere to sit and rest, short of setting your bottom in the shallow water. Add to that the solid field of sawgrass, which is named for the razor-sharp edges of its blades. Then fend against cottonmouth snakebites by wearing heavy pants. Add it all up, and the walk one way across the flat terrain could take an exhausting two hours.

After I had made the trip a few times with my assistants, a television crew from West Palm Beach asked to accompany us. The reporter, Glen, and his cameraman, Jason (not their real names), wanted to film a wading bird colony, and we were studying one of the few remaining in that droughty year.

I phoned Glen beforehand to brief the pair on what to bring. I instructed, "Bring several quarts of water per person and wear a wide-brimmed hat, long-sleeved shirt, long pants, and old sneakers. Carry only what is absolutely necessary. It will be mercilessly hot and humid. You have no idea how hard it is to slog through shallow water and muck. It will sap your energy as fast as you can trip over an alligator."

For years, my field clothing included camouflage garb. Sneaking up on birds requires more than stealth. It requires blending in with the trees by disguising the body's shape, which the camouflage design does. Furthermore, I worked in wetlands, especially steamy, subtropical ones, toiling in soggy clothing all day. I needed rot-proof garb. The only garments I found tough enough to survive tree-climbing, thorns, abrasion from carrying gear, and constant saturation were the U.S. Army's BDUs (Battle Dress Uniforms). I had tried hunters' clothing, and the fabric fell apart after one season. The Army clothing not only lasted many seasons, but the pants had drawstring hems to keep leeches from crawling up my legs, and the clothes even came sized to fit little women. Lord & Taylor never got a penny from me, but I knew where every Army–Navy Surplus store around was.

As I am not the military type, self-consciousness gripped me when I had to interact with the general populace while wearing my camouflage field garb. The local news media often reported that, in some parts of the Everglades, radical groups trained mercenaries for various causes, such as overthrowing Fidel Castro. When I pulled up to a gas station or stopped for an ice cream at the marina after a blistering day, I drew stares of confusion from other customers. Perhaps people were assuming I was a soldierette-for-hire.

Once, when I was back in Massachusetts visiting my friends Joe and Donna Choiniere, Donna admonished their little son for wanting to wear a soldier's battle uniform. I consoled her, "It's not so evil. Even I wear it. Just pretend he's a fledgling field biologist." That seemed to calm her.

I wore the heavy, long-sleeved BDUs summer and winter in the Everglades, and I was wearing them when we rendezvoused with the television crew at the intersection of Tamiami Trail and the levee. Our Audubon crew consisted of the project leader Dr.

Tom Bancroft, assistant biologist Cindy Thompson, and me. Cindy was a hard worker and always ready for any dilemma the fieldwork could dish out.

As we introduced ourselves to the television crew on the levee, I noticed that the cameraman had short sleeves, new leather hiking boots, and no hat. Perhaps he had not gotten my clothing instructions from the reporter. He also had no drinking water. Apparently, he had sacrificed water to carry the thirty-pound video camera. Jason was in his mid-twenties and looked strong and fit, so I didn't fret.

Glen seemed better prepared, with a hat, old sneakers, and a water bottle. He carried the camera's spare battery pack, which weighed about twenty pounds. Tom, Cindy, and I carried water and equipment; Tom carried extra water to share. The three of us were fully loaded, but field-proven.

I was accustomed to men not heeding my advice about going into the field. My guess is that some men think they are tougher than women, so we gals must be exaggerating. If we say something is difficult, it probably isn't. That attitude can backfire. Several years earlier, a newspaper reporter shadowed me for a day in the field to get a story. I had forewarned him to bring a raincoat, because it was likely to rain. In hot weather, which it was, a person may prefer to get a cooling soak. But the raindrops can sting bare skin as you travel on an open boat that is moving at twenty miles per hour. Nevertheless, when the usual afternoon squall came along, the reporter huddled behind a seat on the open deck, trying to keep his bare arms from getting pelted. Cindy and I donned our slickers, traded grins when he wasn't looking, and kept driving in unperturbed comfort.

After the greeting formalities at the levee gate, we caravanned with the television van the fifteen miles up the canal along the levee and parked the vehicles at the place that was closest to the colony. We then launched our canoe into the canal, ferried all five people across the deep water, and left the canoe along the bank. The sun was just rising when we started hiking through the damp marsh, but the air was already steamy. We bulldozed through the thick wall of cattails lining the canal and then through skin-slicing sawgrass.

After only a quarter of a mile, Jason started lagging behind. When we realized that Jason's energy was waning, Tom offered to carry the camera. Jason refused, taking his responsibility for the equipment seriously. Eventually, he traded with Glen for the slightly lighter spare battery. I insisted that I could carry the battery, but Jason would not relent. Granted, I am petite. The battery alone equaled almost twenty percent of my body weight, and I was toting almost that amount in emergency and research gear.

Besides water, food, first-aid kit, clipboard, spring scales for weighing birds, and other measuring equipment, my pack also contained a handheld, marine-band radio. In those days before portable cell phones, the latter was the only way we had to communicate with the outside world. In case of an extreme, immediate emergency, we could call "mayday" and hope that an overflying aircraft would receive the message. Some planes did monitor marine frequencies so that a distress call from a boat would be heard. That we were not on the water made the utility of a marine-band radio marginal.

Against our pleas to turn back with one of our crew, Jason insisted on continuing. He wanted to complete his assignment. Those news crews are a dedicated bunch.

After plodding onward, Jason admitted that he couldn't carry anything and gave the battery to Tom. Even devoid of gear, the cameraman was sorely dragging. Glen was lugging the camera and his own gear. After Tom carried the battery for a while, he passed it to me, so he could help carry Glen's gear. He wouldn't have done that if he thought I couldn't handle the battery plus my own load, because, as the project leader, he would be responsible for my demise.

By the time we arrived at the bird colony, Jason was light-headed and couldn't keep down the water we gave him. He complained of leg cramps. His face was red, but he wasn't sweating. Tom and I knew these symptoms were serious and that he wouldn't make it back on his own.

We had the marine radio, but Glen and Jason had a mobile phone in their van, back on the levee. We opted for the mobile phone approach. Jason wasn't in immediate danger, provided we kept him cool and still. We had time to get to the van, where we were sure to reach help directly with the phone. We couldn't be sure the marine radio would reach anyone, and we would have to relay a message through a pilot to a rescue helicopter. We knew from previous experience in the mangroves how well that form of message-relaying works.

Cindy, Glen, and I started to hike back to the van, leaving Tom with Jason in the shade of the nest trees. How we hated disturbing the birds for so long! The chicks could not survive in the sun with their parents scared off the nests.

Our trio made good progress toward the levee. Then, partway back, Glen began to retch. Cindy stayed with him in a small patch of shade. At least Glen wasn't far from the van. Cindy and I could help him out eventually. I forged the rest of the way alone, with Glen's van keys and directions for telephoning his news editor.

Back at the canal, I paddled the few strokes across the water, unlocked the television station's van, and called the station's editor. Calmly, I described who I was and that we needed a helicopter to retrieve his stricken cameraman.

"He's got heat stroke. He won't make it out on his own," I explained to the editor.

"Oh, he'll be all right in a while. Give him time."

"No, you don't understand. He's got heat stroke. He can't make it out on his own. You need to send a helicopter."

"No need for a chopper. I'll get an airboat out there," he replied.

"There's not enough water for an airboat. That's why we walked. We need a helicopter."

I don't know how many exasperating minutes I spent trying to convince the editor that he needed to send a helicopter. Once again, I felt that I had been caught by the "women always exaggerate" mentality. Apparently, the editor thought that, since I emerged from the marsh on my own, certainly Jason could. Or maybe it was the "if it's really so serious, why isn't she hysterical?" mindset.

Finally, I said, "Here are Jason's symptoms." I rattled off the red-but-dry skin, the heaves, and so on. "Now call a doctor or a hospital and see what they think you should do. I'll wait here until you call me back."

After a deep silence, the editor replied, "Okay, I'll get help."

He called me back soon after and said, "The Sheriff's rescue helicopter is on the way. Do you have the location?" I gave him the LORAN coordinates. LORAN (Long Range Navigation) was the predecessor of GPS (Global Positioning System) for finding locations in the blank areas of road maps.

I paddled across the canal and started traipsing back through the muck to help Cindy bring Glen back. I didn't advance far when I met them walking my way. Glen just needed a rest in the shade, and he recovered quickly. I paddled Cindy and Glen back to the van.

Later, I learned that Glen spent a lot of time outdoors as a birder. He was in good shape, just not used to the midday sun, especially with a twenty- or thirty-pound backpack. Birders often venture out so early in the morning that heat is not an issue.

We watched the Sheriff's helicopter pass overhead and aim toward the bird colony. It disappeared when it plucked up Jason and Tom from the marsh. The helicopter returned soon and landed on the levee where Cindy, Glen, and I were waiting. Everyone was out of the marsh.

The paramedics on the helicopter treated Jason briefly on the levee and then flew him to a hospital, leaving Tom with us. Jason remained hospitalized overnight for observation and was released the next day.

For all the drama of the day, the events were not atypical. Nor was it atypical of what I perceived as the narrow-mindedness of men who dismiss women as helpless. I'm glad Tom never had that attitude. We got a lot more work done that way.

Chapter 7.
Some Day My Ship Will Come In

Biologists will resort to any mode of transportation they can find to study their research subjects. I have canoed, bicycled, snowshoed, scuba dived, and climbed trees. I have also used trucks, motorboats, airboats, all-terrain vehicles (ATVs), airplanes, and helicopters. As someone who disdains the use of motors for the sake of fun and feeling powerful, I prefer the manual way of getting things done. Motorized modes for lifesaving and conservation efforts are often required to fix a problem caused by the same modes of transportation that people use as a matter of choice, not need.

An ATV was my last resort to find a certain tricolored heron in the depths of Big Cypress National Preserve. The heron (one of my National Audubon study subjects) wore a radio transmitter, and the signal that I heard as I flew over the same location lingered for several days. Was the bird dead? I wanted to be sure, and on the ground was the only way. I called the Big Cypress headquarters and asked if a park ranger could take me to the spot.

Ranger John offered his assistance. "Sure, come on up. We'll have to go by ATV," he informed me. "Where you need to go is through cypress trees and into muddy flats. An airboat is useless there."

I had never driven an ATV, nor had I driven a motorcycle. On the two-hour drive from my house on Plantation Key to Big Cypress the next day, I blissfully assumed that ATVs were like motorcycles—I could just jump on the seat behind the ranger, and off we would go.

John was the perfect image of a park ranger—strong, easygoing, and as I saw later, at home in the wilderness. He took me out to the building where the ATVs were housed. All had four wheels. I had only seen three-wheelers before.

"Why four wheels?" I asked.

"The three-wheelers tip over too easily, so the government requires its employees to use four. More stable," he explained.

121

Sensing my naïveté, he queried, "Know how to drive one?"

"Uh, nope. Do I need to?"

"What do you think? You can just jump on the back seat and let me do all the work?" His wry grin put me at ease. How hard could it be? John gave me a crash course. Off we went to find the bird, with John steadily leading the way and me bouncing around in the distance like a bobblehead doll.

Along the way, I watched the ruts that our wheels were gouging in the mud. "How long will these ruts last?" I inquired.

"Probably decades," came the answer. I was shocked.

Big Cypress was a national preserve and, as such, had more lenient regulations about visitor usage than did national parks. ATV use by the public was allowed. I noted the jumble of ATV tracks left by others before us. How long had they been there? Suddenly, I wondered if finding my bird was worth the destruction I was causing. I almost turned back. Instead, I figured my research justified the damage.

Using my LORAN unit, we found the location where the bird had settled for the previous three days. Unexpectedly, my receiver was silent. Around and around, in widening spirals we drove, listening for a signal and looking for any wading birds to no avail.

Eventually, my guilt about destroying the habitat overwhelmed me, and I concluded, "John, that's enough. Let's go back."

I never found the bird. And I never again used an ATV.

In remote, roadless areas, biologists often resort to using aircraft, either single-engine planes or helicopters, as their budgets permit. I used both extensively in the Everglades and other areas of the eastern United States.

Only certain aircraft are suited for biological work. If you are searching for something, and not just flying for transportation as you might to get around in Alaska, then you would need a high-wing plane. That means the wings sit above the windows on the aircraft, and people in the cabin can see the ground. High-wings are commonly used for sightseeing excursions and photographing scenery. In low-wing planes, the wings obstruct the view.

The plane of choice for most biologists is a Cessna 152, 172, or 182. The 152 is a two-place (two-seat) plane with the seats side-by-side. Cessna 172s and 182s have four places (two seats in front and two in back); they are generally designed as family planes, suitable for two parents and two offspring. For most of my work, I used a 172. It was cheaper than a 182, which could carry more weight than I required. But I didn't start with a Cessna.

Before I studied the wood storks in Georgia, I had never flown in a single-engine plane. My introduction to small planes was like stepping back in time. Enter the Piper Super Cub, a tiny, high-wing, two-place plane with tandem seats (one behind the other) and the landing wheel under the tail (called a tail-dragger). From our Birdsville backyard's grassy runway, I climbed into the seat behind the pilot and found a stick for the steering wheel and rudder pedals, the same as the ones for the pilot. Theoretically, I could fly the plane from the back seat if I needed to.

Occasionally, the Piper Super Cub wasn't available and our pilot had to use a Piper Cub. This was one rung down from the Super Cub. I don't know if you can get any lower than a Cub, which doesn't even have an electrical system. This means that it has no radio, no electronic instruments, and no electronic starter. The pilot navigates by a traditional compass and doesn't communicate with any towers or other pilots.

How do you start a plane without an electronic ignition, when you can't turn a key to crank it up? You hand-prop it, and it is not a solo operation. Often, I was the only other person around, such as when we landed at a remote airstrip to gas up or eat our bag lunches. The pilot would start the propeller while standing in front of the plane, yelling "Clear prop!" or simply "Clear!" to warn anyone coming from behind. Then he would whip the propeller counterclockwise by one swift push with his hands, as the engine caught. I sat in the rear seat, dutifully stomping on the brakes until the pilot jumped in the front seat and took over the controls.

Brake-stomping was as necessary as putting enough fuel in the gas tanks. Once the propeller starts spinning, the plane has a tendency to wander forward. The propeller becomes a deadly whirling dervish and is nearly invisible. Sometimes the pilot and I traded hand-propping duties, and I faced the possibility of becoming a soufflé. More than one person has walked obliviously into a spinning propeller. I am glad I never witnessed that colorful event.

Most of the time I curse my minuscule size, but every now and then I cheer it. Flying in Piper Cubs and Super Cubs was such a situation. A chassis much larger than mine would require a shoehorn just to sit down.

Our flights for the wood stork project used three patterns. For one, we flew around scanning for groups of storks feeding—the "oh, I see some!" method. For another, we flew to the colony and followed an unmarked stork as it flew to a feeding location—the "don't lose it!" method. The third way was to fly around in search-pattern transects as we listened with an electronic receiver to find the birds with radio transmitters—the "I hear it!" method. For all three, the object was to find where the birds ended up on the ground, so we knew where to send a ground crew to sample the water.

Finding the birds with transmitters during the field season was no challenge, because the birds were all nearby and we could locate them all in one day. During the winter, the storks migrated south, and we didn't know where they went. I arranged several aerial search trips to find the wintering birds.

The monthly winter trips lasted about three days. The pilot and I would cram overnight bags into the miniature baggage compartment of a Cessna 152 in Augusta, Georgia, and head south through Georgia and Florida. I had mounted the direction-finding antennas on the wing struts, and I would sit in the right seat with my headphones on, listening all day for my kind of music—faint beeps. Hours could pass in silence or static, mostly the latter. Somnolence was close company.

We would fly transects across Florida, coast to coast, east to west and back again, heading twenty miles farther south each time. Our altitude was somewhere around four or five thousand feet. That way, we were likely to catch a signal from a transmitter that might be ten miles away. When I heard a beep, I would direct the pilot toward it. Sometimes we would zigzag to get a better fix on the direction it came from. I could tell from my receiver which antenna, the left or the right, was receiving a stronger signal.

We would fly for the maximum number of hours that the pilot was allowed by the Federal Aviation Administration (eight). Then, we would land at whatever airport we were near and tie the plane down on a general aviation tarmac. We would take a taxi to a nearby motel, plan the route for the next day over dinner, and do the same thing the next day, until we found all the birds or had covered the territory. Three days was usually enough.

Ed was one of the pilots we hired frequently for daily flights. He was a Vietnam veteran, and his flying skills were not the only war memory he carried with him. During the first extended trip we took, we landed at an airfield and went to a restaurant for dinner. The usually courteous Ed did not offer me my choice of seats. Instead, he slipped into the seat against the wall. Not wanting to appear rude, he explained, "Since the war, I always sit where I can see everyone coming and going."

Once, I found four birds scattered to the four corners of Florida, all dining on regional aquatic soups. One was in Okefenokee Swamp, a national wildlife refuge at the north end of Florida. One was in Everglades National Park at Florida's south end. One was in a pond in New Smyrna on the Atlantic coast. One had settled in a water trap on a Fort Myers golf course on the Gulf coast.

In midwinter in Georgia one year, curiosity gripped me. Did all of the Big Duke's Pond wood storks migrate south in the winter or did some linger around Birdsville? We had never looked locally in winter. When we didn't happen to see any, we just assumed they had left, so we stopped our Birdsville flights in October.

One January day, I arranged with our regular pilot, Matt, to fly me over the Birdsville swamps. The day I greeted Matt at the airport was the coldest on record there. In Millen, the temperature dipped to four degrees below zero without the wind chill, as I recall, and that wind was fierce. In the unheated Super Cub, I bundled up in my down jacket, hoping that Matt's fingers could feel the controls.

Matt and I flew transects back and forth, systematically checking a wide area around Millen. As I gazed intently out the window looking for black-edged white specks, Matt asked, "Hey, Su, do you notice anything strange about this flight?"

Having left the flying to Matt, I replied, "No. What?"

"We're flying backwards!" Sure enough, I mentally marked a spot on the ground below and watched it slide forward. Did I mention the wind was fierce? It was too strong for the little plane. Somehow, Matt was able to maintain control, and we finished our survey.

We never did see any storks. That was what I had expected, but sometimes you have to fly the extra mile to confirm a theory.

In later years, I did some of the same aerial work with herons in the Everglades. I was experienced by then, which was a good thing, because most species I studied in the Everglades were much harder to see from the air than wood storks. Going from spotting five-pound birds with five-foot wingspans and mostly white feathers (wood storks) to thirteen-ounce grayish birds with three-foot wingspans (tricolored and little blue herons) required experience and nearly bionic eyesight. Then there were the equal-sized, all-white birds, such as the snowy egrets, cattle egrets, and the white-phased little blue herons. At a distance, they all looked alike.

I never appreciated how easy it was to study the storks while I was studying them. Their feathers always looked dirty. In a mixed flock of great egrets and wood storks, the egrets stood out in their dazzling white plumage among the dingy-coated storks.

One survey I flew periodically covered a good portion of southern Florida in a monthly pursuit of all things wading bird. These "Systematic Reconnaissance Flights" comprised a monumental multi-agency survey performed mostly during the dry-season months and covered an area the size of Delaware. During the wet season, the wading birds spread out over the vast sheet of water and were difficult to count. In the dry season, they concentrated where the water was—a much smaller area to survey.

To reduce the chance that we counted the same birds twice, the survey was conducted by three teams on simultaneous days. The teams were the National Audubon Society, the National Park Service, and the Florida Game and Fresh Water Fish Commission (now called the Florida Fish and Wildlife Conservation Commission). Audubon was responsible for surveying the state Water Conservation Areas, which included Loxahatchee National Wildlife Refuge (because most of the refuge is owned by the state but managed by the U.S. Fish and Wildlife Service). The Park Service surveyed Everglades National Park, and Florida Game and Fish covered Big Cypress National Preserve. I worked for Audubon and later for the Park Service and ended up doing the survey for both groups.

Our plane of choice for these surveys was the Cessna 182. It could carry four adults safely at low altitudes and slow speeds. It was further equipped with a STOL package—an abbreviation for "short takeoff and landing." That allowed us to use an even shorter runway than normal, which was handy when landing on midget airstrips in the middle of nowhere.

When I first started flying surveys over Everglades National Park, I knew we had to turn around at the boundary with Big Cypress National Preserve. Since I was navigating, how would I know where that was? Having the LORAN helped, but I soon found that I didn't need any help. Those ATV tracks in Big Cypress—the ones that persist for decades—are visible from the air. What we couldn't see were the boundary-marker sign posts on the ground. The ATV and airboat drivers could see them and seemed to respect them. They either turned back into the preserve or hugged the boundary. The political boundary between the two parks became starkly visible from the air.

While Cessna 182s sat a rung or two up from the Pipers in sophistication, they still didn't have air conditioning. That would have added too much weight for the engine. With a pilot and three observers flying at ninety knots (about one hundred miles per hour), at an altitude barely above the trees, and in ninety-degree air temperatures, the inside of the plane began to cook after only a few minutes airborne. Within a few hours, I was grateful that I always sat in the front seat, because at least I could direct the air vents so that they blew fresh air onto me. I needed that refreshment. One of my colleagues in the back seat had a sizable critical mass and abundant sweat glands to match.

We flew about eight hours a day for three days to cover the whole area. Even doing virtually nothing but sitting still all day seemed exhausting. The fumes from the engine, the motion of the plane, the heat, the intense mental concentration, and the stagnation of one's circulatory system made it hard to stay alert enough to count hundreds of little blue herons, cattle egrets, tricolored herons, great egrets, and white ibises in one flock. Then the next mixed flock would appear, and the next, and so on.

Our flight pattern must have appeared suspicious to anyone watching. Who but drug runners, looking for a secret drop-off site, would fly low and slow, back and forth, across the remote Everglades? One day, we were flying a transect from which we could not deviate, with us three biologists intently tallying little specks in the sawgrass as we whizzed by. A twin-engine plane drifted alongside our wingtip. The two occupants peered into our cockpit. In midair, *we* were being surveyed.

Were they drug runners trying to tell if we were their competition? Or were they narcotics agents determined to thwart drug runners? Our pilot suspected that the two occupants were not villains, but rather U.S. Customs agents who suspected us of being drug runners. Our pilot tuned into the local flight communication radio frequency to identify us and determine who our escort was. Over and over he called and repeated the information. No one replied. We were torn between being scared off and dutifully carrying out our mission.

Then our pilot radioed the Flight Service station to remind them who we were. He always filed a flight plan, so there should have been no confusion. Flight Service was clear on our identity, but the twin-engine followed our wingtip like a shadow. On and on we flew. Should we be worried?

Eventually, the shadow peeled away and disappeared. Our pilot coolly maintained a straight transect the whole time, and we dutifully kept counting little specks in the shallow water as we figuratively held our breaths. We never knew for sure whether the shadow was friend or foe.

When I worked for National Audubon, I rented Cessnas from a fixed-base operator (FBO) at the regional Tamiami–Kendall Airport in Kendall, just south of Miami and east of the Everglades. For several years, the FBO rented us a red, white, and blue plane known as "Eight-Whiskey-Delta," named for its tail number, N738WD.

Eight-Whiskey-Delta was showing signs of age. The plane had logged thousands of hours for AM radio traffic reports and flight instruction before we came along. It seemed like every time my pilot Chuck Leverich and I went aloft, something went awry. Mostly they were small things, like a broken antenna or a rough engine, and Chuck caught them before we lost work time. Our standing joke when we took off was, "What will go wrong today?"

One day, Eight-Whiskey-Delta's dashboard started to smoke as we flew transects over the Everglades. Chuck followed the standard procedures by shutting down the electronics and flying directly back to the airport without the radio or electronic instruments. We arrived back before any flames started, but we both refused to rent Eight-Whiskey-Delta again.

Often we landed to refuel at small, uncontrolled airfields that had no control tower or flight services, and often no buildings except a shed for fuel. We would have to pump the aviation gas ourselves—literally. You think you've pumped gas? Excuse me, but you have merely put the nozzle in the tank and flipped a lever. We pumped.

The aviation fuel was stored in 55-gallon barrels that were

transported there by pickup truck, a low-budget operation. We placed a hose from the barrel into the wing tank, sometimes using a bandana for a filter, sometimes using no filter at all. With a handle on top of the barrel, one person had to crank constantly to keep up the pressure that pumped the gas up the hose and to the wing tank. Since the pilot usually inspected the plane for loose rivets at every landing, I ended up cranking and cranking. No pumping meant no gas.

Aerial wildlife surveys, radio-tracking, habitat studies, and most tasks related to natural resource conservation involve some of the riskiest types of flying. Air crashes are the most frequent cause of death on the job for wildlife biologists. In Alaska, where flying is integral to the job, between 1990 and 2001, six biologists died in air crashes.

Wildlife-related flying is so perilous because planes must fly low to give biologists the view they need, sometimes right above treetop level. The planes fly slowly, execute sharp turns, and make steep drops and climbs—all risky moves. The pilots must often be watching the animal as well as the controls and other air traffic. They usually can't predict where they need to go, so they can't file a detailed flight plan or know the terrain ahead of time. Sometimes they need to land in remote areas on unpaved surfaces, where of course, the only fuel (if there is any) is in a rusty barrel.

One of my colleagues was in a Cessna that was taking off from a runway in the Everglades to do some wading bird work when the plane crashed and fell about 30 feet. He and his pilot walked away, but not without sustaining minor injuries.

Flight in all types of weather is common for biologists. In South Florida, the climate is frequently hot and humid, creating thin air, a recipe for poor aircraft performance. The propeller doesn't have as much to "grab" onto, so takeoffs require longer runways. This is fine unless you are on a small grass strip with trees at both ends. Thunderstorms occur daily in Florida's rainy season, and thunderstorms anywhere at any time are extremely hazardous to all types of aircraft. The updrafts and downdrafts inside a thunderstorm cell are powerful and swift and can bounce an aircraft around like a kite. Lightning can strike a plane and damage its controls. That we didn't have more serious mishaps was primarily due to our stellar pilots.

I often spent seven drowsy hours as an observer in a plane

on any given day, doing tight circles low over bird colonies to count the nests, following zigzagging birds by sight to see where they landed to feed, and following a signal to find radio-tagged birds. I used binoculars on a regular basis. Holding them still in a bouncing plane took skill. It also took a strong stomach, which fortunately I had.

The radio-telemetry was a major part of my work. I mounted the direction-finding antennas on the struts of the Cessna 172 using cable ties, hose clamps, and duct tape. They always held, but if one of them came off, it would have hit the rudder and made for an abrupt, topsy-turvy landing. In those days (the 1980s), there were no Federal Aviation Administration-approved clamps. If the pilot approved, up we went.

Landing to refuel at airfields other than our FBO provided some entertainment to assuage the risks. Pilots and mechanics would see the odd receiving antennas on the struts and saunter over to us, casually hiding their confusion.

"Do you work for the CIA?" some asked. Mostly, they inquired, "Are you looking for drugs?" Whenever I saw a stranger heading toward our plane, I would wonder what kind of spies he thought we were.

With all the on-the-job flying I did, it seemed wise to learn a thing or two about operating planes in case my pilot ever keeled over with a surprise coronary attack. Flying wasn't something I was inherently interested in. In fact, it was contrary to my conservation ethic. I preferred to locomote by nonconsumptive means, such as walking, biking, and canoeing. However, as I said before, a lot of wildlife fieldwork depends on flying to gather data. I wasn't the showoff type, or prone to try something new just to brag. I needed a practical reason to learn how to fly.

All of my hired pilots, including Chuck Leverich, were coincidentally also certified flight instructors, so they could legally show me maneuvers. I learned rudder and nose control in the Piper Super Cub and immediately felt less nervous about small planes. In fact, they seemed fairly simple to fly.

After several years of flying as an observer, I became serious about learning to fly and enrolled in ground school. I took lessons at the regional Tamiami–Kendall Airport, south of Miami and bordering on the Everglades' east side. Chuck became my primary instructor.

Chuck's amateur interest in the birds made him a superb

pilot for our research needs. Too many times we hired pilots who didn't care about conservation or, worse, thought it was a waste of money. They were the ones who wasted our money by not putting their best efforts toward helping us be efficient.

Chuck was so excited about being part of the *Wild Kingdom* scene that he wanted to learn all he could. I taught him how to use the receiver to track the birds. When I was officially a student pilot, Chuck and I would switch seats for heron tracking. He took the receiver and tracked the birds, and I flew the plane. This relieved boredom and fatigue for both of us, ultimately adding a measure of safety.

After I had been working toward my license for several months, all that remained was to pass the check ride. I had finished ground school and passed the written test and the physical exam. I had flown the mandatory number of solo and dual hours and completed my solo cross-country trips. Cross-county means flying from one airport to another.

A week before my final flight test, my cousin Sheryl came to visit. She needed a break. Her job as a nurse in the emergency room of a major Boston hospital was so stressful that she had to unwind for a while. My little piece of paradise was the perfect place.

That paradise was a rented house on the Florida Bay waterfront on Plantation Key. It had two rooms. One was a long, narrow bedroom with a wonderful cross breeze. The other was a large kitchen–dining–living room combination, also with a cross breeze. Or, you could say it had three rooms, if you include the screened-in porch—my Florida room. So secure was the porch with wrought-iron decorative bars that it would be harder to break into than to smash a window in the house proper and crawl in. Many a guest slept on the studio couch on the porch, lulled asleep by gentle bay waves and the rustling of palm fronds.

Boston winters are harsh, but March in the Florida Keys is delightful—warm and usually rain-free. I picked Sheryl up at Miami International Airport and transported her to a world of flowers, brilliant sun, warm waters, and a slower pace.

Sheryl is seven years my junior and even more petite. We had never spent much time alone together because other family members were always nearby. We passed the week getting to know each other better, lazing in the evening by the water, taking nighttime walks among the fragrant neighborhood blossoms. I had to work several of those days, but I lent Sheryl my car, and she toured some of the island sites. I also had some studying to do. I was scheduled to take my final flight test for my pilot's license the same day as Sheryl's return flight to Boston.

Sheryl and I lamented about how we were still single and stuck in low-level careers, and how we couldn't understand why. We were intelligent, talented, hard-working, well-educated public servants with many interests, and (so we said of each other) pretty nice people. We were also in great shape. So why couldn't we find husbands and better jobs?

That wasn't the week for brilliant answers. I do believe Sheryl achieved her goal of relaxing, and she later married a wonderful man. I remained single, and I'm still puzzling how that happened. I chauffeured Sheryl back to the Miami International Airport on the last morning of March in 1988. She wished me luck on my flight test, we hugged, and I watched her depart on a jumbo jet.

I drove straight from the sprawling airport to the compact Tamiami–Kendall Airport. My flight test with the Federal Aviation Administration examiner was scheduled for 1:00 P.M. I arrived around 10:00 A.M. to prepare my rented Cessna 152.

The Cessna 152 is the perfect-sized plane for my petite frame. The plane can't carry a lot of payload, but I don't usually need to. If my passenger is of normal weight and has no baggage, we'll be fine. However, the little plane doesn't do well in strong winds, because the engine is small and can't outpower a strong wind, like my retrograde flight in the Super Cub. In fact, it can't fly in winds that larger planes can. Thus, it is always critical that the pilot keep track of the wind speeds.

Chuck always coached his students to take a practice flight just before the FAA test to get a feel for the wind that day. I had reserved the plane for the morning so that I would have ample time for that.

My first stop was the Flight Service office to check the weather. A cold front had moved through during the night, and the wind was strong, but it was still under the maximum crosswind velocity that would ground a Cessna 152. I would have to monitor the wind speeds from Flight Service by radio from the plane while I practiced. The clouds were high enough to give me clear visibility, so I proceeded to the FBO to get my rental plane.

The other reason Chuck taught his students to reserve the

132

plane early was to have time to do a thorough pre-flight. The pilot is responsible for checking the tightness of countless bolts and rivets, looking for cracks in the propeller, flexing the ailerons on the wings, kicking the tires, flapping the rudder, and checking for water in the fuel.

Water in the fuel is easy to verify by draining a small portion from the wing tank into a clear plastic fuel tester, because the water sinks and is clearly visible. The last thing you need is to find a problem with the plane while the inspector is watching, because then you must find another plane (if one is available), while he or she waits, glancing impatiently clockward.

The pilot must also check the plane's certifications. Every plane should have five certificates: aircraft air worthiness, aircraft registration, Federal Communication Commission radio permit, operating manual, and weight and balance information. Sometimes the pilot has to hunt for them—in the glove box, in the side pocket, or maybe in the FBO office. Thus, instructors routinely tell students to verify before the check-ride inspector comes that they know where the certificates are and that the certificates haven't expired.

Using a checklist, as all competent pilots do, I performed the preflight and checked the certificates. Satisfied that every nut and bolt was tight and every document in place, I lifted off alone over the Everglades and started practicing the maneuvers. Pilots use some maneuvers commonly during routine flights, and they must be learned thoroughly as a reflex. Examples are takeoffs and landings under various conditions, slips, figure-eights, and S-turns. Others are "oops" moves—when something goes wrong, you had better be ready. These are maneuvers you may never need and hope you won't. Spins and stalls fall into that category.

Stalls are maneuvers that all students must practice because they occur occasionally. Spins are maneuvers that few students practice because they rarely occur unintentionally. A spin is when a plane dives toward the ground, nose down, spinning like a top on its way down. Once upon a time, all students were required to practice spins in the plane with their instructors, but the maneuver is so dangerous that more people died practicing it than by falling into one accidentally. Some planes aren't even designed to withstand spins. Pilots can recover from a spin, even if they never practiced the maneuver. So, the FAA revised the rules to state that practicing spins as part of the in-flight instruction is optional, but ground school instruction must cover the techniques for spin recovery. Thus, I learned the steps for spin recovery in the classroom.

During the check ride, the examiner could theoretically ask me to do any type of maneuver, such as turns, stalls, and even spins to demonstrate that I had control of the aircraft. Chuck had forewarned me that any student who loses control of the plane during the check ride faces certain test failure.

Periodically on this gusty morning, I checked the current weather conditions by tuning to the specified radio frequency. The automated message confirmed the wind was still less than the crosswind velocity limit. I continued practicing power-on stalls and other maneuvers.

Stalls do not refer to the engine stalling. The engine can be running, but a plane can "stall" if it loses the lift on its wings. This may happen when the plane is about to land and has decreased power, when the plane is at too steep an angle, or when the wind shifts. Pilots practice these maneuvers by intentionally causing spins so they know how to handle them if they inadvertently occur.

All maneuvers should be practiced at least fifteen hundred feet above ground level because the plane can lose significant altitude, and the pilot must have plenty of space to avoid hitting radio towers and tall buildings before he or she regains control of the plane. I always started at two thousand feet to have more of a buffer. A pilot should also choose a practice area devoid of other air traffic. The official practice area near Tamiami–Kendall Airport is over the Everglades, so that any crashes wouldn't involve human bystanders. It's a good location for an airport—but not for such innocent by-crawlers as alligators.

Power-on stall can occur during a bungled takeoff. In that case, the throttle would be at full power, but the nose would be so high that the plane can't get the right flow over its wings.

Power-off stalls could happen if a landing goes awry. To practice them, the pilot has to force the plane into a situation where the stall is likely to occur. The setup involves slowing the plane's airspeed by reducing the power to idle speed and extending the flaps. The plane slows and the controls get "mushy," or slow to respond. At a certain point, the stall warning (a buzzer) sounds, and the plane begins to drop. The pilot must regain control of the plane. This is the maneuver that truly tested my fortitude.

I set the plane up for a power-off stall, facing into the wind as if I were landing, then pulling slowly back on the throttle until it was all the way back. The engine was still running and the propeller barely turning, but they weren't doing anything. The plane stayed aloft because it was designed to glide—a great safety feature. It could glide for many miles in a gradual descent until an emergency landing site was spotted.

I extended the flaps to slow the plane down, which is what is needed for landing. For my practice stall, I intentionally tried to slow the airspeed too much.

Sometimes on previous occasions, when I tried practice stalls alone in a 152, I couldn't even set one up intentionally. This is every pilot's dream—it meant that there was less of a chance that I would induce a stall by accident. My advantage is that my mass barely counts. (The only other occupation that I ever considered pursuing, where a low mass would be an advantage, was as a jockey.) The plane has enough gliding ability to keep me aloft even with the engine idling. On several previous solo practice flights, I had pulled the throttle back, set up for a stall with the flaps all the way down, nose in the air, and just kept flying at a preposterously steep angle. I would finally quit trying to stall and switch to some other maneuver.

On this, hopefully, last day as a student pilot, I had to practice everything, so I set up for a power-off stall. I pulled the throttle back, lowered the flaps a notch, and then . . . I don't exactly remember what came next . . . the plane was aiming down . . . the ground was spinning in front of me . . . *what's going on?* After a blur of confusion, it hit me. *I'm in a spin!* It was the one maneuver I had never practiced.

There I was, zooming earthward, mere seconds to react. *I've never practiced a spin. I don't know how to get out of it. Why couldn't I have at least gotten my license before this happened? Now I'm going to die just hours away from being able to say I am a pilot.*

I don't know why this was so important to me. I guess failure wasn't in my blood. *At least I'm over the Everglades and no one else will get hurt.* There no time to radio for instructions.

I was never one to sit and wait for life to happen, so it occurred to me that I shouldn't sit and wait for death either. My brain engaged, and I heard Chuck's voice echoing in my head, telling me of the only time he ever heard of a student passing a flight test after losing control of the plane during a check ride. The female student had inadvertently gotten into a spin. With the FAA examiner sitting next to her, the woman kept her cool, remembered the procedures for spin recovery, and got out of the spin by herself. The examiner was so impressed by her composure and ability to regain the controls that he granted the license.

If she could do it, so can I. I might as well try something. What did they teach me in ground school? Might as well try that. Luckily, I had drilled the simple instructions into my head, probably because I learned in tae kwon do that if something is important, make it a reflex.

"Step One – Power off." I reached for the throttle to pull it back. *Oh, no! It's already all the way off!* Nanosecond pause. *Of course, you idiot, you were doing a power-off stall. Now what?* Logic emerged. *Just skip the step. It's done. Go to the next step.*

"Step Two – Neutral ailerons." I centered the ailerons.

"Step Three – Opposite rudder." I obeyed the voice in my head. I applied the rudder in the direction opposite of the rotation.

"Step Four – Yoke forward." This little motion was one of the hardest moves I've ever made. Even though I thought I was doomed anyway, it went against every fiber in my body to push the yoke forward, because ordinarily, it makes the nose go *down,* and I wanted the nose to go *up.* I clenched my teeth and pushed the yoke forward. Almost instantly, the nose started to float up. It was working! I had drilled the instructions into my brain without ever stopping to contemplate why they worked.

The plane started to level. *What's next?* I pondered.

"Step Five – Hold the controls until the rotation stops, then straighten the rudder."

I was under control! Flying level!

Wait—one more step. There was Chuck's voice again. "Climb! Climb! Climb!"

It's the standard order after any failed maneuver, because you have probably lost altitude and may be dangerously near the ground. I pushed the throttle in and the plane started to climb.

Whew, I think I'm going to make it! I didn't look at the altimeter until I was sure I had climbed above any obstacles. It said fifteen hundred feet. I think I dropped to five hundred feet above the ground before I started my miraculous recovery.

When I rose back to two thousand feet, I circled around a few times to settle my nerves and then headed back to the airport. If anyone was watching, he probably thought I was just practicing spins and maybe even applauded.

I still had a few minutes left to practice, and I had planned to save the touch-and-go landings for last. I did as I had planned, with no emotional residue.

When I returned to the FBO, Chuck was waiting inside. He had come to give me a pep talk before my check ride.

"Chuck, you aren't going to believe this. I just got into a spin!" I blurted.

Taken by surprise, and knowing that I had never practiced one before, he said the only ridiculous thing I've ever heard him say. "Did you get out of it?"

I burst out laughing. "Well, I'm here—aren't I?"

After we finished guffawing over his spontaneous comment, we analyzed what had happened. Chuck thought I might have hit clear air turbulence. Due to the windy conditions that day, it was plausible. Some things Flight Service can't predict. It was also plausible that I bungled the maneuver and dropped a wingtip. The question was, did I feel confident enough to go right back up again and take my test?

The FAA examiner had already arrived, hinting that he wanted to get my test over with and go home to his sick wife. You are supposed to get back on a horse, right? I kept mum and up I went as if nothing had happened.

One after another, the examiner called out maneuvers and I executed them. Slips, figure-eights, turns across a road, power-on stalls, and even power-off stalls. One after another, I did them all. Despite the wind, everything went smoothly. We landed and my very important passenger said, "Congratulations! You're a pilot."

I drove home and phoned Sheryl to break the good news, minus the unplanned drama. Three days later, I received a greeting card in the mail from her. Her handwritten note was both a congratulations for receiving my pilot's license and a thank-you for providing a much-needed break.

On the front of the card was a picture of a ship at a dock with two people standing on the dock. One is declaring to the other, "Some day our ship will come in." Inside the card, the picture showed the other person sighing, "But with our luck, we'll be at the airport."

I've tried the docks and the airports, large and small. I've tried the roads, the trails, the marshes, the swamps, and even the trees. Still, the perfect job and the perfect man have eluded me. Could someone please tell me where I should be?

Chapter 8.
Silent Laughter

The puffin landed on top of a boulder, a little too close to the edge, and toppled down the rock's sloping side, frantically pumping its stubby wings for balance. Losing the battle, it landed in an undignified heap on the beach peas growing at the base of the rocks, shook and ruffled its feathers, then waddled clumsily into its burrow.

I burst into laughter, but silently. Belly shaking, I couldn't risk scaring the birds away. From my tiny blind, I couldn't utter a sound, or the puffins and razorbills would spook. I was used to laughing silently. How many times had I observed some comical behavior while cautiously stalking my research subjects? Or more commonly, watched something wonderfully thrilling and wanted to scream with excitement? I am good at silent screams, too. At least this day, I was inside a burlap blind and could toss my head back and jiggle my feet. Going through the motions would have to do.

Puffins can be so amusing to watch. These birds have explored three earthly realms—air, land, and water—and conquered all. They are birds first and foremost, and so they fly to find food. But since their food is fish, they swim underwater to catch it. And since they live on the barren, treeless northern coasts, they make their nests on the ground, so they must also walk on land.

Few other birds can match this versatility. Puffins must beat their stubby wings four hundred times per minute to stay airborne, but they can fly 55 miles per hour. They must waddle around on land, with occasional stumbles, because their legs are placed so far back on their bodies. Yet they can burrow eight feet into the soil to make a den for their young. Perhaps puffins are most graceful underwater, where we can't see them. There, they can dive 200 feet down. Nature outdid herself when she created an animal that is thoroughly adapted to sky, earth, and ocean.

That would be the most excitement I would have for a few more hours. A puffin would fly in, disappear into its rocky burrow, drop off a load of herring or hake to its lone chick, emerge, and fly off, all within a few minutes. Puffins produce only one chick a year. I pictured that lonely babe crouching in its small, damp, gloomy rock cavity, as I sat alone in my cramped, damp, gloomy burlap blind.

The temperature must have dropped ten degrees in the last half hour. Here it was July, and it was only fifty degrees, normal for the month. Then, too, the wind had picked up. Just how much shelter do you think burlap gives from the wind? I thought the sun had set, but I couldn't tell with the encroaching fog. Any minute the foghorn would blow. And, it would bellow all night, every fifteen seconds, while I tried to sleep next to it in the lighthouse keeper's quarters.

But for now, I would have to concentrate on the puffins. I was watching to see if Number 231 returned. He was carrying a tiny radio transmitter on his back. Or hers? Male and female puffins are feathered alike and share equally in chick-rearing. If you could place them side-by-side, you would be hard-pressed to see that the male was slightly larger.

The transmitter was malfunctioning. So was the bird. As far as I could tell, 231 hadn't returned to feed his chick since we adorned him four days earlier with the transmitter. Meanwhile, his mate was doing double duty. I was getting concerned, although in the last few hours I had reason to hope. I had taken a spotting scope to the puffins' loafing ledge on the island after I had detected a weak radio signal originating from that direction.

The loafing ledge was an outcropping of rocks on the island that caught the sun on rare, fogless days, and gave nesting puffins, guillemots, razorbills, terns, and gulls a place to soak up the rays, dry off, and get away from it all. We humans understand that. The loafing ledge was the Cape Cod, the Fire Island, or the Cape Hatteras of this island. Actually, the whole island is an outcropping of rocks, a 30-acre jumble of bedrock and boulders that juts out of the Atlantic Ocean, 22 miles from the Maine coast and 25 miles southeast of Rockland.

The outcropping is called Matinicus Rock. That's *Rock*, not *Island*. Make no mistake. Aside from a few paths in the lighthouse vicinity, you can't walk anywhere—you jump from rock to rock. Because it is surrounded by ocean, a normal day in summer or winter is foggy, blustery, and chilly.

The Rock has a human history revolving around the lighthouse, originally built in 1827. Lighthouse keepers lived a meager, damp existence, and often died young. Most lighthouse keepers' families lived with them. Tales abound of heroism to keep the light burning amidst brutal storms.

A humorous story persists about one keeper whose wife stayed on the mainland. When the keeper returned to shore after a long stint, his wife wondered why he spoke in short bursts and then paused for twenty seconds. She soon realized that the deafening foghorn had conditioned him that it was pointless to speak during the twenty-second blasts. Nowadays, the lights and foghorn are automated.

The birds I was watching were Atlantic puffins, the smallest of four species of puffins in North America, and all members of the alcid family of seabirds. The other puffins (tufted, horned, and rhinoceros auklet) are found on the West Coast of the United States. Atlantic puffins are found across the North Atlantic to Europe. Most of the population nests in Iceland. In the western Atlantic, puffins nest in coastal eastern Canada and Maine. Hardy birds by any account, puffins rarely wander south of Massachusetts. In fact, the scientific name *Fratercula arctica* means "little brother of the north."

Atlantic puffins are pigeon-sized birds, standing about ten inches tall and weighing about a pound. Their backs and wings are black and their bellies are white, males and females alike. What people notice most about them is the gaudy orange, yellow, and blue triangular, hefty bill, which contributes to its nickname "sea parrot." A cliché photo of a puffin is one showing the bird with its bill packed with slender fish. A puffin may catch ten or more hake, herring, bluefish, krill, butterfish, or lumpfish—one at a time—and hold them in place sideways in its bill, while its rough tongue presses each fish against spines on the palate.

The orange legs rival the bill for visual pizzazz. Their placement so near the tail helps them to act as rudders when the birds dive underwater. Thus, when a puffin stands, it is nearly vertical. Picture how a mallard duck waddles with its body almost horizontal, because its legs are located toward the middle of its body to allow it to paddle on the surface of a pond. A duck can walk to the water and slip in gracefully, barely changing its body position. A puffin belly-flops.

Puffins spend most of their lives at sea and can live for more than thirty years. When they are about two or three years old, they return from the sea to the nesting colony where they hatched. There they loaf around, watching the older birds do their mating rituals and taking notes on proper adult behavior. They also begin staking out a nesting burrow and finding a future mate. During the winters, they disappear across the ocean. When they return at five years of age, they shift into a serious mode and settle down with a mate. Some, however, may not nest until seven years or older.

On some islands, where the puffins find deep soil, they excavate burrows in patches of soil using their sharp bills and the claws on their webbed feet. The burrows are at least two to three feet deep, usually angling sideways into a slope. However, on Matinicus Rock—like Maine's other puffin islands—the soil is usually too shallow for digging, so puffins nest in deep rock crevices. On these windswept, treeless islands, the burrows give the chicks protection from the elements and predators.

The longer burrows present a challenge to researchers who need to retrieve a chick for banding. While I have often been stereotyped into that "small is useless" category and passed over because of my diminutive size, I was in my glory on the Rock. I was often the only person who could fit into the puffin caves or reach into the crevices. I could invade the sanctity of a puffin family and actually see the chick hunkering timidly at the advance of my seemingly huge, featherless body. Without small people to retrieve the chicks, some aspects of this project would have been difficult.

Puffins generally retain the same mate each season and return to the same burrow. They lay only one egg, which hatches in about forty days. The parents take turns warming the newly hatched chick with their bodies (brooding) for the first few days, until the chick's body develops enough to keep it warm. Then, taking turns, the parents fly off, returning periodically with bills full of fish to feed the chick.

At forty-five days, the puffling (baby puffin) waddles down to the water in the dark of night to avoid those bullying gulls that are always hunting for small, warm morsels to eat. Then the puffling dives in. It may not even be able to fly yet. It gradually swims out to sea and typically doesn't return to terra firma for at least two years.

Seabirds choose this island and other rocky islands off-shore because the islands have no land predators, such as raccoons and mink. The only scary monsters are aerial predators, such birds as great black-backed gulls, herring gulls, peregrine falcons, gyrfalcons, and owls.

Evidence shows that centuries of harvesting by native peoples didn't diminish the population, since they harvested relatively small numbers, usually only what they needed. As a species, the puffin's perilous decline stemmed from the early European colonists, who found it child's play to catch the birds on the islands. The blustery islands have no cover other than the burrows, which become traps at the hands of people trying to catch them. A puffin can generally launch into flight only from water or by propelling itself off the edge of a cliff, so people can catch the birds with nets with little effort. Early explorers and colonists snatched the birds for meat and took feathers for the millinery trade. They also collected the eggs for food. The introduction of the shotgun and market hunting by Europeans accelerated the demise of seabird colonies. By the early 1900s, few puffins existed in Maine. Even the Migratory Bird Treaty Act of 1918, which quashed the hunting and sale of birds, didn't restore their populations.

That is why Dr. Stephen Kress entered the scene. In 1973, Steve, then a research biologist for the National Audubon Society, began an innovative program to return nesting puffins to the islands off the coast of Maine. On Eastern Egg Rock, a tiny island where puffins were eliminated by hunting in 1885, he first forced the gulls, which had encroached on the island after the seabirds disappeared, to move elsewhere. Then he dug burrows. He stocked them with pufflings he brought down from Newfoundland with the cooperation of the Canadian Wildlife Service. Seabird colonies were still healthy in Newfoundland.

Steve and his assistants placed the two-week-old pufflings singly in the burrows and hand-fed them fish for the next month, until they were old enough to leave their burrows. After they waddled down to the sea in the middle of the night and plunged in, they were on their own.

Every year, Steve brought pufflings from Newfoundland, patiently raising them, knowing that it would take three years at the earliest to see the first birds return, if any did. He was ready for them. He festooned the island with puffin decoys. How inviting to a naïve puffin! Party time! Eventually it worked, but it took eight years before the birds started nesting. Steve was also successful with this approach at Seal Island National Wildlife Refuge—about six miles east of Matinicus Rock.

While waiting for the puffins to return, Steve used decoys and sound recordings to encourage common, Arctic, and roseate terns to nest at the island. Buoyed by these successes, he modified his methods to also attract Leach's storm-petrels, razorbills, and common murres. All were species that had suffered from excessive hunting and their modern dilemma, competition for habitat with predatory gulls. These successes encouraged yet more species, such as black guillemots and laughing gulls, to return and thrive. Steve's accomplishment of returning nesting colonial waterbirds to Maine remains one of the great success stories in wildlife conservation.

Getting the birds to nest was one great challenge. Keeping them safe from threats in the big ocean would be the next one.

We knew that puffin chicks stayed in their secure little burrows until they were old enough to be on their own. They would emerge under the cover of night, tripping their way down to the chilly water's edge, and plunge in. Would they just keep swimming out to sea? How far? How fast? When did they start feeding themselves? Where did the parent puffins go to find food for their young? How did they navigate hundreds of miles across the ocean to the rich feeding grounds? How did the juveniles navigate back to the same island they hatched from after several years' absence?

Some of these answers held the key to which oceanic areas were vital to our small population of this species. Would a colony be wiped out by commercially overharvesting a certain fishing bank or by an oil spill in a certain area? Even more important to humankind, was the puffins' slow population comeback, despite protection from hunting, an indication that we had overfished the banks for our own food supply?

When I came along, Steve Kress had already been conducting exemplary field research on the Atlantic puffin for more than fifteen years, including the colonies of puffins on Matinicus Rock, Eastern Egg Rock, Seal Island, and other rock piles that puffins call home in the western North Atlantic. His knowledge of these colorful, piscivorous (fish-eating) birds was astounding, but he wanted to fill in the gaps.

In 1989, Steve decided he needed a new approach. He convened a small group of biologists with special skills for an experimental project. The only method for finding the answers seemed to be with the standard wildlife biologists' tool of radio telemetry.

I was also a research biologist for the National Audubon Society, albeit at the other end of the coastline. I had been working in the Everglades studying colonies of wading birds—egrets, herons, storks, ibises, and spoonbills—that fed in shallow water. I had expertise in the field of radio telemetry. I had been radio-tracking birds by airplane, boat, truck, and on foot for five years. I had tested and repaired transmitting and receiving equipment. I had even built my own transmitters from scratch, or I should say from etch, which is what I did to the copper board. I had trapped many birds and fitted them with transmitters.

Steve invited me to work with him on Matinicus Rock and help develop a transmitter for the puffins. Specifically, he wanted one that was "tiny, powerful, and flat." I think I laughed aloud when I read that phrase in his written invitation.

Dr. Mark Fuller, a biologist from the U.S. Fish and Wildlife Service, and his colleague, Holliday (Holly) Obrecht, were experienced in radio telemetry work. Through the Service, they provided the project's funding—oh, so important! If Steve's experimental project worked, he would be able to write a proposal and obtain a grant for the next year. But first, we had to find out if it would work.

Steve had originally invited me onto the team as the pilot who would track the birds. However, most of the puffin tracking would occur over the open ocean, and I was not instrument-rated. He needed someone who could fly farther from shore than I could. I declined the offer and recommended Dr. Colin Pennycuick, the ornithologist at the University of Miami, instead. Colin owned a plane and had soared with vultures and storks in Africa. He would provide the plane and his piloting services, and Holly would do the aerial tracking.

Declining the pilot's role behooved me in the long term. The Rock had no airstrip or regular boat transportation to the mainland. Instead of sitting in a plane all the time, I could hang out on the Rock with the birds, but I couldn't do both. I preferred to be close to the birds.

144

Poor Colin and Holly. Although they stayed in hotels and ate in restaurants (did they really eat lobster every night?), they never saw the up-close-and-puffinal view.

The trip from Florida to Maine was itself engrossing. Colin and I flew from Miami, Florida, to Rockland, Maine, in his Cessna 182 at the start of the project. In the single-engine, four-seat plane, the eighteen hundred miles took thirteen and a half hours of flying over two days. Aside from a refueling stop at Savannah, Georgia, where we sat grounded while it rained 2.6 inches in one hour, the trip was scenic but uneventful. Flying at only a few thousand feet of altitude allowed me to see Americana from a bird's-eye view. The hours passed easily, as I listened to Colin, with his delightful British accent, describe how he soared in gliders in Africa to watch vultures at eye-level.

Rockland was a mere stepping-stone on the trip for me, however. I waved goodbye to the mainland for two weeks and hopped a ride to the Rock on the mail delivery boat. There, I met the rest of the puffin crew, several young up-and-coming assistant biologists who spent the entire summer on the Rock.

Our challenge was to put a radio transmitter on a breeding puffin in a way that would not adversely affect the bird's lifestyle. The bird had to be able to fly, swim, and walk normally. It had to provide for its offspring by diving after speedy fish.

Puffins swim underwater by flapping their compact wings to propel themselves and using their feet as rudders. A dense layer of down covered by sturdy, waterproof outer feathers keeps the birds dry and warm, provided their feathers aren't damaged. The cold North Atlantic waters can chill a bird to death if water leaks through the smallest of gaps in the feathers.

Puffins posed a special problem for radio-tagging. The transmitters were small battery-powered electronic packages that had to be attached to the bird's body. Researchers had put the gizmos on the long legs of sandhill cranes, on the strong wings of California condors, on the long tails of red-tailed hawks, and on the backs of snowy egrets and wood storks. However, finding the right placement for a transmitter had never been accomplished on a puffin.

Puffins have short legs. They have short wings. They have stubby tails. And, the feathers on their backs must lie perfectly flat so their natural waterproofing will work. So, where was the perfect place to attach a transmitter?

Mark Fuller's idea was to tape a tiny transmitter to a few feathers on the bird's back and expect that it would fall off in a few weeks, around the time the battery ran out. That way we would answer the critical question—whether the bird would still feed its young—and the bird wouldn't be condemned to lug the contraption around for eternity.

Our transmitters weighed 4.5 grams (0.16 ounces), about the weight of a cough drop. Small as that sounds, it is equivalent to a 180-pound person carrying a two-pound weight 24 hours a day.

An Atlantic puffin from Matinicus Rock carries
our radio transmitter on its back.

The transmitters housed small batteries that would last about two weeks. A nine-inch antenna extended from the rear of the device. The transmitters had to be sealed against the salt water, since the carriers were diving seabirds. This doesn't sound difficult to do, except that the antenna was supposed to flex, and the bending at the base could open a gap in the seal or weaken the wire. Thus, a spring was built into the base to distribute the bend more widely.

The transmitters were programmed to make a silent signal that could be translated into an audible one by our receiver. As with our wading birds in Florida, each bird had its own radio frequency. A directional antenna, along with some human skill, would determine from which direction a signal was coming. It was a simple concept with many nuances. A good tracker could tell when a bird was far away as opposed to when the battery was weak, whether a bird was really to the left of the plane or the signal was just bouncing off of rocks, or when the antenna was simply facing away and thereby causing a weak signal.

I had always found telemetry to be a fascinating tool through which I learned the answers to many of my questions about wading birds. We needed to make it work with puffins. But their fragile welfare came first.

Thus, my concern for Puffin 231 continued on the fourth day since his disappearance. Later that day, Mark and I went to the blind near the loafing ledge to look for him. Mark scanned each lazing puffin with the scope until he jumped up and exclaimed, "I see him!"

We could identify 231 by the numbered leg band he wore. That meant that at least the bird hadn't died or gone off moping to some private rock. Still, we wanted more evidence of where he had been. If only he had appeared carrying a load of fish in his bill for his chick, we would have rejoiced. Our mission was a flop if we caused a puffin's nest failure. Somehow, we were optimistic that he would resume his parental duties soon, so we made plans to bejewel yet another bird.

Number 231 was actually the second puffin we radio-tagged. The first (number 471) came back to the Rock, but we never saw it return to the burrow to feed its chick.

I returned to a blind by the burrows to catch another puffin. Our low-budget equipment included an upside-down five-gallon bucket that served as a chair. Hours of surveillance caused "blind spine," as we affectionately called the resulting painful posture.

Long hours were a staple of the puffin season. The sun would rise early in offshore Maine, and I would be in the blind on some days at 4:30 in the morning. We changed shifts every four hours. The fewer disturbances we caused to the birds, the better.

Several blinds were set up in different places, and we had many birds to watch. How often a bird returned to feed, how many fish it brought, how long it stayed—these were all nuggets we recorded.

With one hand on my binoculars and the other on a string leading to a hand snare, I had to exercise great patience and self-restraint. If I wasn't careful, I would run out of peanut M&M candies before my blind shift was over. That would be catastrophic. People who had spent any time in the field with me could tell you that I lived on peanut M&Ms during the field season. They provided just the right combination of energy types to keep an active gal bopping around all day in soul-testing conditions. On these cold, damp days, they kept my internal furnace stoked.

I was adept at rationing the tidbits, as long as I was going solo. When other people feigned disinterest in my snack until the bag was almost empty—that was cruel. I have since sworn off artificial food coloring, so my vice has transformed. I still eat chocolate, but only with no artificial ingredients.

Here, I was quite alone, so my stomach wasn't panicking about sharing the edible fuel. But, my trigger finger on the snare was getting impatient. After four hours in the blind, my trigger finger got its chance. The bird I was waiting for (one of the adults from Burrow 86) landed on the entrance rock by the burrow, gingerly stepping over a noose "carpet" trap that I had also set up. The carpet was a fifteen-inch-square piece of chicken wire onto which I had tied several hundred slipknot loops with monofilament (fishing) line.

Theoretically, when a bird stepped on one of the loops, the monofilament would tighten around his foot when he lifted it up. I knew it worked because Steve had trapped other puffins this way. But this puffin was smarter. He ducked into his burrow, dropped off the six or seven two-inch fish he had skillfully nabbed, and emerged from the burrow. As I predicted, the puffin hopped up on an adjacent rock.

I knew the exact route this puffin would take. An individual puffin is a creature of habit, and a few hours of observation from a blind will reveal his or her normal route of entry and exit. Anticipating this route, I had set up another noose carpet on that

148

rock. Once again, he gingerly stepped over the noose carpet. Shucks! That was the easy way to catch him.

Now all that remained was the snare that I had set up on the last rock he would walk on before he flew off for a few more hours. I had strategically placed this thin, nylon line in a twelve-inch circular loop with a slipknot in it. If the puffin stepped within this circle, I had only to pull my end of the string and the loop would close around his legs. I had never personally tried this before. Of course, Steve had. I had caught birds with rocket-powered nets, mist nets, drugs, and various types of cagelike traps. Were my reflexes good enough for this technique? I might have only a split-second to react.

The bird hopped to the top of the rock. Through my binoculars, I tried to see if he was standing within the loop. I thought he was, but I wasn't sure. I pulled the string. He jumped up just as I pulled, probably a knee-jerk response to feeling the snare. He jumped in vain.

I summoned Mark on the two-way radio while I held the captured bird. Mark leaped nimbly across the rocks from the lighthouse to help me put the transmitter on. We adorned the bird with new hardware. Two days later, before we could obtain any useful information from the bird, the radio died. Perhaps water had penetrated the radio's epoxy coating.

Over the next few days, we attached transmitters to several more puffins using different methods, because the first two birds we had tagged weren't doing their parental duties. One of my mottoes is, "If it doesn't work, don't repeat it."

Eventually, we settled on my design of using dental floss to sew the transmitter to the base of the tail feathers. This would prevent the back feathers from getting ruffled, a possibly fatal event if cold water penetrated to the skin. When you have to improvise on a remote island, you use what you can find. Even on a pile of rocks twenty miles out at sea, someone usually has dental floss. It is lightweight, strong, will eventually rot through, and the price is always right.

The tail mounts worked the best as far as minimizing the effect on the bird's health or behavior. However, we lost track of the birds over the ocean because the battery was too small to have a strong signal. In the end, the placement of transmitters proved too risky to the birds for us to continue. We failed to track the puffins to any great distance.

More than fifteen years later, Steve Kress says he doesn't know of anyone that has truly succeeded with telemetry on puffins. He still knows little about where puffin populations go to winter. Some are seen in the Gulf of Maine and in the Grand Banks, one of the world's largest and richest marine fishing areas, located southeast of Newfoundland. Are these birds from Maine or Newfoundland? He adds that the numbers of these feeding birds are inadequate to account for the breeding populations, so there are still fishing sites important to puffins that we don't know about.

For most people, it is sufficient that the puffin numbers are increasing, and now they can take boat tours to watch the ornate birds flit around the nesting islands. What matters to the seabird biologists is that puffins continue to find herring and hake. However, not far away near the Canadian border, puffins in the large colony on Machias Seal Island are finding fewer fish, forcing the birds to eat less nutritious shrimp. Because people also eat herring and hake, the well-being of these puffin colonies predicts the future of these fish stocks for us.

While hard work and sacrifice are needed to find the simplest answer to a wildlife question, often they lead to more questions than answers.

Chapter 9.
Of Gopher Tortoises and Biostitutes

The gopher tortoises are running out of room. These easy-going creatures, lumbering tanks with minor brains and a major mission, are being chased from their homes in slow motion. That alone is a sad tale for the tortoises, but when it also causes the permanent closing of shelters for a myriad of other creatures, the effect spreads like toppling dominoes throughout the underground community.

In southeastern Florida, most of the high ground lies on a narrow strip of land called the Atlantic Coastal Ridge. Barely five miles wide and extending along the coast from Homestead to West Palm Beach and points north, the ridge is bounded on the east by the Atlantic Ocean and on the west by Everglades water pressing against it. Long ago, humans emigrated to the ridge because it was the only dry ground around. About six million people now crowd onto this narrow ridge.

What is good for humans is often good for animals. Thus, the upland species of fauna crowd onto the ridge, because they, too, need dry land. The competition for dry ground in Miami-Dade, Broward, and Palm Beach counties pits man against beast. Gopher tortoises, burrowing owls, and Florida scrub lizards are all facing eviction by the bulldozer.

Not long ago, developers acknowledged gopher tortoises by burying them alive, intentionally or not. Once environmental consciences surfaced and the law rose to protect the tortoises, the standard solution for a developer was to dump the tortoises elsewhere. That never worked well, even when there was enough open land, because the tortoises were not wind-up toys. They were vulnerable to the elements, such as the scorching sun, until they dug a new burrow. Moreover, they would be unfamiliar with the terrain (can you hear them crying, "Where's my favorite prickly-pear treats?"), and there might already be too many tortoises competing for the available food. However, relocation is still the method many developers often do, because the alternative is to entomb the tortoises, and that is no longer a legal option.

151

Laws protecting gopher tortoises (*Gopherus polyphemus*) vary throughout their range, which extends from southern South Carolina to eastern Louisiana, including Florida, Georgia, Mississippi, and Alabama. The gopher tortoise has been listed by the U.S. Fish and Wildlife Service as federally threatened in Alabama, Louisiana, and Mississippi since 1987. Individually, the states have their own forms of protection for rare species. South Carolina, for example, lists the tortoise as endangered. Florida listed it as a species of special concern until 2006, when the species was upgraded to the more serious threatened status.

With tortoises thus protected, developers cannot simply level a parcel and destroy the tortoises and their habitat. They have to help the affected reptiles. One way they can do this is by agreeing to mitigate—that is, set aside some acreage that the tortoises can live on so that the developer can smother whatever live tortoises are left on the rest of the land.

Enter the consulting companies, ready to show developers how to wade through the morass of environmental permits, both state and federal, and ready to solve the dilemma of how to handle those pesky tortoises. One day, I had the chance to become a contractor-to-the-rescue.

My National Audubon research project on wading birds in the Everglades was ending, and I was offered a job with an environmental consulting company. I had served not-for-profit employers, including governments, conservation organizations, and academic institutions, for my entire career. They are a good fit for someone who doesn't place much value on the almighty dollar. The consulting company was a business, and their goal was to protect the environment while enabling development. I had positive reports about them from a friend who worked there.

Nevertheless, I had always been suspicious of consulting companies. Environmental consultants were paid to make sure the developers got what they wanted, as long as it was within the law. Did these biologists really care about the land? Did they create the best plan for the wildlife or for the developer? I had even borrowed the term "biostitute" (origin unknown) when I referred to such a consultant.

The decision whether to accept the position churned in my mind like the contents of a cement mixer. Could my preconceived ideas be wrong? The arrangement did seem suited to me. I could choose to work part-time and draw a decent salary while I concentrated on my dream of writing a book, and I could walk right into this flexible job without moving elsewhere.

To stoke the flames, a memory from high school nagged at me. My schoolmate Allison worked in the summer at a local thoroughbred horseracing track. Allison suggested I, too, get a summer job there and offered to arrange it. I was morally opposed to exploiting animals for profit, so I declined her offer. She responded with logic that cornered me.

"Isn't it better if you are there treating the horses like royalty than to have a careless jerk or a racing zealot with shady practices in that position?" she reasoned. "Huh? So, what do you say?"

Checkmate. I spent that summer and the next one at the track pampering the horses. My job was called hotwalking. Before your mind falls into the gutter, it means that I walked the sweaty horses, one at a time, around the stable to cool them off after they raced or exercised with a rider. I made a practice to go to the track with empty pockets, except a dime for an emergency phone call. Even if I had an inside scoop on a race, I never bet a penny. I took the weekly pay but never gave the race people my money.

If the trainers employing me were crooked, I had no hint. One trainer, noting my strength and diminutive size, even offered to train me to be a jockey. The vocation would have required me to quit college and travel extensively, while lining the pockets of the horse owners if I did my job well. I didn't ask Allison her opinion on that.

Assuming the worst of the consulting company, I could use the same logic—better that I was there than some uncaring nine-to-fivers. And, if the company had all good folks, I had no worries.

The small family-owned company operated out of South Miami, but its territory spanned from Palm Beach County to the Florida Keys. Our staff of six worked with local, state, and federal laws to develop plans to help landowners comply with environmental regulations. My role included surveying for wetland jurisdiction, endangered species and other species of concern (such as gopher tortoises), and seagrasses (grasslike plants that grow underwater in shallow seas). Most of the time, I was assigned to gopher tortoise duty.

Gopher tortoises are ponderous land turtles. Their domed shells, like the army helmets they resemble, protect the tortoises' body, because they can draw their heads, tails, and legs inside. Younger tortoises need this ability to avoid being chomped by such toothy predators as raccoons, foxes, and opossums. Large tortoises, which can exceed fifteen pounds, have few natural predators other than humans. Hatching tortoises are vulnerable to red imported fire ants, those same little beasties that sent a flock of wood stork biologists into maniacal frenzies in Birdsville, Georgia.

A gopher tortoise forages for food in Boca Raton.

The reptiles plod across the high, dry ground in broad daylight, which is usually where and when people occupy. Thus, human-versus-tortoise encounters are common. Certainly, the burrows are easy to spot. Doing a survey to document the presence of gopher tortoises was more like an afternoon stroll at a resort than bona fide fieldwork.

The plots we studied were always small (often ten to twenty acres), because those were the only undeveloped sites left. These open sites were in Palm Beach County for the same reason, because Broward and Miami-Dade counties were built out. That meant our three-person survey crew frequented Boca Raton, West Palm Beach, and other such upper-crust communities. We were rarely out of sight of a high-rise condominium or a pricey hotel.

A typical survey consisted of waking up when the rest of the civilized world did, driving an hour or more in an air-conditioned car on smooth (but traffic-choked) Interstate 95, walking around outside for a few hours looking for burrows and tracks (granted, it was in the sun in the heat of the day), carrying only a clipboard and a water bottle, returning to the air-conditioned car and driving to a restaurant for lunch, driving to another site for a few hours of walking and observing and taking notes, and then driving home, after stopping at a store for ice-cold refreshments. We would arrive back at the office in late afternoon, type some data into a computer, and quit with the rest of the world. It hardly seemed fair. Did this qualify as fieldwork?

Furthermore, gopher tortoises have neither fight nor flight reflexes, making them exceedingly easy to study. When faced with an adversary, they simply "clam up," a poor expression for a vertebrate. However, they withdraw their head, legs, and tail into their shells and hope the predator has to work too hard for a meal and thus leaves the tortoise alone. We couldn't have been dealt an easier research wild animal.

Tortoises have stumpy hind legs and forelegs with flattened, shovel-like feet for digging. Each gopher tortoise burrow has a mound of excavated soil at its entrance, called an apron. The burrow opening is slightly wider than the tortoise, or about nine inches wide for an adult. It is flatter from top to bottom, unlike the round burrow openings of armadillos and pocket gophers. Tortoise burrows may reach ten feet deep and forty feet long in the easy-to-dig sandy soil, which is why the tortoises must live on a ridge where the water table is not near the surface. Their fossorial (digging) talent is what earned the reptiles the colloquial name of "gophers."

Water percolates easily through this loose soil, so the surface vegetation is scrubby, almost desertlike. The tortoises feed on prickly-pear cacti, gopher apples, other native fruits, and leaves that grow in the open sun. Gopher tortoises attain breeding age when they are about ten to fifteen years old and live at least forty years. They bury their leathery eggs in mounds near their burrows.

Gopher tortoises, prairie dogs, beavers, and alligators all have one thing in common: they make the world a better place for many creatures. Herein lies my reason for so admiring them. Beavers and alligators create ponds that provide water, safety, and food for aquatic animals. Tortoises and prairie dogs create dry shelter to the otherwise homeless fauna by digging burrows, which happen to be just what hundreds of other species of animals need for protection from predators and the elements.

None of these four-legged engineers is altruistic, but the effect is the same. Ecologists call these do-gooders "keystone" species. Like the high central stone that holds an archway together without mortar—simply by its presence—the tortoise, the prairie dog, the beaver, and the alligator hold their biological communities together.

More than three hundred species of invertebrates have been reported living in the gopher tortoise burrows or using the aprons. Many vertebrates depend on the burrows, too, such as Florida mice, cotton rats, burrowing owls, indigo snakes, gopher frogs, and lizards. Sometimes the freeloaders take up residence side-by-side with the diggers and sometimes after the burrow is vacated. The temperature and humidity inside the burrows are mild and nearly constant year-round. Without the tortoises to maintain the burrows, many of these coexisting species would perish.

The prairie dog (*Cynomys ludovicianus*) burrows into the rock-hard soil of the grasslands from Canada to Mexico. Hundreds of species of mammals, reptiles, amphibians, and insects seek refuge in active or abandoned burrows. Even birds, like the burrowing owls of the Great Plains, depend on the burrows, because the prairie sod is too hard-packed for them to dig themselves. Burrowing owls that live in Florida may dig burrows where the soil is looser, or they may occupy gopher tortoise burrows.

In the treeless, open prairie, the big rodents' burrows are often the only shelter around. Besides providing shelter for a myriad of species, prairie dogs add yet more value to the ecosystem. They turn over the soil, bringing deep, fertile earth to the surface to help plants grow. Their burrows provide drainage into the compacted ground, so rain can replenish the groundwater instead of running off the surface. Prairie dog grazing keeps the grasses more concentrated with nutrients, a vital favor to cattle, horses, bison, and any herbivore that munches it. Since grasses grow from the base, grazing the tips doesn't kill them. Instead, a grazed plant gushes forth extra nutrients from its roots to the blades to help them regenerate.

Is there a downside to the presence of prairie dogs, such as the risk of livestock breaking a leg in a burrow? That rumor was started a hundred years ago with no factual basis. Bison, horses, and cattle can easily see and avoid stepping in burrows, especially if the prairie dog town is active. In the active towns, the grass is shorter and the big rodents keep the area surrounding the burrow openings clear of vegetation. A problem is more likely to occur if the prairie dogs die. Then the grass will grow around the burrow openings, concealing them from grazing livestock. Huge herds of bison and pronghorn antelope have lived in harmony and thrived with prairie dogs for millennia.

Across much of North America, beavers (*Castor canadensis*) are the innkeepers of the woods. These largest of North American rodents weigh from 35 to 70 pounds. They feed on the bark and twigs of alders, birches, willows, and other hardwood trees. Beavers are the only animals besides humans that alter their environment on a large scale. With legendary engineering skills, they erect stick dams and lodges. The dams are astonishingly sturdy and functional. They are constructed at the right height to keep the water level in the pond exactly as the beavers need it, allowing heavy rainfalls to flow over gradually. The ponds provide shelter for minks, ducks, fish, turtles, crayfish, snakes, amphibians, insects, snails, and plants. So many plants and animals depend on the wetlands created by beavers across this vast continent that beavers are the unequaled model of a keystone species.

Many endangered and threatened species depend on wetlands that beavers construct. The beaver is so beneficial to its wetland neighbors that boreal toads even find a place to winter in beaver lodges. All told, thousands of species depend on wetlands that would not exist if not for the beavers.

The list of beaver dam virtues is impressive. Downpours and spring snowmelts are slowed by the system of dams along a stream, thus preventing erosion from rushing waters and flooding in valleys. Sediment is trapped closer to where it originated, instead of piling up downstream. Water that is slowed and trapped by the ponds is held at higher elevations, close to where the rain fell, thus storing it for future dry spells and protection against drought. Some of this water percolates down to the groundwater and replenishes the water table. Without beaver ponds, most of the rain and snowmelt from higher elevations would rush downhill, leaving the slopes scoured and parched. Much of the ecology of North America, from Alaska to Mexico, was shaped by beavers and can only be maintained by them.

Beavers played another prominent role in our history as the object of exploration and settlement by Europeans. Native Americans traded beaver pelts to the sixteenth-century sailors, who carried them back to Europe, launching the craze for beaver coats and hats. In the 1820s and 1830s, an average pelt could bring fifteen to twenty dollars, a hefty sum in that era. As the clamor for *Castor* couture continued, beavers became scarce, and trappers plunged ever westward and northward, especially into the current northern states and southern provinces. Not only were their pelts valued, but beavers were the source of castoreum, an oil from glands near the base of their paddle-shaped tails. Castoreum is an ingredient in some perfumes. Beavers use it to mark their territories.

The population of beavers prior to European contact is estimated at around sixty million. As the trappers depleted an area, they moved westward and northward. Gradually, the beaver populations declined, until the species vanished from much of eastern North America by the mid-1800s. By the early twentieth century, trappers had to venture into far northern Canada to find enough beavers to support themselves.

The loss of wetlands corresponded with the loss of beavers. However, through careful conservation management and protective state laws, beavers have made a remarkable comeback. The current population is roughly two million. No other species of animal was so important to the early exploration and settlement of North America by Europeans, and no other animal has so shaped the habitat from the Arctic to the subtropics.

In the southeastern swamps and marshes—the flatland devoid of beavers—the alligator (*Alligator mississippiensis*) is the reigning keystone species. The reptile scoops out and maintains depressions in the marsh that remain wet during the dry season. Aquatic animals that normally can spread throughout the marsh in the wet season crowd together in the only watering holes left, those that the alligators maintain for themselves. One alligator hole, even as small as a living room, can harbor fish, turtles, frogs, watersnakes, crayfish, and amphiumas and sirens (both amphibians), as well as a multitude of other animals. The tight quarters provide enough habitat to support the aquatic fauna into the next wet season.

Clearly, gopher tortoises hold the key to a healthy upland ecosystem in the Southeast. When they disappear and their burrows collapse, hundreds of other species lose their homes.

Competition for habitat is only one cause of the decline of the tortoise all over the Southeast. Early settlers found the tortoises were an easy supply of meat. More recently, immigrants from Haiti and Cuba also eat them. Occasional tortoise hunters will pour gasoline down their burrows and force the hiding animals out. This practice is illegal. In fact, the tortoises are protected all over their range now, but that doesn't mean poaching doesn't occur. The protection also doesn't save them from other threats, such as motor vehicles that crush the slow creatures when they cross roads.

In 1991, a highly contagious upper respiratory tract disease (*Mycoplasma agassizii*) started killing tortoises on the west coast of Florida. Relocating the reptiles away from construction became more problematic and restricted. The risk of spreading the infection to other tortoise populations was great, so relocations of the animals were preceded by quarantines and veterinary examinations.

While I was working for the consulting company in 1990, we still relocated tortoises. Before the bulldozers came, we had to locate suitable land where the tortoises would be moved to, ensure it wasn't already occupied, and get permission from the landowner to dump the scaly diggers there.

The day before the scheduled razing of the land, we would try to trap the tortoises alive as they entered or left their burrows. If we could do that, we could just haul them to the new site and drop them off next to holes a few feet deep, which we clumsily dug to give the little guys a semblance of a haven until they could dig their own.

If we failed to find a tortoise, we would direct the operator of a tractor with a huge digging claw to gouge out the burrow. The operator, perched high in his air-conditioned cabin, tried to delicately scoop out the dwarfed tortoise—which we assumed was somewhere in the ten- to forty-foot-long tunnel—without so much as scratching its shell. At best, it was an exasperating process. Sometimes, it was worse. If we failed again to find the tortoise, we either buried it accidentally forever, or we sentenced it to return to find its burrow paved over and its food supply scarified.

What happened to the hundreds of other co-habitants who shared the tortoise burrows? Most were buried alive; others died while wandering desperately in search of a room at another inn.

Undeveloped land to receive transplanted tortoises is fast dwindling. What will we do when there is no land left for them and their cohorts? How many species will go extinct?

After six months with the consulting company (where I opted for longer hours, greedily grabbing larger paychecks), I never even started writing a book. I gradually saw that private enterprise wasn't my calling, although the company treated me well and was as conservation-minded as consulting companies can be. Perhaps my dissatisfaction was as simple as longing for real fieldwork, the kind that keeps you outside all day in the middle of nowhere, covered in mud and sweat, and delivers you physically exhausted at the end of the day. More likely, the motivation was knowing that I was doing something of lasting value for the great outdoors.

Thus, I quit after six months and went to work for Everglades National Park's Research Center. I was, once again, a public servant—like the lowly gopher tortoise—except that I chose my lot. The scant pay, the inflexible schedule, and an arrogant boss made me sometimes regret that decision. Still, I would prefer to think that those creatures who make a better world for others, even by happenstance, ultimately inherit the Earth, but the odds favor the ones with the biggest egos.

Chapter 10.
Male Gators Like it Hot

"Is it true the Everglades are infested with alligators?" the reporters asked.

"Just like your yard is infested with robins." What else could I say about something that is supposed to be there and in plentiful numbers?

The reporters' phone calls that reached me after ValuJet flight 592 plowed into the Everglades in 1996 were fraught with misconceptions. The plane crashed north of Everglades National Park in a water conservation area that was part of the Everglades system. The ValuJet incident gave good public exposure to the alligators. Even though the poor creatures had *their* lives turned upside down, too, the carnivores hadn't retaliated on the passengers or rescuers. Their reputation as man-eaters suffered.

At the time of the crash, I was working at Loxahatchee National Wildlife Refuge in the northern Everglades, about forty miles north of the crash site. Nevertheless, having previously researched alligators in Everglades National Park, I was a magnet for reporters.

As a biologist in Everglades National Park before my refuge stint, I investigated alligator nesting success. The occupation was fascinating, albeit sometimes risky. Oddly, the risk came less from the alligators than from other aspects of the work, such as the helicopter flights. A field team was composed of a researcher (me), a helicopter pilot, and a gator guard. All the gator guard had to do was keep the gators away from the researcher.

Summer—the rainy season—was our field season, when the gators had enough water to spread out and build their nests. We reserved a helicopter for six days, the time it would take to crisscross the 600,000 acres of marsh and locate every nest we could.

The equipment we carried included a clipboard for recording data, a meter stick for measuring nest heights, a National Park Service two-way radio, a two-inch-diameter plastic pipe that was ten-feet long, and all of our crash- and fire-protective flight clothing.

The clothing consisted of a jumpsuit (or shirt and pants) of flame-retardant Nomex material, Nomex gloves, and a three-pound crash helmet with a face visor. The crash gear and special training were required for all Department of the Interior employees who flew on such hazardous flights.

Dire events can happen when a helicopter flies at low altitudes, on an irregular path, and then lands in shallow water instead of an official, paved landing pad. To see the alligator nests, we had to fly less than five hundred feet above ground level. Normally, pilots are not permitted to fly this low because of the danger of hitting buildings, communication towers, and birds, but we were Park Service people on Park Service land. Many birds fly barely above ground level, so our pilot needed sharp reflexes to avoid colliding with them. We would land the helicopter in the water near each nest, thanks to the pontoons attached to the skids. A pontoon made a convenient platform to carry the ten-foot pole.

At flight-safety training classes, we had learned practical tips, such as don't walk into the helicopter's tail rotor; don't raise your hands or hold anything resembling a pole vertically while standing under the main rotor, and other self-preserving information. Before I was hired, someone really did raise the pole into the main rotor and caused twenty thousand dollars of damage. We also learned to crack the door open and wedge an empty shoe in the opening if we were heading for a crash into deep water. Water pressure, even in a canal, can make it difficult to open a closed door.

What was the ten-foot pole for? That was our only protection from the other potential hazard—the maternal reptiles. Whoever accepted the dubious honor of protecting me became my gator guard and used the pole for defense. More on that later. The gator guards often were other biologists from the research center who were hungry to learn more about alligators or who wanted to see a part of the marsh they otherwise couldn't access. Sometimes the assistant would be an intern or a volunteer. No Tom Sawyer whitewashing was needed. I always had a covey of eager helpers.

I keep the mother alligator at bay at her nest in Everglades
National Park while my gator guard takes the photo.
Hatched eggs are in the foreground. (Photo by Tom Cawley)

During one survey week, we carried an additional passenger in the helicopter. Local freelance video photographer Rich Kern wanted to film the nests up close. Rich was producing a thirty-minute documentary about alligators in the Everglades.

As usual, the helicopter landed in a field near the research center to collect our team and gear. Rich, the pilot, another biologist, and I took off on a sweltering July day, dressed head to finger to toe in hazard-duty gear. In addition to the aforementioned risks of flying in a field situation, the location exacerbated it. The South Florida air is hot and humid, which decreases air density and therefore decreases lift—what an aircraft needs to keep it aloft.

We lifted off and proceeded to fly transects across the park in our cumbersome outfits. Heading west, we searched the ground below for nests, then turned north for a few seconds before heading east. The vast sawgrass marsh, interspersed with tree islands and willowheads, spread out below. Back and forth we traversed, landing at each nest we spotted, until we reached the northern park boundary.

The water in the sawgrass marsh of Everglades National Park is generally ten to thirty inches deep, at the lower range during the dry season and at the upper range in summer. The substrate is soft, but not shoe-sucking muck—most of the time, that is. Other plants that grow in the shallow water include water-lilies, bladderwort, pickerelweed, and spike-rush.

Everglades tree islands are clumps of trees on higher ground, usually above water, ranging from less than an acre to hundreds of acres. Tree islands form several different ways, depending on their location in the Everglades. One intriguing way they develop is from the peat. Peat is an organic soil layer formed from decomposing plants, as opposed to disintegrating rocks that build most soils. Occasionally, a slab of peat separates from the bottom and floats to the water's surface, presumably from marsh gas emanating from under the peat layer as vegetation decomposes. The moist, fertile, floating peat mat is the ideal surface for wind-borne seeds to alight and germinate.

I was in my glory on floating peat mats, for I could walk on them like a child on a trampoline, bouncing up and down, quaking the mat without fear of breaking through. Those were the rare occasions when my slight mass allowed me to go where no man had gone before. Many times I had watched amusedly as male heavyweights shuffled gingerly across a peat mat, only to stab through anyway.

The real entertainment ensued when I worked at Loxahat-chee National Wildlife Refuge, and the unfortunate soul was someone on the opposite political side of the Everglades restoration issue, whom I escorted regularly to sample water for phosphorus. Since the public was not permitted in that part of the marsh, I had to accompany him as he scooped water into jars. We landed the helicopter at numerous locations around the marsh. Poetic justice was served when the hefty man was forced to crawl across the peat mat, as I strolled upright, secretly giggling.

The process of forming tree islands continues when several of the floating mats drift around on the water, bump into each other, and merge into a larger mat. As seedlings grow on top, more wind-blown debris lands on the mat and clings, adding to the mass of material. When the water level drops in the dry season, the mat drops as well. If the water disappears, the mat becomes anchored to the substrate over the following months. Then, when the water rises in the next rainy season, the mat remains anchored and becomes a tiny island. Thereafter, it catches more floating debris and more peat mats and grows to cover many acres.

The flow of the water through the Everglades is imperceptible to the human eye but not to the island. The subtle energy sculpts it into a teardrop shape with the wide end upstream, easily recognizable from the air. Debris accretes on the upstream end. Decades ago, this shape was distinctive enough even from a boater's level for him or her to know which way was north (upstream). Early froggers and fishermen could navigate by studying the shape of the tree islands. In the decades since construction of the levees reduced the flow of water, the tree islands have been losing their teardrop shape. Now they are expanding in all directions into nebulous masses. Were humans the only ones that navigated by tree islands? Are we causing confusion to the migrating birds?

Willowheads (clumps of willow trees) were the landmarks I aimed for from the helicopter on my quest for alligator nests. As we flew across the seemingly endless sawgrass marsh, I scanned for blotches of willow trees in the surrounding sawgrass. Willows grow in water deeper than other trees do, and the deeper water provides security for the female if she feels threatened. Alligators even make their own depressions (gator holes) to store water during the dry season. The deeper water provides more prey, so mother gators won't need to hunt far from the nest. Furthermore, the holes offer assurance that there will be sufficient water during the upcoming months, even if it barely rains. In addition, the nearby willowheads provide the vegetative cover that is so important to gator families.

Once I had spotted a willowhead, I scouted for nearby mounds of vegetation that stood out from the surrounding habitat like small haystacks. From the air, gator nests are easy to spot if they are in the open, but the presence of willows or shrubs could camouflage them. A telltale sign would be a beaten-down trail through the emergent vegetation. The trails indicated that an alligator had repeatedly visited that same location.

A female alligator builds a nest by biting off blades of sawgrass and other grasslike plants and piling them in a mound three to four feet high and seven feet wide. Partway through, she leaves a cavity and lays her eggs in it, then covers the eggs with more vegetation. The harsh South Florida sun rots the moist leaves and they decompose. The decomposition process causes heat to build in the mound, creating a natural incubator for the eggs.

Florida red-bellied turtles often lay their eggs in the side of the nest, taking advantage of the same incubating conditions. I have also found red imported fire ants using gator nests because they present the only above-water substrate around. I pitied the poor alligator hatchlings from such nests, because their thin skin made them defenseless targets for the hungry ants as soon as the reptiles hatched. A mother alligator's protection extends only to what she can see.

Since alligators don't sit on the nest to incubate the eggs, the heat in the rotting mound helps the embryos to develop. This imitates what a parent bird's body does when it broods its clutch of eggs. But unlike for birds, the heat of the alligator's nest also determines what gender the alligator embryos will become. This amazing process is known as environmental sex determination, or ESD, and is common in the reptile world.

Gender is determined in mammal and bird offspring by genetics (the male and female chromosomes). However, the gender of many reptiles depends instead on environmental temperatures. If the temperature in the chamber surrounding the alligator egg is above 91 degrees Fahrenheit in the first few weeks of incubation, the embryo will become a male. If the temperature is less than 85 degrees, it will become a female. If the temperature is in between, the embryo could become either a male or a female. Moreover, the temperature can vary between the top and bottom of the nest, so each nest should have both genders. Both sexes require the same amount of time to incubate, an average of 56 days in South Florida.

The same process of gender determination works for turtles, although the sexes are reversed: females are generally produced above 86 degrees and males are generally produced below 78 degrees.

Temperature is so critical in this process that small changes can tip the ratio of males to females. What do you think a few degrees of change from global warming would do to the alligator population? How about the sea turtles (loggerheads, greens, and leatherbacks) that nest on beaches along the Florida coasts? Or another group of reptiles—the dinosaurs?

Some scientists think that dinosaurs had the same environmental sex determination process for their eggs. If a global catastrophe, such as a meteorite or a volcanic eruption, caused widespread cloud cover that changed the atmospheric temperature by a few degrees, the result could have been all males hatching, all females hatching, or insufficient embryonic development for any hatching. Was temperature the cause of the dinosaur extinctions? If so, we could be heading for a modern mass reptilian extinction.

In Florida, and in low latitudes around the world, sea turtles nest on sandy beaches that are warmed by the sun's rays. An introduced tree called the Australian-pine has been invading the beaches of eastern Florida and shading the sea turtle nests, thus cooling the eggs. Normally, the only trees that grow along those beaches are slender palms and short trees, such as sea-grape, that cast little shade. Technically, palms aren't even trees. They are more closely related to grasses, which is why they don't have branches.

The Australian-pines are tall, densely canopied, and can grow thickly wherever they take root. These trees are not true pines but are members of the Casuarinaceae family. The cones resemble pine cones, hence the name. The tree is native to coastal regions in northeastern Australia, southeastern Asia, and the intervening islands.

Sea turtle resource managers in Florida must remove the encroaching Australian-pines to let the sun back onto the beach. Simply killing them won't work, because the woody hulks would still cast shade. Australian-pines also thrive around alligator nests in Florida. The hulks must be dismembered there, too, but it is harder to access them in the marsh than along the beach.

Alligators face other threats to their survival. Although no shortage of alligators exists in the Everglades, normal-sized ones are scarce. To put it another way, there is a passel of puny gators in the Everglades. Do you want to see a really big alligator? Then go to Louisiana, Georgia, or even Mississippi, but don't expect to see them in the Everglades. Most of the female alligators I saw were six to eight feet long. The males were eight to ten feet. Farther north, they average about two feet longer.

Water may be everywhere, but just the presence of water is not enough to grow a healthy alligator. If that water doesn't come at the right time, in the right quantity, at the right speed, at the right depth, and at the right quality, the aquatic prey won't grow. And if the prey doesn't grow, neither will the alligators. So goes the food chain, and alligators are at the top.

In Florida, people often confuse the American alligator with the local American crocodile (*Crocodylus acutus*), a threatened species that is smaller than its cousins on other continents. The easiest way to differentiate an alligator from a crocodile is by where you see it. If it is in fresh water, it is probably an alligator. If it is in salt water, in the mangroves, or on the beach, it is probably a crocodile. There is no need to fret about how to distinguish the species unless you are hunting alligators, because neither is known as a people-eater. Alligator hunting is carefully regulated in Florida to prevent the accidental killing of crocodiles.

Now let's return to the nest survey. From the air, our crew would spot a nest and land the helicopter a few hundred yards away. We had to land far enough away to keep the propeller wash from blowing the nest apart. The nest measurements didn't take long enough to warrant shutting the helicopter's engine down, so the pilot had to remain with the aircraft. The gator guard and I would slosh through the water toward the nest, scanning the water's surface for the telltale snout of the mother alligator. We usually found her as expected, silently watching over her mound of buried treasure, only her eyes and nostrils protruding above the water.

After the female builds her nest and lays eggs, she guards it until they hatch. A female alligator defending her nest is not something you want to disturb, but the possibility of arousing a mother was a necessary risk to accomplish our task.

The gator guard's job was to keep an eye on the female and watch for other gators and cottonmouth snakes. Most gators would keep a ten-foot distance, hence the length of our plastic pole. Although the reptiles were protective of their nests, they were also wary of us. The gators we encountered didn't know what to make of us. They had probably never seen humans before. After all, we were in the middle of the park, where the public wasn't allowed. If perchance another biologist or a ranger had ever passed that way, then maybe they had seen humans once before.

Alligators are naturally shy of humans. The ones that are habituated to the presence of people are generally the most dangerous, such as ones that live in canals near houses and often receive handouts from people or steal bait from fishing lines. People create the monsters.

When a person stands in shallow water, as we did on our nest surveys, he or she towers over the big reptiles. Yes, even I, though I stand barely five feet tall with ramrod stance, deceptively dwarfed them. The gators we encountered usually didn't know what to do about us intruders, so they played it safe by cowering back. Oh, there was a lot of hissing and an occasional bluffing lunge, but generally, they kept their distance.

Only a few mad moms were so agitated by our presence—hissing and lunging repeatedly—that I never began the measuring process and retreated instead. Even though I didn't think they would attack, I had sampled enough nests to gather adequate data, and I felt nefarious about distressing the gals. If the cooperative ones were similarly distraught, they didn't show it. To my knowledge, there has never been an attack on a human by a female gator defending her young. We pushed the envelope, and we all still have ten fingers and ten toes.

Still, the possibility existed that we could have been bitten. Our only weapon was the plastic pipe. Since firearms were allowed in the park only by law enforcement rangers, we had invented a substitute. Centuries ago, Korean farmers became adept at using common farming implements as weapons when Japanese occupiers forbade them to possess real weapons. Grain threshers became nunchucks and bucket-carrying poles became bo staffs. Those tools are serious weapons nowadays, mostly used in martial arts competitions. The scenario of creating weapons from common items has often been repeated throughout history and in many cultures.

Brandishing that plastic pipe, the gator guard would stand sentry, scrutinizing the water for nearby submerged gators. If one was spotted, the guard would simply keep an eye on it, unless it came within ten feet of us. Then the guard would gently bop it on the snout with the tip of the pole. Almost invariably, the scaly gal would slink backward a few feet and stay there. The ones that actively stood their muck and wouldn't back off were the ones that caused us to retreat.

We always preferred to see the mother gator rather than not see her. If we didn't see her, we knew she was nearby, probably skulking underwater, eyes and snout hidden by blades of grass, slowly inching closer. Those moms will always remain a mystery, because I took the required measurements, nervously looking over my shoulder, and skedaddled before any confrontation occurred.

On our survey day, whether or not the mama gators showed themselves, my task was to measure the depth of the water around each nest, the height of the nest (which was usually about two feet above the water), and the height of the egg chamber above water. Then I gently scooped off the top layer of the nest, revealing the egg cavity. I counted the eggs and noted how many were fertile.

A fertile egg has a faint band around the middle of the shell that is more opaque than the ends. Thus, the band looks a little whiter. This area is where the embryo attaches to the shell. We didn't need to shine a light to see through the egg, like the old-fashioned candling technique used with chicken eggs. Some alligator eggs were infertile and would never hatch. I didn't take the temperature of the egg chamber, because we weren't studying the sex ratio of the offspring. Later, I would return to count the fertile ones that had hatched, and thus I could calculate the hatching rate of the fertile eggs.

Measuring the hatching success rate each year allows scientists to track trends over several years. Are the alligators hatching as many eggs as they should, or is the rate dropping? If it worsened, we would need to find out why the nests were failing.

Because the eggs were temperature-sensitive, I had to remove them one by one and place them carefully around the rim of the nest in an order that could be reversed. Each egg had to return swiftly to its proper place.

Later in the season, I would return to collect three eggs from each nest, one each from the top, middle, and bottom of the egg chamber. Fortunately, I didn't need eggs from all nests, just a subset of them. The temperature varied slightly between the top and bottom of the nest, so I needed a representative sample. The goal was to estimate the age of the embryos so I could arrive at an approximate hatching date. For example, if the average embryo age in a nest was 48 days on August 15, the eggs would hatch approximately eight days later, or on August 23 (because the average hatching age is 56 days).

To age the embryos, I would need to keep them alive, keep the temperature constant (but not cold), and get them to the laboratory as soon as possible. I lined a food cooler with dry grass and nestled the eggs in the grass. Each egg was marked on its shell with an identifying code based on where it came from.

After collecting the eggs, I took the cooler home with me so that I could drive straight to the laboratory at the University of Miami the next morning without wasting time going back to the research center. The lab contained a collection of alligator embryos for which someone had already determined the ages. The embryos were in glass jars of formaldehyde, lined up on a shelf by embryo age, looking like jars of increasingly larger pickles. In fact, we called the embryos pickles, not to be funny, but because they were effectively pickled. My task was to open each of the eggs and compare the embryo to the pickles (yes, that would kill the embryo).

One night, after returning home from the field with a cooler of eggs, I was awakened by a plaintive whimpering sound. *Unh, unh. Unh, unh.* It came from the direction of the cooler in my living room. I crawled from bed, opened the cooler, and in the faint ambient light, I could see two beady eyes attached to a miniature reptile. *Unh, unh, unh!*

It was August 21, close to most of the nest hatching dates, but I thought this nest was built late because I hadn't seen it on an earlier survey. Oh, well. That was one egg I didn't have to age. But rather than making my job easier, it created a dilemma. What's a gal to do with a live baby alligator?

Soon I realized that our disturbance of the nest so close to hatching would simulate the mother opening the nest cavity. The rest of the babies would think it was time to hatch and whimper for their mother to come and get them. I looked at the broken shell. It was marked "SVLT," the abbreviation for Shark Valley Lookout Tower, a tourist attraction at the north end of the park.

Early the next morning, I phoned Rich, the video photographer. "Hey, you wanted to film a nest hatching, right? Have I got just the one for you! But, we have to go right now."

"I'm ready!" he exclaimed.

We rendezvoused by earth-bound motor vehicles on the Shark Valley Lookout Tower Road and slogged through the marsh for about a half mile. I was right. The mother alligator had torn open the top of the nest and the babies were hatching. Rich's camera whirred away.

I didn't think to bring my hatchling back to return it to its family. Was it the lack of sleep? Was it my lack of confidence that

I was right about the rest of the nest hatching? Then I would have been stuck carrying the baby around with me all day, because the mother wouldn't be stimulated to take care of only one hatchling.

Perhaps subconsciously I wanted to find an excuse to keep it. Have you ever seen a baby alligator? Thousands of tourists fell in love with them and bought them, live or stuffed, by the bucketful until the 1960s. Because no regulations existed on killing alligators, wanton extermination was underway. That fad contributed to alligators becoming one of the first species ever listed under the Endangered Species Conservation Act of 1966, the precursor to the Endangered Species Act of 1973. That one law was all that was needed to bring the species back from the brink of extinction and allow it to be delisted twenty years later.

Habitat loss wasn't a problem then as it is now. Simply making it illegal to harm an alligator stopped enough of the mortality to allow the species to make a dramatic recovery. If only it were so easy to save other species! But alligators now face habitat destruction, chemical and mercury contamination, loss of prey, and other threats.

As long as I was going to keep the little tyke, at least temporarily, I could learn something about alligators. To simplify my note-taking for observations, I would name it. The shell was labeled "SVLT." Hmmm. I sounded it out: Svelte. Now there was a good name for an alligator.

Svelte was eight inches long, black-skinned with bold yellow bands. The bands would gradually fade through the years as the little guy got older, but he would always be black like all his cronies. He still had the yolk sac attached to his umbilical area. It took a week for that to disappear. During that time, he obtained his nourishment from the yolk, as he would have in the wild.

I kept Svelte in a glass tank and caught small fish for him in a minnow trap. Sometimes he would have to settle for store-bought bait shrimp or frozen fish. I never knew if Svelte was a male, because I didn't know the temperature in his nest, and there is no way to know by a small gator's appearance. I let him crawl around my yard in Homestead so that he could exercise and soak up the bone-building sunlight.

Months later, when I could return to the area from which he came, I slid all thirteen inches of his leathery physique into the water and waved goodbye. I will never know if he survived, but I wouldn't bet on it. Too many predators relished the young reptiles.

Meanwhile, I continued to check the nests in the study area until the third week in September, when all had hatched. Hatched nests are easy to spot from the air. When the young are ready for their debuts, they start that pathetic whimpering sound—*unh, unh, unh.* The mother hears it and starts biting off the top of the nest, opening up the egg chamber. She has to, because the hatchlings aren't strong enough to dig themselves out from the compact, decayed morass of grass. Having lost its haystack shape, the gouged-out nest can be recognized from the air.

Some of the eggs do hatch on their own. Others need the tender crunch of the mother's jaw to help them along. As incredulous as it sounds, that tremendous force, the same one that can crush a big turtle's shell, can be disciplined enough to crack a four-inch-long eggshell and not harm the live contents.

When all the young have hatched, the mother may decide to move the brood to another location. What was a good spot for placing a nest isn't always the best spot for raising a clan. Again, with mouth slightly agape, she will employ that motherly discipline and carry the young gently in her jaws to a better home.

All this fieldwork was necessary to determine what was happening to the population of alligators, an indication of the health of the entire Everglades. As I noted earlier, alligators are a keystone species, one that supports many other species by the way it modifies the environment or regulates the local species diversity. Ducks drink the water in the alligator holes and feed on the aquatic fare there. Otters, bobcats, raccoons, wading birds, and many other animals drink and hunt in the lively pools that the gators maintain. So important are alligators that, in places where alligators disappeared, some resource managers have resorted to blasting holes in the bedrock to create pools where aquatic species can survive the November to April dry season.

While the Everglades may appear to be a useless place unless you have fins or webbed feet, its benefits reach far. The water that covers the marsh in the rainy season is flowing slowly southward into Florida Bay and adjacent estuaries. The nutrients carried with that water, compliments of the plant and animal by-products, support one of the most productive seafood nurseries in the United States. Because of the Everglades and smaller marshes along our coasts, we enjoy shrimp, lobsters, crabs, oysters, and a profusion of fish on our dinner plates.

Although alligators have a fierce reputation, I waded in their midst from South Carolina to Florida for fourteen years, many times alone, and never suffered an incident. My personal rule was to never swim in ponds, lakes, or canals, or anywhere that the water was chest deep on me or more. I also never waded in water around concentrations of humans, where it was likely that the alligators had lost their fear of us. Yes, there was that one close call when I had to jump into deep water to save the heron that later became known as 151. In that instance, my observant partner, who was in a canoe, bopped the behemoth on the snout with his paddle, driving the reptile silently away. It was only a few feet from me and probably was merely investigating the mysterious alien.

Rich Kern finished filming after a few days in the field with us. He produced a great documentary on alligators in the Everglades, featuring a cameo of me studying a nest in the marsh. The video was subsequently sold in nature centers all over Florida, and it was shown in the visitor centers of national parks and national wildlife refuges. When I started working at Loxahatchee a few years later, the staff from the refuge's visitor center already recognized me. Fifteen years later, the video was still being shown at the refuge, including, to my eternal embarrassment, a scene where I tripped and fell in the water.

Chapter 11. The Florida Bay Boaters' and Manglers' Club

"Hello, how are you today?" I called cheerfully to the fishermen pulling up to the dock.

"Lousy!" barked one of them from behind the steering wheel of the seventeen-foot Bayliner.

I had heard this answer a dozen times that day, each time from a different angler. Without further conversation, I could guess what had gone wrong on his outing.

It was a Saturday in the village of Flamingo, situated on Florida Bay within the borders of Everglades National Park. This southern Florida community had been one of my favorite destinations since I first visited it on a vacation ten years earlier—a placid enclave brimming with bobcats, dolphins, alligators, snakes, frogs, and other wildlife. The sum of the village consisted of a marina, lodge and rental cabins, campground, restaurant, visitor center, ranger station, gas station, post office, and employee residences.

I had come to spend the day, as I did every Saturday and Sunday, conducting a creel survey as a biologist with the Everglades National Park Research Center.[5] How lucky could a gal get? My job required me to spend two days a week hanging around the edge of Florida Bay, chatting with anglers and watching birds when no anglers were in sight. Just the trip to Flamingo was delightful. I had to drive across fifty miles of spectacular Everglades, past the famed Anhinga Trail, Mahogany Hammock, Pa-Hay-Okee Overlook, and many other places that attracted tourists from around the world. If I embarked early or dawdled after my shift, I could stop and scout for wildlife anywhere along the way. It was a dream job for a field biologist, or so I thought. I didn't know I would learn a lesson that would haunt me for years to come.

The creel survey involved interviewing each boater as he or she returned to the dock after fishing on Florida Bay. The bay is widely recognized as the sportfishing capital of the United States. Much of the bay's best fishing lies within the jurisdiction of the

National Park Service, which monitors the health of the fishery stocks. The Park had conducted the survey continuously for twenty years and accumulated a valuable set of data.

As each boat arrived at the dock, I would ask the anglers a prearranged set of questions about what they caught, record the answers on paper, and then enter them into a computer later in the week. The anglers were not required to participate, but they rarely declined.

The task sounds simple and stressless. In the beginning, the only hitch was my stinky ambience at the end of the day. Handling dozens of dead fish to identify or measure them caused an accumulation of fish slime on my clothes that kept everything but the mosquitoes at a distance.

Usually, merely being in Flamingo relaxed me. But I felt my ire intensifying, as I continued my conversation with this grouchy angler.

"Did you have trouble with your boat?" I asked the gruff man, trying to mask my sarcasm, since I knew that wasn't the problem.

"Naw, I just didn't get my limit of redfish."

I'll call him Sam because I never asked for names for the survey. Sam had given the standard fisherman's answer. Just hearing it spiked my blood pressure. Here he was in a glorious place—the dream of anglers all over the country—with a fine boat, top-of-the-line fishing gear, glorious weather, and the luxury of leisure time, and he was miserable because he didn't catch as many fish as he wanted. Or the right sizes. Or the right species. In other words, he lost out on bragging rights to his wife and buddies. I doubt he even needed the fish for food. I don't believe, however, that Flamingo anglers differed from anglers elsewhere across the country.

I counted to twenty silently and continued aloud, "I'm doing a survey for Everglades National Park to help manage the fisheries. If you don't mind, would you please tell me everything you caught today—everything you kept and everything you threw back? How many of each species?" I was careful to spell out what I needed.

"Sure. I kept two redfish and three seatrout and threw back five undersized seatrout. Frankie here kept a snook, three mangrove snappers, and five seatrout."

"Is that everything?" I asked incredulously. "You didn't catch any ladyfish or jacks?"

"Oh, the *trash* fish. I didn't know you wanted to count the *trash* fish. Yeah, we threw back a bunch of both. You can't help but catch 'em and they're good for nothin'."

He growled it as if he then needed to wash his mouth with soap. *Trash* fish? The sound of the word in my ears was like a nail scraping across a chalkboard. I had heard this answer as often as I had heard "lousy."

Gritting my teeth, I replied, "Yes, I did say that I wanted to know everything you caught and everything you threw back."

What part of that hadn't he understood? I continued the survey, grabbing a chance to slip in some environmental outreach.

"You know, the ones you call trash fish serve a purpose," I explained. "They're part of the food chain that keeps Florida Bay and the sport fish healthy. Without them, the whole fishery would collapse. Some of the small fish eat algae, which could seriously cloud the water. The fish you catch eat the trash fish. Nothing is really a trash fish, because they're all important."

Without looking up, the anglers continued unloading their coolers and gear from the boat. Were they even listening to me? I asked to see their keepers so I could confirm the identifications, and Sam and Frankie obligingly opened their coolers.

As if on cue, as if it was part of the survey, Sam and Frankie started jabbering about the giant that got away. A monster redfish (as they called red drum) would make a good story for the guys at the bar if they could just catch it. Oh, the fight it put up! Their eyes glazed over as they recalled the scene to me—the fish tugging on the line, swimming in circles, and the two men laughing while one struggled to hold on to the fish. The line finally snapped, and the fish swam off with a hook in its mouth.

The two men resumed their scowls. "This place ain't what it used to be. Thirty years ago we got our limit every day," Sam lamented, referring to the ego-building species.

I tried to picture how much of a dent that would make in the population. I knew the size and bag limits were set to prevent overfishing, but it's what is thrown back—not what is kept—that concerned me.

At the park, we assumed that the post-release mortality of the fish was ten percent. Post-release mortality is an estimate of the number of fish that die after being released into the water as a result of handling by anglers. Thus, one of every ten fish released dies from the handling. A fisheries biologist I knew estimated this figure to be more like twenty-five percent—one fish dies of every four that are caught and released. That statistic does not include fish that survive but are physiologically so acutely stressed that they don't reproduce that year. The intense fighting on the line can cause a buildup of lactic acid, so even if the fish escapes, its muscles will be sore and stiff or its blood pH altered so that the chemical imbalance can cause death even three days later.

Fishing in Florida Bay is a year-round activity. Boat ramps and docks are located in many places around the bay outside Everglades National Park. The effect of decades of fishing by hundreds of people on any given day, with the fish they keep and between a tenth and a quarter of the fish they return to the water dying, adds up to a good reason for the fishery to be declining.

Water pollution and habitat disturbance also contribute to the fisheries' decline. However, most of Florida Bay is within the national park, so much of the habitat is protected from those factors. Nevertheless, merely the presence of hundreds of boats churning up the shallow seagrass beds destroys the fishes' habitat.

When I saw the anglers' livewells (small onboard tanks), I realized that the post-release mortality numbers didn't include initial mortality, which also was significant. Initial mortality happens when a fish dies before it is released. A common practice among anglers is to keep a livewell on board for legal-sized fish they catch; at the end of the day, they select the largest and throw the rest back. The rejects, which sit for hours in the hot tanks gasping for every breath, may die in the misnamed livewells before they are released. This form of killing fish is legal, as long as you are still in the process of fishing and the fish are within legal limits. If the shock of being yanked from cool bay water and dunked in tepid livewell water isn't lethal, returning the fish suddenly to the cool bay certainly could be.

Fish have a coating of mucus on their scales that protects them from disease-bearing microorganisms. When scraped by a landing net or touched by dry hands, the coating is compromised, paving the way for the fish to contract a disease. When a fish is caught in a landing net and the hook is removed with dry hands, the fish is immediately exposed to risks, even before it is tossed in the livewell. Just the act of pulling a fish quickly out of deep water can disrupt its buoyancy system by rupturing the swim bladders, and it can cause the gills to bleed. These forms of indirect killing are legal.

People who fish from shore have an alternative to a livewell that is unfortunately no better. They keep their fish on a stringer, so-called because a string is threaded through the gills and mouth. The fish are held underwater, preferably alive, so that they don't spoil as quickly as leaving them onshore, or so the anglers can release the runts if they catch trophies. The stringer is harmful because the gills are delicate structures containing the capillaries that absorb oxygen. Rough handling of a fish by the gills can hinder its ability to breathe. For example, holding a fish by the gills for a photograph, rather than by its jaws, will likely cause this injury.

The fish released straight from the line fare slightly better, especially when the angler uses the fish-friendly technique of wetting his hands before touching the fish, working quickly and gently, and holding the fish underwater when releasing it. Unfortunately, anglers rarely practice this method.

I recall only one man I interviewed who ventured bayside regularly and truly seemed grateful for a day on the water. He was always cheerful and polite. He paddled out in a well-used canoe and never complained to me about anything, no matter what he didn't catch.

Many of the anglers were straightforward, listened to my questions, and did admit to catching the less-than-desirable fish. I encountered few women fishing during my creel surveys, and, for the most part, they let their men do the talking, so I don't know how they felt about fishing. In general, most anglers were men and seemed to care little about the fish as living animals. Therefore, I propose that a better name for those fishermen would be "manglers."

Besides the entertainment and food factor the fish provide, some manglers seemed to need to release their machismo on the closest member of the opposite sex. That unlucky gal was often me. Here are typical repartees on any given day:

(First Example) Me: "Hello, sir. I'm with the Park Service, and I'm gathering information to help the fisheries. May I ask you a few questions about the fish you caught today?"

Mangler A: "Sure, sweetheart, and you can clean them for me, too."

(Second Example) Me: "Good afternoon, gentlemen. I'm with the Park Service, and I'm collecting information about the fish in Florida Bay. Would you mind answering a few questions about the fish you caught?"

Mangler B: "Only if you promise to keep me company when I go out again tomorrow, sugar."

Ironically, the federal government protected me from sexual harassment and innuendos from other federal employees, but I still had to endure it from the public. To be fair, I should note that I never brought these encounters to the attention of the park's managers and, to my knowledge, they were not otherwise aware of it.

On my long drive home at the end of the day, I reflected on the comments from Sam and Frankie and the other manglers. A warm day with flat water, good friends, an expensive boat, a cooler of fish for dinner, and these people were still griping. My morning's bliss swung to despair by day's end.

What caused these people to take so much for granted? Why did they think that the Park Service should be doing a better job of providing fish for them? Did it ever occur to them that generations of anglers keeping the largest fish have caused a downward shift in fish sizes? When anglers keep only the large fish, few fish grow to large sizes. There are more small ones, and they compete with each other for the same-sized food and thus grow abnormally slowly.[6]

After each survey day, I left Flamingo tense and distraught, contemplating how many people have lost their connection with the fish. A subject I had never dwelled on was taking a whole new perspective.

For thousands of years, fishing was necessary for survival in many cultures. Fish provided protein that was relatively easy to obtain. Later in history, fewer fishermen caught the fish and sold them to villagers at markets. Eventually, large-scale commercial fishing methods were developed. Most families did not have to do their own fishing anymore, so they lost the skills.

When leisure time increased, the old-timers tried to teach the younger generations how to maintain the old ways, but they could not use the excuse that it was necessary, so they tried to make it fun. After all, it was supposed to be playtime. Thus, fishing became a sport.

However, one important aspect of fishing was different. In the early days, the goal of fishing was to kill the fish, because it was your food. It didn't matter that your rough handling caused the fish to die. That was actually good, because then you wouldn't have to kill it yourself. The gentle treatment of just-caught fish for release wasn't part of what Granddaddy was taught, so he didn't teach it to his followers. The next generations learned how to capture fish, but not how to treat them so they would survive if released.

A long time ago, anglers kept just about everything they caught if it was edible. They didn't have the luxury of time to sit and wait for the perfect fish. Subsequent generations became choosier, and anglers threw back many fish, because there seemed to be an endless supply. Current generations are even pickier about what species they keep. What they don't want become their so-called trash fish. If you want to raise my hackles and see steam pouring from my ears, just tell me you caught some trash fish. I will assume you know absolutely nothing about the lives of these important animals.

When I see people wasting fish, I think about my own philosophy of fishing. I eat fish, and I have occasionally stuck a pole in the water, usually on an overnight canoeing trip. My purpose was to obtain food. I wasn't taught how to fish by a family member, but rather by an old-timer friend, Dalton Philpott, who was born in a log cabin with many siblings in the Appalachian Mountains of Virginia. He fished to live, not the other way around.

Most other people I know learned to fish from their father, older brother, or grandfather. Our society endorses taking children fishing as a demonstration of quality parenting. The same enthusiasm is not displayed as much for taking children bird watching, hiking, or canoeing. Perhaps this is because the parents are doing what they learned.

I can see how novice anglers learn that the fish exist for people's enjoyment. Sam and Frankie will probably teach their sons that fishing for recreation is what real men do when they want to impress someone equally gullible.

In no way is this attitude confined to South Florida. Read a story in any sporting magazine about fishing, and you will see the same careless perspective. It is pervasive throughout cultures wherever people fish in leisure time. The fish are treated as toys that were placed there for the anglers' enjoyment. In fact, sometimes they were. Hatcheries all over the United States raise fish to stock them for sportfishing, where the angler must release all the fish he or she catches. This practice is a sign that fishing is now a game.

My fishing philosophy quickly changed once I was exposed to the concentrated conversations with hard-core anglers at Flamingo. I am grateful that I had that experience to open my eyes. Since then, I think about how traditions started, and then I decide for myself if they are worthy of continuing or have lost their purpose. Growing up in the American culture, I was taught many things and abided by them for years without according them a second thought.

For example, I was taught that courteous people reply "bless you" when someone else sneezes. Some sources state that the tradition started around fourteen centuries ago in Europe, when a sneeze or cough was a symptom of the bubonic plague, and you were doomed without God's intervention. Thus, people said "may God bless you" to a loved one.

Plague is now curable with antibiotics. A sneeze happens because you have dust in your nose, an allergy, or a common respiratory infection. Blessing someone is perfunctory, and even rude. Why draw attention to someone's itchy nose?

More to the point, shouldn't the ritual be reversed? The sneezer should bless the person on whom he sneezes. After all, the sneezer just cast his germs into the air and may make everyone sick who is within range. Come to think of it, instead of saying "bless you" to a sneezer, we should say it to the fish we catch: "Bless you, fish, for without God's intervention, you are doomed."

I give this example merely to point out how often we do things that once were justifiable and now are ridiculous. "Catch and release" is another often unquestioned, although more modern, tradition. In 1972, an organization called B.A.S.S. (Bass Anglers Sportsman Society) realized that the large number of tournaments around the country put tremendous survival pressure on bass and other fish species. To prevent these losses, B.A.S.S. justifiably introduced the catch-and-release concept of fishing and imposed the rules for their bass tournaments. However, many years later, they still found that "zero percent to over thirty percent" of fish in catch-and-release tournaments died before the weigh-in.[7] Obviously, the dead fish couldn't be released alive.

To reduce this initial mortality, B.A.S.S. developed and published methods for the gentle handling of fish. Unfortunately, these beneficial methods don't seem to have caught on in mainstream fishing. Most of the time, people still practice the standard catch-and-release (or what I call catch-and-distress) fishing. Anglers should learn how to protect fish during handling, especially if they intend to release them, so that the fish have a greater chance of surviving. The most basic tips are: 1) set the hook quickly; 2) don't tire the fish; 3) handle the fish only with wet hands and nets; 4) cut the barb off the hook and back the hook out of the mouth; and 5) return the fish to the water quickly, releasing it there.

We need to take such care because fish are animals. They have brains, pain receptors, and strong survival instincts. Scientists consider fish to be a class of animals on the same level as other vertebrates (mammals, birds, reptiles, and amphibians). The federal Endangered Species Act treats all types of animals, including invertebrates, equally. So why don't the humane laws for the ethical treatment of animals apply to fish?

The federal Animal Welfare Act[8] defines an animal as "any live or dead dog, cat, monkey (nonhuman primate), guinea pig, hamster, rabbit, or such other warm-blooded animal. . . ." Fish, reptiles, amphibians, and invertebrates are not covered.

The Animal Welfare Institute, champion of faunal rights, barely mentions fish in its book *Animals and Their Legal Rights.*[9] It makes no mention of fish in its book *The Animal Dealers: Evidence of abuse of animals in the commercial trade 1952–1997,*[10] although it does include reptiles. Certainly, the aquarium fish trade is an enormous commercial establishment, and pet fish are abused at an alarming rate.

The philosophy of excluding fish as animals is pervasive. I am reminded of it every time I visit a small county park near where I live in Virginia that has a signpost with three signs:

A sign at a Fairfax County (VA) park contradicts itself.

Fishing is legal at the park and trout are stocked annually. Clearly, Fairfax County does not consider fish to be animals. It is little wonder, then, that the anglers don't either.

Perhaps we treat fish differently because they aren't soft and fluffy, like mammals and birds. They don't have huge brown eyes that gaze mournfully at us. The only time we see a fish's eyes is when they are out of water—glazed from exhaustion or desiccation—nothing cute there. And, of course, while a scared fawn bleats, or a wounded bird squawks, a dying fish is silent. Beauty may be skin deep, but sound penetrates to your brain.

However, I suspect that the treatment of fish as objects also has to do with their mysterious underwater lifestyles and our inability to watch their daily activities. Most people have seen terrestrial animals in their natural surroundings, especially if they are common species. We can watch birds and mammals gather food, build nests, and raise their young. We can walk through a field and watch deer grazing or birds hunting for insects. At a pond, we see frogs calling to mates on lily pads and turtles sunning themselves on logs. Even in the most crowded American city, pigeons and gray squirrels can scrounge a living while giving benchsitters some visual enjoyment.

But how can we watch a fish in its natural surroundings? Most people see fish only on a plate in their most lifeless, boring forms. If we are lucky, we can squint through the glare of a pond's surface water and see a shadow darting around. Without donning a snorkel mask, we would be unlikely to see the fish clearly and view it as a living animal. Fish in an aquarium are a poor substitute, but they do help the understanding.

I should not ignore another reason that people feel the need to go fishing—pressure from the fishing and tourism industries. Anglers spend more than $40 billion a year on equipment, transportation, lodging, and other expenses associated with the sport.[11] These industries push the right buttons on the right people, who place more value on fishing than they otherwise might.

I often hear people say that fishing is fun. I could never comprehend what the fun is. I can enjoy the outdoors without harassing wildlife. Fishing isn't fun for the fish. They fight for their lives. Playing with a dog or cat is fun for the pet, but only if you don't hurt it. If you do, you are likely to be bitten or clawed. Animals will defend themselves or flee when the activity ceases to be fun. The difference with fish is that they can't defend themselves because they have no claws and they are on the end of a pole with a hook in their mouths or suffocating out of water. Underwater, they do try to flee, and that is what rouses the manglers' thrill.

Fish can be caught in many ways, but a hook-and-line is the most common legal way in most places. Monofilament line is environmentally destructive by strangling countless animals unintentionally and taking about six hundred years to degrade. Hook-and-line fishing kills sea turtles, dolphins, wading birds, pelicans, and many other animals that become hooked or entangled. Others die slow deaths by infection or lose an appendage because the fishing line stanched the blood flow.

The bait from fishing lines attracts alligators to popular fishing areas. The reptiles become dangerous, condemned nuisances when they expect food from every human that ventures near, including children. Indeed, an alligator by a fishing hole is more dangerous than one in a remote area.

Society has convinced many people that sport hunting—that is, shooting game animals when you don't want the meat—is unethical. Yet sport hunting for fish has not achieved this level of rejection. I use the word "hunting" for fish because fishing is a form of hunting. Hunting means to search for and pursue wild animals with the intent to capture or kill them. That's what fishing is, except it's done below the water.

Just as we must be taught to hate something, we must be taught why we should fish. Those who learned to fish for food see it in a practical light. Fishing is an age-old method of obtaining highly nutritious food. In modern society, fishing has become a game; people teach others that fishing is a form of entertainment—hence, the term "game fish" is quite appropriate. I wish that people who fish would do so only when they need food; that they treat their captives with care; and that they wouldn't leave hooks, monofilament line, and exotic bait species behind.

I am not blind or ungrateful to the many anglers who work hard to protect habitat for the fish. My issue with them occurs if they treat the fish like inanimate objects or if they protect the habitat with the ulterior motive of having better places to fish for fun. Doing a good deed with the intent of later doing harm is akin to giving someone a watch and later stealing it back. Catch-and-release is the converse—doing harm with the intent of repairing it—and is akin to stealing the watch and then returning it as a gift.

Some day, another generation of biologists will stand at the dock and ask, "Hello, how are you today?" and the cheerful angler will answer, "Wonderful! I had a lovely day on the water with my family. I kept two seatrout because they'll make a great dinner tonight. Then I stopped fishing so I wouldn't injure any more fish. Then we just enjoyed the day on the water. We watched some ospreys build a nest and even saw some dolphins. There are more fish out there now than I remember when I was young."

The sooner we begin to equate fish with mammals and birds, the sooner that day will come. First, we must realize that fish are not an inferior class of animals called "toys."

Chapter 12. The Wind in the Walls

Be careful what you wish for—it may come true. I knew that. But, I still wished that I didn't have to go to work that day. It wasn't laziness on my part, but the dread of dealing yet another day with self-centered fishermen in Florida Bay for the sportfishing creel survey. My experience had revealed that many anglers were obnoxious, spoiled, and, in some cases, lewd.

Only five weeks remained until I commenced my new job at Loxahatchee National Wildlife Refuge at the northern end of the Everglades. The last two of those weeks I had planned as a salubrious vacation in the Cascade Mountains of Washington, so now I was ticking off the final three weeks of my frustrating job.

I worked weekends, because that was when most people fished and, therefore, the most efficient time to gather data. On Saturday morning, August 22, 1992, I drove as usual down the long, scenic road to Flamingo in Everglades National Park. I knew there was a hurricane churning in the Atlantic, east of the Bahamas. Late August to early September is the peak of the Atlantic hurricane season, so I scrutinized the forecasts. During the day, I kept my Park Service radio tuned to the NOAA (National Oceanic and Atmospheric Administration) weather station.

At five o'clock in the afternoon, the National Hurricane Center issued a hurricane warning for southern Florida. That message mandated the rangers to pull all patrol boats from the water and stow them safely. The National Park Service would have to close Everglades National Park immediately, asking all the campers, anglers, and other visitors to leave and seek shelter elsewhere. Thus, it didn't look like I would have to drag myself to work on Sunday.

After I finished questioning the anglers around six in the evening, I stopped at the research center to safeguard my files from the impending wind and water. Then I went home and started preparing my house for the big blow.

My house in Homestead, Florida, was owned by senior park biologist John Ogden and his wife, Maryanne Biggar. It was built as the carriage house for the main house, where the Ogdens lived. The structures had been built in the early 1900s and had weathered many storms. John referred to mine as "Palm Cottage," a cheerful way to verbally dress up a drab abode.

While most houses are built above ground level to prevent flooding, my cottage was nearly at ground level to allow the smooth entry of carriages. The flimsy tin roof seemed destined to peel off even in a minor (Category 1) hurricane and prevented me from qualifying for renter's insurance. Other than that, the two bedrooms, bathroom, and kitchen–living area were typical for a small cottage.

But the hurricane heading my way was no Category 1 storm, and it was colossal. Although I should have continued battening down the home hatches, I took a break to attend a welcome party for the new Everglades National Park superintendent. Despite the threat on the horizon, the party's host felt obligated to carry on in honor of his new boss. About two hours after I arrived, anxiety over the approaching maelstrom seized me. I departed the festivities early to continue my preparations, such as food shopping and fueling my car.

On Sunday, I arose at sunrise and turned on the television news. After seeing the current track of the storm and that it had strengthened to a Category 3 (winds of 111 to 130 mph), I began a feverish, nonstop preparation that ended fourteen hours later. You wouldn't believe how much there was to do, even for my three-room cottage. Something as easy as filling the bathtub with water that may be needed for drinking or washing becomes time-consuming because, if you are like me, first you have to clean the tub. Ditto for all the other "simple" things. Fortunately, much of my preparation was worth the effort and saved what survived.

Throughout the day, I teamed up with the Ogdens. We disassembled their outdoor television antenna and mine. We closed the heavy metal hurricane shutters on their house, which doubled as window awnings. Palm Cottage had no shutters.

To prepare efficiently, I tried to think like the wind. What could I damage? The two propane tanks outside the front door looked like fine targets. I closed the gas valves on the tanks, despite the gas company's pat warning not to do so when I phoned for advice, because I wasn't qualified. I also roped the tanks to the house, a gesture I recognized as perfunctory but did anyway.

What if the roof came off? What if the windows blew out? I covered my television and computer with tarps and placed them in the center of a room away from any windows. I built a two-inch-high pallet with scrap wood from the garage and placed packed suitcases and other possessions on top, also covered with a tarp.

Maryanne came over during the day to inform me about a potential problem. "You know, since the floor of this place is barely above ground level, we've had some floods in here. If the yard starts flooding, water could come inside under the front door. You might want to put some towels behind the threshold."

That sounded wise and simple. I laid the towels down. I wanted to be totally prepared.

During the day, the newscasters reported hurricane updates of the storm, which had increased to a Category 4 and then a Category 5 (winds greater than 155 mph). My stomach knotted. The storm reportedly diminished to a Category 4 before it hit land, but years later, that assessment was rescinded.

We lived about five miles inland, the farthest inland the authorities had ever extended a mandatory evacuation zone. But evacuate to where? Nowhere was guaranteed to be safe. The hurricane shelters couldn't accommodate the millions of people along the coast. The number of evacuation routes for hundreds of thousands of cars could be counted on one hand. One accident or one breakdown would snarl traffic, and we would be trapped in the open. The Ogdens' house had weathered storms gracefully for nearly a century, and they were staying put.

At seven o'clock in the evening, I packed a duffle bag of valuables and irreplaceable photos and appeared at the Ogdens' back door, dragging the duffle and a lightweight blanket. Also seeking refuge with the Ogdens was a family with two children and two dogs who had evacuated from the Keys. The storm missed the Keys; in hindsight, they would have been safer staying home.

We drank rum-and-colas in the living room to ease the suspense. At every radio weather report, the forecaster repeated the arrow-straight route of the storm, heading due west on the 25.6 degree latitude. John and I knew we were close to that latitude. Every time we heard the coordinates, we looked at each other, questioning. Just how close? We had to know exactly.

I returned to my house briefly to retrieve an aviation map. When I located 25.6 degrees north, I gasped. I brought the map back and showed the others.

"Look—we're at 25.5 degrees! That's only six miles from the center's path!"

That revelation didn't help morale. We resigned ourselves to a mighty turmoil. At midnight, everyone scattered to their respective rooms to attempt sleep. The storm was not expected to hit until seven or eight o'clock in the morning.

I slept on the couch in the Ogdens' living room. The Odgens' beagle Sadie and basset hound Chessie kept me company. At three o'clock Monday morning, I bolted awake when the ceiling fan stilled. The old house had no air conditioning. With all the shutters and windows closed, the air became instantly stagnant and oppressive. I sensed that the electric power had died. The howling wind outside filled me with dread.

The others woke at the same time. The six other two-legged figures and the four four-legged ones appeared from the shadows and merged in the sitting room. The storm had picked up tremendous forward speed and arrived hours earlier than expected. My transistor radio broadcasted constant static, rendered useless by the intense atmospheric disturbance from the lightning.

Although it was still night, we could see outside through a tiny, shutterless kitchen window because of the nearly continuous lightning. The electricity in the storm was unequal to anything I had ever seen before or have seen since. It flashed almost continuously, yet I couldn't hear the thunder over the roar of the wind.

Squinting through the tiny window, I saw the power lines to my cottage snap. When some shuttered windows upstairs in the big house shattered and branches began battering the outside walls, I backed away from the window to an interior room.

The wind was deafening. More likely, the sound was the effect of the wind—flying debris of all types slamming the house. The wind flexed the house so much that the doors shifted out of their frames. The front door, which had been bolted, blew open and one of the kids' dogs disappeared outside. Surely the dog didn't voluntarily run out into the maelstrom! Did the wind suck him out?

The fury before the eye of the storm lasted a few hours. The eye is the dead-calm center of a hurricane, arriving suddenly and ending just as suddenly. When the eye appeared at about 5:00 A.M., we breathed a sigh of relief, thinking that the worst had passed, because what could be worse than what we had just experienced?

I opened the back door and stared into the darkness long enough to see that the silhouette of my cottage had changed. Most of the roof was gone. The whole neighborhood seemed alien. Trees were toppled or stripped bare.

I wanted to check the damage to the inside of my house, but the wise Ogdens pleaded in unison, "Don't go! It's not safe!"

"Okay, I won't go inside. I'll just go closer. I need to see what's left," I begged.

"Just go as far as the gate, so you can see better, then come right back," one of them conceded.

They had lived in the hurricane belt long enough to know the hazards of venturing out into the eye of a storm, which can end with no warning when the opposite wall of the storm hits. Even in the calm of the eye, downed power lines dance with devilish energy and gremlins roam all over, waiting to trip or cut someone. The Ogdens also understood that people who are in shock often do irrational things.

I obeyed their request and took a quick peek from the gate at the halfway point. I returned to the big house, weak and subdued, my fears confirmed.

As the storm traveled on its due-west path, the north winds on the west side struck us first, mutilating all but the strongest structures. Then the eye came, and calm descended for a few minutes. When the eye passed, the winds came from the opposite direction. Whatever had not been ripped out by the north wind succumbed to the even fiercer south wind.

Nothing I could imagine could match the fury of the storm's second half. The roar was constant. The whole eleven-room house shook. We were gathered in the central sitting room with a fireplace when the brick chimney cracked in half . . . the top crashed through the second floor . . . into the sitting room . . . destroying the upstairs bathroom . . . creating a void where the roof once was . . . the wind came barreling in . . . we were underneath the chimney . . . the ceiling started to collapse . . . we scrambled into a tiny study room . . . seven people and the three remaining dogs . . . huddled through the rest of the storm . . . singing "My Favorite Things" to calm the children . . . or ourselves . . . leaning and pushing with all our strength against the door to the study to keep it from blowing open . . . for hours.

The only reason the chimney hadn't fallen to the first floor was that the house was constructed of Dade County pine, a variety of slash pine (*Pinus elliottii* var. *densa*) that is known for its strength and resistance to rotting and insect damage. The trees grow only on rocklands around Miami. The wood is so valuable for building that most of the trees have already been logged, and the variety is nearly extinct. Only a few, small, highly stressed pine stands remained even before the storm.

As we huddled in the small study, taking turns to force the door closed, we smelled a suspicious odor. Something had hit a gas line under the house and caused a leak. Fortunately, we were using flashlights, not candles. There was little danger of an explosion—the house was quite well ventilated by then.

The winds decreased around nine o'clock in the morning, and, after a series of rainy squalls passed, I ventured outside. The destruction that met my eyes resembled a nuclear holocaust that I had seen in photos. Almost everything was bare. There was not a leaf on a tree. The image will forever be engraved in my mind.

And, oh, how quiet! Not a single bird, not a car, not even a cricket. No leaves for the wind to rustle. Dead quiet. Except you could hear someone talking a block away, since there was nothing left to block or absorb sound. I've heard that happens in the Arctic, too.

The missing dog had hunkered under the van in the driveway and was shaken, but otherwise unhurt. We seven humans survived without a scratch. Sadly, a twelve-year-old girl three blocks from our houses was crushed to death by a beam falling in her bedroom. A National Park Service employee I knew, who lived in Homestead but worked at Fort Jefferson National Monument (now Dry Tortugas National Park), was fatally crushed under his collapsed house. Most of my local friends lost their homes.

My cottage had new skylights, many small ones that twinkled like stars in the daytime. The knotty pine boards that comprised the sturdy tongue-and-groove ceiling, so uncharacteristically attractive for an otherwise plain dwelling, held in place perfectly. But, here and there, the wind had sucked out the knots, leaving tiny windows to the sky.

Palm Cottage in Homestead sits sadly after Hurricane Andrew in 1992.

My fear of the cottage's floor flooding from the yard did not materialize. The storm passed so quickly that the ground was able to absorb the rain. Yet that was little comfort. In a great ironic twist, the floor flooded *because* the towels were there. When the roof blew off, the rain fell into the house through the new skylights. With the door's threshold blocked by the towels, the water could not drain out. An inch of water soaked the carpets.

In the space of a few hours early that Monday morning, a whole society collapsed. Rules evaporated. Years would pass before life returned to sort-of-normal.

The sustained winds had reached approximately 165 miles per hour, and the highest reported gust was 204 miles per hour, but all the anemometers in the peak wind areas flew the coop below that, so who knows? When all the calculations were revised fourteen years later, the National Weather Service proclaimed Hurricane Andrew a Category 5, the strongest storm category, based on the barometric pressure. Based on the winds, it is the third most-powerful hurricane ever to hit the United States.

The days that followed the storm blurred together for me. Clocks and calendars were moot. I worked day after day from sunrise to sunset in the blistering heat, helping people put temporary roofs on houses, hauling trees, clearing debris, riding my bicycle to check on friends. A tree in the driveway blocked my car and the roads were cluttered with debris, but I could get my trusty bicycle through.

I lost seven pounds in seven days, a significant amount on my small frame. I had food, but there wasn't much time to eat. I was doing heavy physical labor, and the stress just melted the rest off.

With a giant hole in the roof of the Ogdens' house, John and Maryanne were afraid a county inspector would condemn their home. Their gracious invitation to shelter the family from the Keys was fortuitous. As luck would have it, the father was a carpenter. He threw himself wholeheartedly to the task of stabilizing the tattered house, or, as we suspected, enough to satisfy the overworked inspectors.

Before the man could start, however, we had to remove the chimney from inside the house. Bucket by bucket, in dozens of trips, I hauled about a half ton of chimney bricks out of the Ogdens' upstairs bathroom, carrying them through the hall, down the stairs, and into the backyard.

Not a shade tree was left in southern Dade County, nor any ice, nor a cold drink. The scorching atmosphere reminded me of doing fieldwork in the middle of the Everglades.

The quiet lasted only a day. After that, noises gradually increased until there was a constant round-the-clock din: hammers, chainsaws, generators, military and news helicopters landing in any field they could find, even cargo planes landing nearby. The activity continued nonstop for weeks.

One day, I saw a map of the hurricane's path on the front page of the *Miami Herald*. I gasped. The center of the hurricane went right up our street. Everglades National Park also took a hard hit, especially the main entrance area. Biscayne National Park, which was in the direct path of the storm's landfall, was almost totally destroyed—its buildings a total loss, the docks and trails useless, and the vegetation a tangled jumble. Big Cypress National Preserve's southern end received significant damage. Fort Jefferson lost an employee. All told, the South Florida parks were stressed to the maximum to help their staffs, prevent further damage and injury, and make repairs.

National Park Service offices from across the country were magnanimous in responding and made me grateful to be working for the agency. Indeed, the Fish and Wildlife Service and other bureaus of the Department of the Interior were astoundingly helpful. Employees from all over the country arrived to help. The Park Service provided a medical trailer for first aid. I went for a tetanus booster and saw my blood pressure reach a new zenith.

The Park Service also availed us of a food service trailer, where hot meals were served three times daily for employees who had nowhere to cook. The Park Service even provided small home generators to some families.

While many private-industry employees lost their jobs when businesses closed down, we didn't even lose pay. Everglades National Park remained closed for several months, but I know of no jobs that were lost.

Fortunately, I could switch my brain into camping or fieldwork mode to handle the aftermath. No electricity? I don't need it. No running water? I'm used to it. Climbing roofs to fix them? That's easier than climbing cypress trees, especially without fire ants.

Looking on the bright side, I was planning to move from Homestead to live near my new job at Loxahatchee Refuge at the end of September anyway, so I just had fewer things to move. Just like when I started out after college, everything I owned fit in one pickup truck.

One of the first things that Maryanne did when it was safe to walk outside was to survey the damage to her amazing collection of orchids and bromeliads in the yard. The plants were strewn everywhere amidst fallen branches, pieces of roofing, and every other type of debris you can imagine. Maryanne was a botanist and had nurtured the plants for years, only to have them scoured from the branches and tree trunks. Even though we helped gather them and tie them to the trees, the dearth of shade would probably consign them to fatal desiccation.

While hurricanes seem indiscriminately destructive, goodness lurks in every hurricane's heart. This may be hard to fathom in the face of other recent hurricanes, such as Katrina, Rita, and Wilma. The purpose of hurricanes, however, is to maintain the balance of Nature. As the sun heats the oceans in the summer, the ocean temperature rises. While the warmer waters are nice for human swimmers, the water may become so warm that the marine organisms become stressed or even die.

Nature's answer is to carry the heat away toward somewhere cooler. Thus, a huge air mass forms from the warm air that rises above the tepid water, and this air mass drifts off with the prevailing winds toward cooler regions, usually the North Atlantic Ocean or a land mass. In cooling the waters for marine-life survival, Andrew was almost certainly a success, although the benchmark is difficult to measure.

Other benefits of hurricanes are the sweeping of accumulated litter from the ground to allow seeds to sprout, the dumping of needed rain before the dry season begins, and the flushing of estuaries that have become choked with vegetation. These effects were at least partially accomplished. Much of the damage to the native vegetation was severe, but the trees are slowly regrowing. Damage to the non-native vegetation, such as Australian-pine, was worse because they weren't adapted to such winds.

All told, the direct effects upon wildlife appeared to be minimal. Some sea turtle nests were destroyed, but most were located farther north or south of the severe damage. All 23 of the radio-collared panthers in the area were eventually accounted for by the National Park Service. Since many alligator nests had already hatched, an insignificant number were destroyed. Most of the crocodile nests were south of the severe damage, although some probably succumbed. Wading birds, eagles, and most other birds were long since done nesting. The worst effect would be on two types of invertebrates that were already endangered. Fortunately, the Schaus' swallowtail butterflies and *Liguus* tree snails enjoyed much assistance in the ensuing years by scientists determined to keep them from going extinct.

Truthfully, the terrible environmental effects had more to do with human interference than with natural events. When people left paint and varnish in their carports or sheds, for example, these toxic materials blew into the canals. Rusty nails, metal roofs, broken glass—all are hazardous to living beings. Downed power lines, leaking oil tanks, lawn furniture that became projectiles—these, too, caused extreme damage.

The Australian-pines that the South Florida Water Management District had so proudly planted along the canal banks decades earlier to stem erosion had snapped like matchsticks, causing flooding from major water backups in the canals. The damage the fallen exotic trees caused was so extensive that the Water Management District never wanted to deal with them again. At great cost to the taxpayers, they felled the remaining

Australian-pines, so that they would never have to worry about the weak trees again.

Weeks after the storm, eighty bonfires were burning around Homestead to get rid of the debris piles. Clean air laws were disregarded. The air quality was worse than a city in China.

Non-native rats feasted on the piles of garbage, 25 years' worth of which was created in one day. Captive non-native animals in zoos and private yards were left to roam free when their pens were destroyed. Seeds of non-native plants were spread far and wide by the winds that blew across the peninsula. Without the interference of civilization, the hurricane would have zipped through, leaving environmental benefits and little irreparable damage.

Financially, the loss of personal possessions was extensive. Certainly, the damage to structures across the county was obvious. What about the contents? I have a feeling some of those losses are exaggerated in every storm. For example, the roof of my cottage peeled off, drenching everything inside with rain. My stereo receiver and speakers, already twenty years old, took a soaking. Weeks later, when they were dry and I had moved my surviving possessions to an electrified house, I tested them. They sang out as if they were new, and now, fifteen years later, they still warble beautifully. The reason is that most electronic circuit boards are coated with oil that protects them from moisture. If the unit is completely dry and clean when you turn it on, it should experience no ill effects.

Another example of an indefatigable gadget was my little Royal Dirt Devil vacuum cleaner, which was also soaked in the heavenly shower. After the storm had passed, I set the Dirt Devil in my sunny yard to dry. Then down the street I went to patch a roof, and while I was absent, a typical afternoon thunderstorm passed by, drenching the Dirt Devil again. For three days in a row, I left the vacuum cleaner out in the sun to dry, and every afternoon it rained. In the end, there was no damage to the unit, and I still use it.

The upshot is that many people probably discard electronics and other soaked items without trying to salvage them first, needlessly increasing the damage estimates, filling the landfills, and consuming more resources for replacements.

Some of the storm's effects, seemingly minor, didn't hit me until weeks later. The lack of electricity caused the loss of all frozen specimens at the research center, which were being stored until the biologists could preserve them permanently. Among them was a black-legged kittiwake (a type of gull) that I had stashed there four months earlier.

I had been doing some fishing surveys on the islands of Dry Tortugas National Park (Fort Jefferson) on April 7, 1992, when someone brought the kittiwake to me, alive but with a fishhook lodged in its throat. Black-legged kittiwakes are fish-eaters of the open ocean and are often the victims of commercial long-line fishing. The birds also follow ocean vessels, feeding on the small fish, crustaceans, or other sea life churned up by the engines or bycatch tossed out by fishing vessels. The scientists Forbush and May[12] reported that "thousands have been caught in the past by fishermen with hooks and lines baited with pieces of fish offal. The birds thus taken were eaten or used for bait."

Judging by its first-year winter plumage, the bird had probably hatched the year before. That may have explained why it was so far south that late in the spring. It should have been farther north and in the Atlantic Ocean. It must have become lost.

The kittiwake in my care was beyond hope of saving. We had no facilities for animal first aid on this remote, sixteen-acre island, almost seventy miles west of Key West. We also had no way off the island until the Park Service supply boat *Activa* arrived the next day. I kept the bird warm and quiet overnight. Before dawn, it lost its grip on life.

Black-legged kittiwakes weren't on the park's bird check-list and, upon conferring later with Bill Robertson (now deceased), I learned what a valuable find that bird was. Bill was the undisputed fountain of ornithological knowledge for Everglades National Park and Fort Jefferson National Monument. Only three other kittiwakes from Florida were in permanent scientific collections. Mine would have been the fourth. I can't imagine how much other valuable scientific information was lost in those freezers because of the hurricane.

Worse than any material loss that I suffered was the storm's effect on the manuscript of my first book, *Exploring Wild South Florida: A Guide to Finding the Natural Areas and Wildlife of the Everglades and Florida Keys*. The hurricane hit three weeks before the deadline with my publisher, Pineapple Press. In one night, every place I had just written about was flattened. My manuscript, although safeguarded on computer disks in several locations, including my bank's vault, might as well have been drowned in the storm surge. I had just written about this wonderful area to visit, only to have it transform into a giant garbage dump. None of the parks would be open for months. Depression set in. I was a lost soul. I was afraid to call my editor because I didn't know what to tell her.

After I'd spent two weeks in mourning for my manuscript, an astute friend, who lived safely out of the hurricane zone and the accompanying psychological traumas, pulled me out of my rut.

"You know," he said, "all the other books on the shelf are obsolete now. Maybe you can do something simple to fix it up without a lot of rewriting?"

"How?" I wondered aloud.

"I don't know, but you'll think of something."

Slowly, it sank in. In my posttraumatic stress, simple solutions had not occurred to me. Mine had the chance of being the first book on the shelves that was current. I made a plan. I would add a section about the general effects of the storm. I would leave the original sections as they were and add a paragraph to the end of each that described the effect that Andrew had on that area. Months later, when the parks reopened, people could identify the changes. My editor agreed, and the resulting book became the most useful one on the shelves.

In the long run, I got my wish on that August 24. I never had to return to my exasperating job in Flamingo. In fact, I never had to return to work at the park at all, because it was closed until after my transfer date. What a price to pay!

Chapter 13.

"I Love You" in the Everglades

"What exactly do you want to see?" I queried the film crew, as we loaded their camera gear onto the airboat.

"Just give us your standard tour. We don't have any particular agenda. We'll know it when we see it," answered the producer.

On this day in early 1997, the film crew from Charles Kuralt's television show *An American Moment* arrived at Loxahatchee National Wildlife Refuge. They had arranged with the refuge manager to film in Florida's Everglades by airboat. I was assigned the enviable task of operating the boat and playing tour guide.

An American Moment was exactly that—sixty seconds of Charles Kuralt showing something engaging about our country. Mr. Kuralt wasn't present for the tour. His part was dubbed in later from a studio.

I gave the Kuralt film crew my standard airboat safety briefing: "Don't stand up while we're moving—this isn't a surfboard. Wear your floatation vest—you won't believe how fast this heap of sheet metal can sink. Don't stick your arms out of the boat, or you'll get sliced by sawgrass or stung by puss caterpillars. Hold on to your hat and anything else that can fly back into my face—I don't drive so well blindfolded. Don't try to talk to me when we're underway. I'll nod dumbly as if I heard you, but I can't hear a thing with the engine running. It has no muffler. And please, please, please, let me know way ahead of time when you want me to stop. This thing has no brakes."

For the record, I didn't invent any of my warnings for effect. Puss caterpillars (*Megalopyge opercularis*) really do exist—inch-long hairy moth larvae with stinging spines filled with venom. They hang out on branches and eat the leaves, and they can latch onto you when your boat bulldozes through low brush. They won't kill you, but they'll raise some painful welts. Now you know why we wear long sleeves in the summer in South Florida.

As the senior biologist at this northern Everglades refuge, I spent many hours in airboats, conducting wading bird and snail kite surveys, monitoring water and air quality, and checking research plots around the marsh. I was one of only a handful of women airboat operators in the Everglades.

The primary way we accessed the 147,000-acre sawgrass marsh was by water. However, the water was so shallow that motorboats would hit bottom anywhere except in the deeper pools at the southern end. Sometimes we rented a helicopter with pontoon floats, but that was dreadfully expensive on our government budget. We needed cheaper transportation that cruised on top of the water. An airboat was the most appropriate craft.

An airboat is like a primitive airplane, or a reptile that hasn't yet evolved into a bird, except that airplanes were invented before airboats. I got the hang of driving the flat-bottomed aluminum boats quickly because I already knew how to fly propeller planes. Planes and airboats work on similar principles of physics for steering and forward momentum. The air passing by the propeller causes thrust, and the air passing around the rudder provides steering. One difference is that an airboat is pushed forward by a propeller at the rear of the boat while an airplane is pulled by a propeller in front. Another is that an airplane needs lift—hence it has wings.

I drive an airboat in Loxahatchee NWR. (Photo by John Green)

When a small plane crashes in the Everglades, some local airboat owners race to the scene. Not exactly paramedic types, these are unscrupulous scavengers. They are not seeking the cargo. They want the engine. Those Lycoming engines work so smoothly in airboats. A used propeller is a nice bonus.

Airboats can glide over water barely two inches deep. An airboat's engine sits in the stern, exposed to view but protected in front by a wire cage to keep people and flying objects from hitting the propeller. Most airboats, including ours, use airplane engines and propellers, like the ones that powered the single-engine Cessnas I flew. Other airboats may have car engines, which are cheaper and easier to obtain. Car engines are heavier, however, and make balancing the boat difficult.

Because an airboat is steered by airflow from the propeller over the rudders, the propeller must be turning to be able to steer the boat. If the engine quits, you lose control suddenly but forward momentum only gradually. Thus, until the boat stops on its own, it is out of control. Furthermore, like a plane but unlike a motorboat, there is no reverse gear. If you drift into a corner, you had better have enough room to get the boat out yourself, either by pushing it out with a pole or by wading in the water. Grabbing onto branches works in a pinch—but watch out for those puss caterpillars!

In general, much can go wrong on an airboat. All are top-heavy, but some are more so, depending on how high the seats are placed. One of our boats had seats raised about four feet above the deck to give a better view across the high cattails and sawgrass. Even low-seated workboats have little draft (the part under the water) to balance the top. This makes them prone to flipping if the driver hits a bump too hard or turns a corner too fast.

Even if the boat doesn't flip, injuries are common. I have been thrown twice and was injured both times. My neck constantly reminds me of the vertical whiplash I received when the boat I was riding in hit a bump too hard.

Unlike motorboats, airboats have little buoyancy and can sink in seconds if too much water flows over the sides. One of our refuge boats sank at a most unfortunate time. A colleague and I were escorting a film crew from a French public television station around the marsh in two airboats. My colleague drove the photographer and his hefty video camera in a boat with high seats. High seats are generally favored by biologists to see above the sawgrass for wildlife surveys, but they create a tipsy situation by making a high center of gravity. The photographer needed to see above the sawgrass, too. I drove the airboat with the low seats to carry the producer and several other television crew members. Our two boats traversed the marsh and entered a canal on the far side. Adjacent to the canal was densely packed cattails, well beyond the density of a healthy marsh. The cameraman wanted to film the difference between the cattails and the surrounding marsh, so my passengers and I waited while the other boat disappeared into the cattails. We didn't see the drama unfold around a bend in the canal, but later we heard the story.

As the other boat broke through the cattails and entered the canal, it turned in the deep, open water apparently at the same time the cameraman leaned over with the weighty camera. The boat tipped sideways, and a small wave from the boat's wake overshot the gunwale (the boat's rim). The boat sank in seconds, and one hundred thousand dollars of camera gear and glorious footage of endangered snail kites went with it. Praise to the flotation vests—no one was injured.

In 1996, Steve Martin, a biologist with the Florida Game and Fresh Water Fish Commission, drowned while on duty ostensibly because his airboat had a car's engine. He was alone on the Kissimmee River when the engine apparently failed. The theory I heard is that he climbed aft to the engine to try to fix it, and his weight plus that of the car engine tipped the boat backwards, trapping him underwater inside the cage that shields the propeller.

The first airboat was designed in 1920, but the idea didn't catch on until 1933, when the boats were used for frogging. Frogging was popular with low-income people, who would catch sizable pig frogs at night by torchlight in the marsh and sell the legs to restaurants the next day. Airboats are noisy and disruptive to wildlife, but sometimes they are the only way to get around. Although I've heard of airboats with mufflers, I've never met one. I wore two layers of hearing protection at all times—the small foam plugs and the bulky headphones.

I gave the Kuralt film crew the standard Loxahatchee tour. Vast shallow areas with emergent vegetation interspersed with tree islands comprise the bulk of the refuge. Loxahatchee contains some of the only remaining examples of the relatively untouched northern Everglades.

Our first stops were in the pristine Everglades, of which little is left. Here, the water has low nutrient levels, which sounds sickly but is exactly what the marsh evolved to need. The water, tinted brown from the tannins in the decaying leaves, is still clear enough to read a newspaper on the bottom.

Typical plants that grow in low-nutrient (oligotrophic) waters are water-lilies and bladderworts. The bladderworts are floating plants, not rooted to the bottom, so they must obtain nutrients from the water. Small air bladders on their floating roots capture tiny organisms, such as protozoans, cladocerans, nematodes, and rotifers. Once inside the bladders, the organisms are liquefied and digested. Thus, the plants are considered carnivorous—little green meat-eaters, like sundews, pitcherplants, and Venus flytraps. Even though the latter three plants are rooted to the soil, that soil is so poor that the plants supplement their nutrient needs by eating flies.

I showed the film crew the empty shells of apple snails, victims of hungry snail kites. The snail kite, an endangered crow-sized raptor, feeds almost exclusively on these two- to three-inch freshwater snails. The kite's bill is hooked, the better to reach into the curved shell and sever the muscle that anchors the snail's body in place. Look above a mound of empty shells under a tree and you'll find the perch of a snail kite, and if you're lucky, the kite will be there. The kites carry the snails back to the perch to eat and then drop the shells.

Among the 250 species of birds that use Loxahatchee Refuge are such ducks as blue-winged and green-winged teals, ringnecks, mottled ducks, wood ducks, pintails, and fulvous whistling ducks. Waterfowl are the only animals allowed to be hunted by humans on the refuge besides fish. Waterfowl have depended on the Everglades since the marsh was geologically created. For some species, Loxahatchee is their winter home. Others stop and rest during their migration between northern North America and South America. So important are wetlands like the Everglades for supporting migrating waterfowl that many refuges across the country were established just to protect the wetlands.

With the Kuralt crew, we skimmed over to the polluted marsh, the subject of intensive ecological restoration work. Many stakeholders were involved: federal, state, and local agencies Seminole and Miccosukee tribes; conservation organizations;

farmers; anglers; and other groups affected by the declining Everglades. The cameraman filmed the cattails that thrived on high-nutrient (eutrophic) water, laden with phosphorus and nitrogen from fertilizers that washed in from the agricultural lands to the north and west.

On parts of the refuge, thousands of acres of nine-foot-tall cattails grew so densely that a duck on steroids couldn't swim through them. We couldn't even drive the airboat through. No light could penetrate the water to nourish the aquatic plants that fish feed on. The character of the western marsh had changed from a diverse and lively community to a monoculture in which only a few songbirds and insects could find some use.

Although cattails are native to the Everglades, they historically grew only in small, isolated patches near seasonal wading bird roosting and nesting colonies. The water near these heavy bird concentrations has higher levels of phosphorus from the birds' droppings (sometimes called guano). Other places in the marsh were reacting as if they were sitting under wading bird colonies—as if they were receiving huge doses of guano.

One of the research sites we visited was established by internationally known wetlands ecologist, Dr. Edward Maltby, of the Royal Holloway University of London in England. Ed, the author of *Our Waterlogged Wealth: Why waste the world's wet places?*,[13] is sought by governments all over the world to advise them on restoring their countries' ravaged wetlands. Even the Vietnamese government invited him to help restore its war-torn lands.

Ed had set up a site immediately downstream of a tree island that hosted five thousand pairs of nesting white ibises in 1988. That was a particularly large colony for the refuge. At that time, no cattails grew just downstream of the tree island. By 1993, cattails were well established, and they had spread downstream every year during the study. The site was far enough away from the influences of agricultural pollution for us to be confident that the nutrient input came primarily from the birds' droppings. It was a good location to study how fast the cattails spread after the addition of the phosphorus, but just as importantly, how long the cattails lingered after the nutrient input was gone. Then we could determine how long it would take to heal the Everglades once the unnatural addition of phosphorus was halted.

Ed arrived from London every year with a dozen or so college students who, as part of their ecology studies, helped him measure annual changes in the marsh. I eagerly anticipated their visits, for their excitement at exploring the wilds of the Everglades was contagious. Few of the students had ever been to a subtropical marsh, and fewer had physically immersed themselves. They assumed that, since it was hot and not primitive Africa or South America, they could wear bathing suits in the water. That wading around in the leech-laden, saw-bladed muck was not the prime place for bare skin was blissfully irrelevant to them.

The mere mention of an alligator sighting would set the students to tittering. Occasionally, a nervous student would refuse to get out of the boat. One year, an alligator appeared at the edge of the study site, floating silently and watching us. As we moved to each point along the transect, the alligator stealthily advanced with us. Seeing the reptile advance, the students gasped, "It's coming after us!"

I pointed out that the alligator moved only when we did and always kept the same distance from us, like a slow dance. Eventually, I convinced them that the alligator was curious, but that it wouldn't breach its comfort zone. It would get as close as it dared to see what we were doing in its domain. If the students were afraid, they still got the work done.

After chronicling the changes at the Maltby site for the Kuralt crew, I cruised the boat by some tree islands, with their stands of native red bay, dahoon holly, willow, wax myrtle, and cocoplum trees. More than two thousand tree islands, ranging in size from 0.4 to 160 acres, dot the marsh. They formed from the separation of the underlying peat, which is almost one hundred percent organic material. In this context, organic means that it is composed of decaying animal or plant matter, not rocks that are breaking down into their mineral components. The Everglades peat reached its greatest thickness—sometimes as much as fifteen feet thick—in Loxahatchee Refuge.

Another stop on the tour was at one of our "bucket stations." We had five such stations at five areas of the refuge to test for possible phosphorus sources. The environmentalists believed the excess phosphorus in the water came from fertilizers applied to the sugarcane and other crops upstream from the Everglades. The runoff from rainfall and irrigation flowed directly into the

Everglades. We collected marsh water samples at various locations to determine how much phosphorus it contained.

The farmers had a different story. They argued that the phosphorus fell from the sky. They claimed that nutrient was in the air, maybe from smoke particles or industrial emissions, and was either absorbed by raindrops before they fell to the ground (a phenomenon known as wetfall) or fell as dust (known as dryfall).

We devised a way to find the answer at the refuge. Measuring the wetfall and dryfall can be tricky, but we designed a clever setup for those scenarios. We built a platform at each of four sites in the marsh and one on dry land, away from overhanging trees. On top of each platform, we placed frames that held two coverless five-gallon buckets. A flat board (the "roof") covered one bucket at a time. The roof moved automatically from one bucket to the other if the sensor determined that it was raining. The flat, metal sensor had a low-level electric charge running through it. As long as it wasn't raining, the dryfall bucket remained open to the air, collecting dust, leaves, and the occasional hapless frog. As soon as the first raindrops began to fall, they would hit the sensor, causing a water contact between two metal plates and completing the electric circuit. The roof would move over the dryfall bucket and expose the other to the rain. When the rain stopped, the sensor would dry out almost immediately, breaking the electric current. That triggered the roof to move back to the rainfall (wetfall) bucket, keeping it from collecting dryfall.

The sensors were powered by solar panels assisted by rechargeable boat batteries. Once a week, an assistant or I would go to each station, retrieve the buckets, and replace them with clean ones. Using laboratory protocols, we cleaned each bucket and collected the contents into sample jars for testing by Florida International University. By examining the quantity of phosphorus that fell from the sky during a given period and knowing the amount of rainfall during that period from rainfall gauges, we could calculate how much phosphorus came from the atmosphere. We compared that level to that from water collected from the marsh and determined that not enough came from the sky to account for the nutrient levels found in the marsh water. The rest must have come from the land upstream, and that was the agricultural land.

Demonstrating to visitors, such as the Kuralt crew, how the buckets worked was always entertaining. I could pour a few drops of water onto the sensor and the roof would move. In a minute, it would move back, because the sensor had dried. Occasionally, I would remind myself that, five years earlier, if someone had told me that I would some day have fun studying phosphorus, I would have screwed up my face and retorted, "Boring!"

After the bucket demonstration for the television camera, I swung the boat over to the canals and levees that blocked and diverted water from its natural path. Most were constructed in the 1950s for flood control. Loxahatchee is like a bathtub now—you put water in the north end (from pumping stations or rainfall) and it flows down a gradual slope to the levee and water-control structure drain at the south end.

All the while the camera was rolling, I was rattling off monologues about all that was good and evil in the marsh. Part of the tour included my sermon about the harmful effects of non-native plants that were introduced into the ecosystem. These plants came from another place, usually another continent, and they didn't belong in the Everglades. Some species, such as melaleuca (*Melaleuca quinquenervia*), were deliberately planted, and some, such as Old World climbing fern (*Lygodium microphyllum*), were inadvertently released. Exotic species become unmanageable pests in their new habitats because no natural enemies exist for them there.

In a truly natural setting, a plant or animal species evolves in balance with the other species around it. One species keeps another in check, so nothing ever takes over completely. That's what natural harmony is all about. Animals are controlled by other animals that hunt them, but a predator never hunts all of its prey to extinction. Plants have insects, fungi, and other animals that feed on them to keep them in check. When the natural control is missing, a non-native species is likely to grow out of control, sometimes causing a native species to go extinct.

Much of the refuge was and still is being overgrown by invasive non-native species. Melaleuca, a eucalyptus relative from Australia, is one of the worst. This species was introduced to Miami in 1906 and has since spread all over South Florida, growing equally well in standing water or on dry land. Among its vices are its ability to soak up tremendously more water than the smaller native plants, the way its presence changes the water chemistry, and the flammability of its wood.

Picture dense stands of trees growing where sawgrass once stood. Next, picture an airboat trying to get through. Now picture a crew of biologists and laborers killing millions of these melaleucas, one by one. That's what we did, using hatchets and chemicals that were deemed safe for a sensitive aquatic environment. The refuge's exotic-plant-control crew labored year-round. In the brutal heat and relentless humidity, the crew hacked a girdle (a horizontal gouge in the bark) around each tree trunk and applied the chemical. Sometimes they chainsawed the tree down and then applied the chemical to the exposed cambium (the growth layer under the bark). They waded in water all day, as thunderstorms came and went, often so fast that there was no time to seek shelter.

It's hard to believe that such a beautiful tree could be such a nuisance. It's also hard to believe that a tree we tried desperately to kill was the same species that the Vietnamese government wanted Ed Maltby to save. Melaleuca is native in Vietnam, and Agent Orange (an herbicide used in the Vietnam War) had seriously denuded the natural forests. The government wanted to restore the forests.

The other plant pest mentioned above is the Old World climbing fern, a vining fern that also came from Southeast Asia (courtesy of humans) and has since covered whole tree islands. The delicate little fronds look innocent enough, but they could have emerged from a horror movie. The vines grow seemingly endlessly and wrap themselves over the tops of trees. The Old World climbing fern is an indeterminate grower, a highfalutin term that means it will keep growing as long as it has nourishment and something to cling to. Like kudzu, a vine that is smothering the South, climbing ferns will ascend tall trees and drape down the other side or creep along the ground. This is significant because the vast majority of the world's plants have maximum growth limits. Once they reach the size they were genetically programmed for, they slow down to imperceptible growth rates.

When I first learned we had climbing ferns on the refuge, I thought they would grow only on tree islands. That was bad enough. But the day I found some growing up blades of partially submerged sawgrass was one of the worst days of my life at the refuge. Only then did I realize that the plant could spread anywhere.

The fern's coverage was so extensive that I could spot ravaged tree islands from an airplane three thousand feet in the air. The fuzzy character of the vines and the yellow-green color blanketing an entire stand of trees made them easy to distinguish.

We had no way of controlling the fern. Its tiny spores floated on the updrafts of fires, so prescribed burns (a common plant-control method) merely spread the plant. Herbicides would have killed the native species, too. Water level management can often control plants, but this one grew in floods or droughts. Yanking out the thirty-foot-long vines was impossible. My failure at finding a control for Old World climbing fern was a source of bitter disappointment to me.

All this I explained to the Kuralt crew, and after two or three hours and about twenty miles of cruising, the crew announced they had enough footage. I aimed the boat toward the boat ramp. When we were less than a mile from it, I spotted the glint of sunlight reflecting from a party balloon tangled in the sawgrass. Since most of the refuge is off-limits to the public, we normally saw no litter except what wafted in on the wind. Balloons were the most common trespassers.

I am referring to helium-filled, Mylar balloons used for special occasions, such as birthday parties, anniversaries, and graduations. They say "Happy Birthday," "Congratulations," or another salutation. When any of our staff spotted a fallen balloon, we always retrieved it. Usually, the airboat driver would steer closely enough for a colleague to reach out and snatch it up. We practiced our airboat rodeo skills that way.

I steered toward the balloon. Not wanting to ask the television crew to do our work, I stopped the boat, hopped out, and waded the few yards to the shriveled balloon. As I was slogging through the water, I explained why balloons were almost the only litter we found, how people don't realize that they are littering when they release a balloon, and what damage they do. Balloons can drift for miles before floating down to solid earth—or liquid ocean.

The open-ocean dumping grounds concern many environmental experts. When the balloons land on the water, they resemble the shiny blobs of jellyfish, a staple food of some sea turtles. Since Mylar doesn't degrade, it can float for years. The same is true of plastic bags, which are just as persistent in the environment and just as attractive to hungry sea turtles. When a sea turtle eats a balloon or a plastic bag, the turtle's digestive system becomes blocked, eventually causing the creature to starve to death.

I knew about sea turtles from another aspect of my job. Hobe Sound National Wildlife Refuge, about forty miles northeast of Loxahatchee, was under our jurisdiction. Thus, I was also the senior biologist for Hobe Sound. Hobe Sound is a coastal refuge, located north of West Palm Beach and south of Jupiter. Its 1,035 acres are a mix of sandy beaches, old scrub dunes, and mangroves. The beaches are a favored nesting place for three species of sea turtles: loggerhead, green, and leatherback. The loggerhead is a federally threatened species, and the other two are endangered.

Once upon a time, sea turtles were a staple food for coastal people. The reptiles could live in watery corrals for months with little or nothing to eat, providing edible protein when other meat was scarce. Sailors kept sea turtles on ships so that they had fresh meat while at sea. The eggs were an important source of protein when turtles were plentiful and still are in some countries, even though the eggs are scarce. Now that sea turtles are so rare, an important food source for people is disappearing.

Every year, starting in March, the female turtles come ashore to lay their eggs. Hobe Sound hosts some of the highest concentrations of loggerhead nests in the world. In a stretch about three miles long, approximately fifteen hundred nests are made per season, but this figure varies from year to year. Usually fewer than thirty green sea turtle nests are found and even fewer leatherback nests.

Since acquiring the land in 1971, the U.S. Fish and Wildlife Service has been monitoring the nesting of these sea turtles. Traditionally, we hired a summer employee to walk the beaches every morning at sunrise and record the new nests. The tracks left by a turtle as she dragged herself across the sand would be erased by the employee after he or she recorded the information, so that no nest was counted twice.

The turtles almost always come ashore in the dark so that diurnal predators won't see the delectable eggs she is laying. Using her flippers, she scoops out a cavity in the sand, lays the eggs, and buries them in the warm sand. Several months later, the babies hatch. Unlike alligators, the mother turtle is long gone and will probably never see her offspring. Each hatchling, about the size of a York Peppermint Pattie, will head immediately toward the relative safety of the ocean. By dawn, a pile of shells resembling broken ping-pong balls and dozens of wispy tracks are the only traces of the wee ones.

The life cycle of the sea turtle—part on land, part in the ocean—makes life confusing for agencies that protect endangered species. Under the Endangered Species Act, the U.S. Fish and Wildlife Service has jurisdiction over terrestrial and freshwater plants and animals, and the National Marine Fisheries Service has jurisdiction over marine species. So, who has jurisdiction over sea turtles? The answer is that the two agencies share the responsibility. When the turtles are at sea, the Fisheries Service has jurisdiction. When they are on land (the nesting beaches), the Fish and Wildlife Service has authority.

The party balloons and plastic bags generally affect the adult sea turtles. This cause of mortality is a serious problem, but it is not the major cause of the decline of sea turtle populations. Most of the mortality is caused by the destruction of nesting beaches for development, illegal digging of eggs by humans, predation by mammals (raccoons, armadillos, opossums, and others) that have been attracted to an area by human disturbance, drowning of sea turtles in fishing nets, and artificial lighting along beaches that disorients the hatchlings. However, with some species of sea turtles dangerously close to extinction, every death counts.

Party balloons trigger other problems more obvious to landlubbers. Groups of balloons tied together and released sometimes become tangled in power lines and cause power outages, especially if they have metallic ribbons. Their effect on both the sea turtles and the power grid caused several states to pass legislation regulating the release of balloons into the atmosphere. In 1990, Florida passed a law prohibiting the outdoor release of ten or more balloons filled with a lighter-than-air gas (such as helium) within a 24-hour period. Biodegradable and photodegradable balloons, such as latex ones, are exempt, provided they do not have strings attached. Virginia and California have similar, but less restrictive, laws. All of the balloons we found in the refuge were of Mylar material and at least two years after the law was passed in Florida, so even small quantities were littering our land.

I picked up the shiny balloon and held it up for the film crew to see. "I Love You" was emblazoned on it. I brought the sopping thing back to the boat, wringing it out as I walked. The producer handed me a wireless microphone and instructed, "Put the balloon back and say that all again." I figured they had some film left to use up. I dropped the balloon back in the marsh and performed "Take Two."

Mr. Kuralt passed away on July 4, 1997, shortly before the segment aired on CBS-TV, but not before completing his role. When the show aired, I expected the usual "Oh, my, look at what is happening to the Everglades water," or "Can you believe how the melaleucas have taken over?"

Instead, there I was, scooping up an "I Love You" balloon and telling the world that litter that's thrown *up* is still litter. I cheered. All the other media were presenting the standard Everglades stories, so often that people stopped listening. This was one message that no one else was venting.

The show's film crew was right—they knew what they wanted when they saw it. If only the people who sent "I Love You" messages into the Everglades actually did love the place.

Postscript – I drove an airboat around the Everglades for six years until I traded it for a desk in Washington, D.C. My glory days of fieldwork were over.

Epilogue.
Do We Need Nature?

My parents were born and raised in cities—my mother in Boston and my father in New York. Their generation grew up thinking that Nature would always be there—you just had to leave the city to find it. In their eyes, they did not need to protect the environment for their children. If their children grew up preferring city life, they need not worry—there would always be cities. If their children favored suburbia, that also was guaranteed for the foreseeable future. The need for wilderness was not obvious. How could my parents know that their suburban-raised daughter would possess a mutant gene that kicked in at age fifteen, driving her to become an ardent conservationist?

On the afternoon of September 11, 2001, Shenandoah National Park (about sixty miles from Washington, D.C.) experienced an unusual influx of visitors for a weekday. Rangers noted that the visitors expressed a need to escape emergency sirens around the Pentagon and the horror of the scenes on the television news, a need to be soothed by the peace of Nature.

In the days that followed, Shenandoah and other natural areas around the country experienced increases in visitation. Rocky Mountain National Park in Colorado posted a three percent rise over the same period the previous year, despite the ban on air travel.

When the smoke cleared from the World Trade Center, the Pentagon, and a field in Pennsylvania, our nation rallied together with the strength of our shared freedom—a freedom we had started taking for granted. This freedom was molded from a foundation of abundant natural resources, which we were also taking for granted. How did we get to this point?

In the 1400s, Europe was becoming crowded and re-sources were scarce. Timber for ships, houses, and fuel was disappearing, as were furs for coats and blankets. Gold and silver were in demand. The favored sources for these material riches were Cathay (China), India, and the East Indies islands.

At the same time, the Christian monarchies in Europe

were feeling threatened by the burgeoning power of the Islamic nations of the eastern Mediterranean, which were blocking trade routes to the Orient. Christian rulers set out to expand their sovereignty and to find another route to the rich eastern lands.

Enter Christopher Columbus, who sought wealth for his family and a position of nobility that his explorations could bring. The gold, spice, and human cargo that Columbus brought back from the Caribbean island of Hispaniola on his first voyage convinced Queen Isabella of Spain to finance more voyages. It gained the captain great respect. Henry Hudson, sailing for England and the Netherlands, was searching for a northwest passage to Cathay through the Arctic Ocean when he sailed along the eastern coast of North America and paved the way for the Jamestown and Plymouth colonies.

Our nation was born on some of the most diverse and fertile lands in the world. Upon these shores weary explorers collapsed, survivors of harrowing voyages, bent on finding Nature's riches at any cost. They came from Spain, England, Italy, the Netherlands, France, and other European countries. They sought timber, furs, ores, spices, whales, and slaves. They found these and much, much more in the New World—enough to make it worth the perilous sail across the North Atlantic. The dream of freedom came later, when word of a bountiful land drifted across the Atlantic.

Although the rich continent that the European explorers found was not the object of their destination, it was nevertheless a treasure. The varied wealth was so vast it seemed infinite. Even better, since the New World populace had no centralized government, the European nations considered it their right to claim the land and all it contained. Here lay an entire continent ripe for harvesting.

Settlers found unfamiliar species so numerous that no one dreamed they could ever disappear. Sixty million bison, ranging from Alaska to Mexico and almost coast to coast, provided everything that cattle could, even where cattle could not survive. Beaver, then found in every current state except Hawaii, gave trappers a reason to forge ever farther inland into unexplored territory and brought fabulous wealth to the traders. Four billion American chestnut trees in the eastern continent yielded food and lumber of such great quality that no other tree could match it.

However, in fewer than four hundred years, the settlers nearly exterminated the bison and beaver. Only through extreme efforts did enlightened people return them from the brink of extinction.

What about the American chestnut? This eastern tree had lightweight wood that was easy to split and virtually rot-resistant, making it ideal for building houses and fences. The straight trunks were often branchless for fifty feet—a boon for market value. Hollow trees stood for decades, providing dens for squirrels, bears, and many other animals.

The nuts were tasty, high-protein food that brought rural settlers much-needed nourishment and cash from selling the fall crop to cities by the boxcar-load. Chestnuts also fattened deer, turkeys, bears, squirrels, and barnyard pigs, all staple meats of Eastern rural settlers.

Foresters estimate that one of every four hardwood trees east of the Mississippi River a hundred years ago was a chestnut. Their massive size—towering one hundred feet high and reaching a diameter of ten feet or more—made them the most significant trees in the eastern forests by biomass alone. Like the beavers, prairie dogs, and alligators that create inviting conditions for other species, the presence of American chestnut trees ensures the presence of many other species. This firmly qualifies the tree as a keystone species.

In 1904, a fungal blight accidentally brought from Asia on commercial nursery plants struck the eastern forests, but only the American chestnut was affected. Within twenty years, nearly all mature chestnut trees were dead. Across nine million acres, the ghosts of the massive trees lingered for decades, their rot-proof skeletons a haunting reminder of the catastrophic loss. Today, occasional trees sprout from the remnant root system, but they die of the lingering blight before they mature. Species that relied on the chestnut tree declined and the homesteaders fell on hard times. The fatal blight caused a chain reaction from wildlife population crashes to human poverty in Appalachia that devastated the region. An entire ecosystem, including the people, had been tied to the chestnut.

Another striking example of the often invisible relationship among species is the demise of the dodo. This flightless, fruit-eating bird lived on the island of Mauritius in the Indian Ocean. Prehistorically, the island had never known mammalian inhabitants or any other ground-dwelling predators. Mauritius was never even visited by humans until the 1500s, when Portuguese traders landed there en route to the East Indies. The island became a popular stopover because the fifty-pound birds were easy to catch and provided fresh meat for the sailors. Later sailors brought and released pigs and monkeys as food for subsequent ship stopovers. Rats hitchhiked along. These mammals raided dodo nests, which contributed to the decline of dodo populations from hunting by the sailors. In less than two hundred years, the dodo became extinct. But the tragedy did not end there.

Three hundred years after the last dodo died, a scientist noticed that one species of tree on Mauritius was dying off. In fact, only a few remained, and they were all about three hundred years old. Why were they not reproducing? The scientist eventually theorized that the trees' reproduction had depended upon the dodo. The bird fed on the tree's fruit, which possessed a tough seed coat. The bird's digestive system had etched the hard seed coat enough to allow the seed to sprout after being defecated onto the ground. No other animal on the island served that function. After that discovery, scientists fed the seeds to turkeys and were able to germinate some seeds. The tree was saved from extinction. In our ignorance, what less-conspicuous species that were associated with the dodo did we miss?

History shows that when natural resources are scarce, people fight over them. Witness the countless water-rights clashes between neighbors and the oil that drives one nation to invade another. Imagine if the United States in Columbus's or Hudson's day was barren. Would settlers have flocked to a desert or tundra? Obviously not, because the New World has both, and they are still sparsely populated compared to the lush woodlands. Only when we import natural resources from elsewhere (water from canals and deep aquifers or food from distant farms) do we have population booms in the desert. We settled where we did because of the bountiful natural resources, and we financed our world-power strength with them.

These bounties allowed us to become a nation of consumers, never seeming to have enough motorized vehicles to conquer the terrain, electronic devices to accomplish our work, clothes to flaunt every day of the week, or knickknacks to clutter the mantle. We are rapidly spreading these values to other cultures for our own economic gain. These values will not likely change until we deplete the materials.

Material wealth is composed of matter, and the physicist Albert Einstein postulated that matter can neither be created nor destroyed. Thus, it can only change form, so it just shifts around the Earth. What Einstein left out is that, in a sense, matter can be destroyed, if it is rendered useless to humans. Thus, we can diminish our stock of usable matter, but we can never truly increase it.

How is it that our country's per capita wealth is increasing, if matter can't be created? This phenomenon can happen only two ways—if we take it from someone else or we take it from the Earth. All too often, we take it from the Earth.

The world's collective ingenuity has not yet solved some basic global problems. Contaminated water prevails around population centers, hunger annually starves millions of children, invasive species cause 130 billion dollars of damage annually, and vicious contagious diseases arise for which we have no cures. We still cannot halt the chestnut blight that erupts in the young trees just as they approach maturity. How can we trust our cumulative brainpower to find a way to live without Nature?

We cannot know what our children will want, despite our efforts to guide them on a certain path. I was not taught to embrace Nature. Yet the impulse was a part of me, a remnant of my primitive ancestors, something in my soul that emerged at an early age. Not a mutant gene at all, I believe, but a latent one. Perhaps this primordial legacy lies deep in the souls of all humans. Some are fortunate to find it, to know the whole of their being. Others do not yet recognize this part of themselves. When they do, what will remain for them?

Notes

[1] The game begins when two players, facing each other, pound their closed fists (one for each person) three times in quick succession on a table or the floor. Then they pound once more, this time forming their hands in one of three symbols: flat hand for paper, fist for rock, and two fingers for scissors. Scissors win over paper (worth a point), because scissors cut paper and thus destroy it. Paper wins over rock, because paper wraps around a rock and blunts it. Rock wins over scissors, because rocks blunt the scissors' blades, rendering the scissors useless. A tie occurs when both people produce the same symbol. We played in sets of 10 points, with a point for each winning shoot.

[2] Howlett, Carl C. 1973. Hampden: its settlers and the homes they built. Yola Guild of the Federated Community Church, Hampden, MA. 139 pp.

[3] When a band is recovered from a dead bird, the band should be mailed to the Bird Banding Lab, Patuxent Wildlife Research Center, Laurel, MD 20708 USA. If you capture a live bird that already has a band, such as at a banding station, do not remove the band. Write the number down, release the bird, and call the Bird Banding Lab at 800-327-BAND from anywhere in Canada, the United States, and most parts of the Caribbean to report the band number and relevant information regarding the bird.

[4] Jewell, S.D. 1987. Larval dermestid infestation of nestling Wood Storks (*Mycteria americana*) in Georgia. Oriole 52:11–13.

[5] The opinions and views expressed in this chapter and elsewhere in this book are the opinions and views of the author and do not necessarily represent the opinions or positions of the United States Government, the Department of the Interior, the National Park Service, or Everglades National Park.

[6] Loder, Natasha. 2005. Point of no return. Conservation in Practice 6(3):28–34.

[7] Gilliland, Gene, Hal Schramm, and Bruce Shupp. 2002. Keeping Bass Alive: A Guidebook for Anglers and Tournament Organizers. B.A.S.S. Montgomery, AL. 44 pp.

[8] 7 U.S.C. §§ 2131 et. seq.

[9] Animal Welfare Institute. 1990. Animals and Their Legal Rights: a survey of American laws from 1641 to 1990. AWI. 441 pp.

[10] Drayer, Mary Ellen (ed.). 1997. The Animal Dealers: evidence of abuse in the commercial trade 1952–1997. Animal Welfare Institute. 395 pp.

[11] American Sportfishing Association. 2008. Sportfishing in America — Economic Engine and Conservation Powerhouse. http://www.asafishing.org/asa/newsroom/newspr_010808.html.

[12] Forbush, E.H. and J.R. May. 1939. Natural History of the Birds of Eastern and Central North America. Houghton Mifflin Company, Boston. 226 pp.

[13] Maltby, Edward. 1986. Our Waterlogged Wealth. Earthscan Paperbacks and the International Institute for Environment and Development; London. 200 pp.